Anton Shekhovtsov

RUSSIAN POLITICAL WARFARE
Essays on Kremlin Propaganda in Europe
and the Neighbourhood, 2020-2023

With a foreword by Nathalie Loiseau

Bibliographic information published by the Deutsche Nationalbibliothek
Die Deutsche Nationalbibliothek lists this publication in the Deutsche Nationalbibliografie; detailed bibliographic data are available in the Internet at http://dnb.d-nb.de.

Bibliografische Information der Deutschen Nationalbibliothek
Die Deutsche Nationalbibliothek verzeichnet diese Publikation in der Deutschen Nationalbibliografie; detaillierte bibliografische Daten sind im Internet über http://dnb.d-nb.de abrufbar.

Cover picture: Created by Anton Shekhovtsov using Midjourney AI.

ISBN-13: 978-3-8382-1821-2
© *ibidem*-Verlag, Stuttgart 2023

Printed in the United States of America

Soviet and Post-Soviet Politics and Society (SPPS)　　Vol. 271
ISSN 1614-3515

General Editor: Andreas Umland,
Stockholm Centre for Eastern European Studies, andreas.umland@ui.se

Commissioning Editor: Max Jakob Horstmann,
London, mjh@ibidem.eu

Soviet and Post-Soviet Politics and Society (SPPS)

ISSN 1614-3515

Founded in 2004 and refereed since 2007, SPPS makes available affordable English-, German-, and Russian-language studies on the history of the countries of the former Soviet bloc from the late Tsarist period to today. It publishes between 5 and 20 volumes per year and focuses on issues in transitions to and from democracy such as economic crisis, identity formation, civil society development, and constitutional reform in CEE and the NIS. SPPS also aims to highlight so far understudied themes in East European studies such as right-wing radicalism, religious life, higher education, or human rights protection. The authors and titles of all previously published volumes are listed at the end of this book. For a full description of the series and reviews of its books, see www.ibidem-verlag.de/red/spps.

Editorial correspondence & manuscripts should be sent to: Dr. Andreas Umland, Department of Political Science, Kyiv-Mohyla Academy, vul. Voloska 8/5, UA-04070 Kyiv, UKRAINE; andreas.umland@cantab.net

Business correspondence & review copy requests should be sent to: *ibidem* Press, Leuschnerstr. 40, 30457 Hannover, Germany; tel.: +49 511 2622200; fax: +49 511 2622201; spps@ibidem.eu.

Authors, reviewers, referees, and editors for (as well as all other persons sympathetic to) SPPS are invited to join its networks at www.facebook.com/group.php?gid=52638198614 www.linkedin.com/groups?about=&gid=103012 www.xing.com/net/spps-ibidem-verlag/

To fallen defenders of Ukraine

Contents

Foreword

I started to hear about Anton Shekhovtsov's work as early as 2020. Europe was facing the brutal surge of the COVID-19 pandemic and in parallel another unprecedented epidemic, the Infodemic, as it was rapidly being called by the few who really cared.

It was obvious that fear had allowed the weirdest of all conspiracy theories to circulate at full speed and that the massive development of social media, accelerated by the diverse episodes of lockdown, had allowed unverified opinions to spread faster than ever. All of this could have been spontaneous and mirrored the high level of anxiety among European public opinions. But there was more in it that needed some analysis: there was a deliberate effort to manipulate European audiences, coming from two state actors working in parallel and using similar narratives: China and Russia. On information manipulation, Russia was the master and China was learning, and learning fast.

This was the moment when the European Parliament decided to set up a special committee on foreign interferences in our democracies. I was already chairing the Subcommittee on Security and Defence, but decided to get involved as a whip for my political group, Renew Europe, in the new special committee as soon as it was established. For me, foreign interferences were simply another sort of warfare, a hybrid one, that was being fought against different countries, mainly democracies, by a handful of authoritarian regimes.

This warfare was taking many forms, approximately everything but direct military confrontation: manipulation of information was an obvious one, and interference in electoral processes was starting to be investigated both in the US and the UK. Elite capture had been going on for decades, through direct relations with both individuals and political parties. Cyberattacks were on the rise.

I met with Anton Shekhovtsov and rapidly discovered that we were interested by the same phenomena. Still, he had something that I was missing: a first-hand experience of Ukraine. His reasons to be fighting Russian influence in Europe were existential. He understood long before the Russian war of aggression of 2022 what hybrid warfare was able to achieve. From the Russian annexation of Crimea, to the blurring of the downing of the MH-17 flight, to the complacency of so many European politicians towards Russian propaganda, he had every reason to be concerned and to share his knowledge.

His knowledge was very significant. On the strong relations between the Russian regime and far-right political parties in Europe, he had documented contacts, links, trips, joint events. On unexpected aspects of Russian interference in Europe, he had brilliant research, such as on the role of the Chechen leader Ramzan Kadyrov in the aftermath of the assassination of a French school-teacher, Samuel Paty. But his research was – and is – going much further and digging much deeper than hints and pieces of evidence related to Russian interference in Europe. Where some commentators only see anecdotes, Anton Shekhovtsov analyses patterns of influence and hybrid warfare. Where many in Europe still do not realise that the objective of manipulation is to weaken and divide our democracies, he knows from experience that Ukraine is a lab: what took place in 2014 was not met with sufficient reactions by the West. The reality is that we allowed the 2022 full-scale aggression against Ukraine to happen, because too many among us wanted to believe that the annexation of Crimea had taken place voluntarily and that the destabilising of Donbas was only the responsibility of Ukrainian separatists. All this was pure manipulation, but too many in Europe were ready to accept it at face value.

Since 2022, we realise that hybrid warfare is just the first step in a serious confrontation. We have come to learn that new instruments can be used to try to blackmail developing countries, such as energy dependency, food safety or the weaponisation of migrants.

I am convinced that Anton Shekhovtsov still has a lot of research to carry out. But I am delighted that he managed to gather some of his most recent and interesting pieces into this book. I hope it will help bring about the necessary eye-opening of public opinion in Europe with regards to the war, which is hitting our continent hard, though with too little attention to the nature of Russian political warfare.

Nathalie Loiseau
Member of the European Parliament
Minister for European Affairs of France (2017-2019)

Acknowledgements

Most of the essays comprising this book were written over the course of my cooperation with two organisations, the European Platform for Democratic Elections (EPDE) and Free Russia Foundation (FRF).

The EPDE is an international association that supports experts and citizens standing up for transparent and equal suffrage wherever it is at risk in Europe. Together with the EPDE, we have strengthened the previously fragmented field of research into the use of biased election observation as part of authoritarian regimes' political warfare against democracy in Europe and its neighbourhood. I am grateful to the EPDE's team, namely Stefanie Schiffer, Adam Busuleanu and Kira Mössinger, for their enthusiastic support of my work.

The FRF is an international organisation founded by Russian citizens united by their vision of a free, democratic and peaceful Russia. In 2020, the FRF and I launched *The Kremlin's Influence Quarterly*, a journal that provided analyses of attempts by the Putin regime and its accomplices to exert malign influence in Europe. I thank the FRF and, in particular, Natalia Arno, Grigory Frolov and Natalya Lunde for our fruitful cooperation in this important area.

I highly appreciate insightful conversations with Antoine Arjakovsky, Roland Freudenstein, Jacopo Iacoboni, Anastasia Kirilenko, Nathalie Loiseau, Pavel Luzin, Marian Madeła, Marie Mendras, Dirk Schuebel, Silvia Stöber and Nicolas Tenzer addressing various aspects of the developments discussed in this book.

I wish to thank Vladyslav Galushko and Open Society Foundations for their valuable support of my studies of Russian political warfare.

I am also grateful to Andreas Umland for his long-standing guidance and agreement to publish this volume in his critically acclaimed book series "Soviet and Post-Soviet Politics and Society".

Last but not least, I wish to express my deepest gratitude to my family and friends for their moral support during my work on this book.

Anton Shekhovtsov
18 July 2023
Vienna

List of Tables

List of Figures

Abbreviations

ABW	Agencja Bezpieczeństwa Wewnętrznego (Internal Security Agency)	Poland
AfD	Alternative für Deutschland (Alternative for Germany)	Germany
AFRIC	Association for Free Research and International Cooperation	Russia
ANC	African National Congress	South Africa
BBC	British Broadcasting Corporation	United Kingdom
BRICS	Brazil, Russia, India, China, and South Africa	International
CENI-M	Commission Electorale Nationale Indépendante (Independent National Election Commission)	Democratic Republic of the Congo
CGTN	China Global Television Network	China
CIS	Commonwealth of Independent States	International
CIS-EMO	Commonwealth of the Independent States-Election Monitoring Organisation	Russia
DPR	"Donetsk People's Republic"	Ukraine
DRC	Democratic Republic of the Congo	Democratic Republic of the Congo
ECAG	Europejskie Centrum Analiz Geopolitycznych (European Centre for Geopolitical Analysis)	Poland
ECDHR	European Council on Democracy and Human Rights	Poland
EFDD	Europe of Freedom and Direct Democracy	European Union
ENEMO	European Network of Election Monitoring Organisations	International
EU	European Union	International
FDG	Foundation for Democracy and Governance	Belgium
FDNV	Foundation for the Defence of National Values	Russia
FPÖ	Freiheitliche Partei Österreichs (Freedom Party of Austria)	Austria

FRELIMO	Frente de Libertação de Moçambique (Mozambique Liberation Front)	Mozambique
FSB	Federal'naya sluzhba bezopasnosti (Federal Security Department)	Russia
ICES	International Expert Centre for Electoral Systems	Israel
IFBG	International Foundation for Better Governance	Belgium
ISIS	Islamic State of Iraq and Syria	International
LN	Lega Nord (Northern League)	Italy
LPR	"Lugansk People's Republic"	Ukraine
MEP	Member of the European Parliament	European Union
MMA	Mixed martial arts	
NATO	North Atlantic Treaty Organisation	International
NBC	Nuclear, biological, and chemical	
NGO	Non-governmental organisation	
OSCE	Organisation for Security and Cooperation in Europe	International
OSCE ODIHR	Office for Democratic Institutions and Human Rights of the Organisation for Security and Cooperation in Europe	International
OSCE PA	Parliamentary Assembly of the Organisation for Security and Co-operation in Europe	International
OWP	Obóz Wielkiej Polski (Camp of Great Poland)	Poland
PACE	Parliamentary Assembly of the Council of Europe	International
PoR	Party of Regions	Ukraine
PSL	Polskie Stronnictwo Ludowe (Polish People's Party)	Poland
RPF	Russian Peace Foundation	Russia
RT	Russia Today	Russia
SADC	Southern African Development Community	International
SD	Sverigedemokraterna (Sweden Democrats)	Sweden
SVR	Sluzhba vneshney razvedki (Foreign Intelligence Service)	Russia
UMP	Union pour un mouvement populaire (Union for a Popular Movement)	France
UN	United Nations	International
UNGA	United Nations General Assembly	International
WHO	World Health Organisation	International

1. Conceptualising Malign Influence of Putin's Russia in Europe

Influence and power in international relations

Influence, as the Cambridge Dictionary defines it, is "the power to have an effect on people or things",[1] and it would not be an exaggeration to say that all states, to one degree or another, try to exert influence on other states.[2]

As its definition implies, influence is closely linked to power which represents the ability to influence how someone or something behaves, develops or thinks, or to cause someone to change their behaviour, belief or opinion when that would not have occurred otherwise. In the context of international relations and on the basis of the close connection between influence and power, Joseph Nye introduced the concepts of hard power and soft power.[3] Hard power is the ability to exert influence over other nations through coercion that implies using military threats, sanctions and/or bribery. In turn, soft power is the ability to influence through affinity and attraction with resources such as a nation's political values, culture, and foreign policies.

In recent years, as authoritarian regimes increasingly challenged the democratic West, experts developed new terms in an effort to identify those aspects of power and influence that made the challenge of authoritarian regimes especially distressing.

In 2013, elaborating on Nye's concept of soft power in relation to Putin's Russia, James Sherr argued that, when discussing the country's influence abroad, a better way would be to talk not of soft power but rather of soft coercion. Sherr defined the latter as "influence that is indirectly coercive, resting on covert methods

---

1   "Influence", *Cambridge Dictionary*, https://dictionary.cambridge.org/dictionary/english/influence.
2   I am grateful to Thomas Garrett, Maria Snegovaya and Melissa Hooper for their useful comments on the earlier draft of this essay.
3   Joseph S. Nye, *Bound to Lead: The Changing Nature of American Power* (New York: Basic Books, 1990); idem, *Soft Power: The Means to Success in World Politics* (New York: PublicAffairs, 2004).

(penetration, bribery, blackmail) and on new forms of power, such as energy supply, which are difficult to define as hard or soft".[4]

Christopher Walker and Jessica Ludwig also found it difficult to identify particular influence techniques used by authoritarian regimes such as Putin's Russia and Xi's China as related to either hard power or soft power. Therefore, they wrote of sharp power to characterise malign, aggressive, and manipulative aspects of influence operations of authoritarian states in democratic societies. Unlike soft power, sharp power "is not a 'charm offensive,' nor is it an effort to 'share alternative ideas' or 'broaden the debate.' It is not principally about attraction or even persuasion; instead, it centers on manipulation and distraction".[5]

Mimetic power is another useful concept to employ in discussions about the approaches of authoritarian regimes to wield influence in the democratic West. Mimetic power can be defined as the ability to influence Western nations by creating the impression that authoritarian regimes are normal members of the international community and emulating what authoritarian regimes perceive as Western soft power techniques.[6] The idea behind mimetic power is that, for example, Putin's Russia is no better and no worse than any other Western country: even if Moscow behaves in an apparently questionable way, it is still normal because Western capitals allegedly do the same.

Another power-related concept that is useful for analysing influence of authoritarian regimes in democratic societies is dark power. The term appeared in 2007,[7] but was not properly conceptualised until very recently. Mark Galeotti offered arguably the

4   James Sherr, *Hard Diplomacy and Soft Coercion: Russia's Influence Abroad* (London: Chatham House, 2013), p. 2.
5   Christopher Walker, Jessica Ludwig, "From 'Soft Power' to 'Sharp Power': Rising Authoritarian Influence in the Democratic World", in *Sharp Power: Rising Authoritarian Influence* (Washington: National Endowment for Democracy, 2017), pp. 8-25 (10).
6   Anton Shekhovtsov, "Mimetic Power: How Russia Pretends to Be a Normal Member of the International Community", *openDemocracy*, 31 October (2018), https://www.opendemocracy.net/en/odr/mimetic-power-russia-international-community/.
7   Charles S. Maier, "Dark Power: Globalization, Inequality, and Conflict", *Harvard International Review*, Vol. 29, No. 1 (2007), pp. 60-65.

most significant contribution to the conceptualisation of dark power:

> "If soft power is the ability of a state to get its way by attraction and positive example, then dark power is the capacity to bully. [...] If you are going to be a bully, then be a fearsome and formidable one. That way, rivals are deterred from challenging you, and are inclined to pacify you with deals and exemptions".[8]

Drawing on the discussions of dark power by Galeotti and ourselves,[9] we can define it as the ability to influence preferences and behaviour of other nations through projecting an image of a state inherently antagonistic to their political values. Wielding dark power is about producing an image of a country that opposes the "Western hypocrisy" of liberal democracy, has the right to behave irresponsibly on the international stage, and is able to corrupt democracy in other countries.

The above-mentioned interpretations and definitions of sharp power, mimetic power and dark power suggest that these concepts are related to deception as an instrument employed by authoritarian regimes in their relations with democratic states. Hence, it seems natural that these types of power can be linked to specific forms of what the Soviet forces called *maskirovka*, "a set of processes employed during the Soviet era designed to mislead, confuse, and interfere with anyone accurately assessing its plans, objectives, strengths, and weaknesses".[10] One Soviet military dictionary argues that these forms include concealment, imitation, simulation, demonstrative actions, and disinformation.[11] Although the Soviet

---

8   Mark Galeotti, "Russia Pursues 'Dark Power' and the West Has No Answer", *Raam op Rusland*, 15 March (2018), https://raamoprusland.nl/dossiers/krem lin/894-russia-pursues-dark-power-and-the-west-has-no-answer.

9   Anton Shekhovtsov, "How Vladislav Surkov Joined the Russian Order of Dark Power", *Political Capital Institute*, 8 April (2019), https://politicalcapital.hu/rus sian_sharp_power_in_cee/publications.php?article_read=1&article_id=2382.

10 Timothy C. Shea, "Post-Soviet Maskirovka, Cold War Nostalgia, and Peacetime Engagement", *Military Review*, Vol. 82, No. 3 (May/June 2002), pp. 63-67. See also Charles L. Smith, "Soviet Maskirovka", *Airpower*, Vol. 2, No. 1 (Spring 1988), pp. 28-39.

11 *Sovetskaya voennaya entsiklopediya*, Vol. 5 (Moscow: Voenizdat, 1976), s.v. "Maskirovka".

forces originally applied the concept of *maskirovka* only to particular aspects of kinetic warfare, they would later use it to describe political, economic and diplomatic measures. In the context of this paper, we can argue that mimetic power corresponds to such forms of *maskirovka* as imitation and simulation, while sharp power and dark power draw upon disinformation and demonstrative actions.

Malign influence

Nye wrote that a nation is more likely to produce soft power or, in other words, to implement the ability to influence other societies through affinity and attraction "when a country's culture includes universal values and its policies promote values and interests that others share [...]. Narrow values and parochial cultures are less likely to produce soft power".[12] From this we can conjecture that influence emanating from soft power is normatively positive: when a state tries to influence the behaviour of another state by appealing to shared universal values and common interests, it effectively strengthens the universal value system thus contributing to the building of a global culture of human rights and achieving long-term balance and stability in international relations.

In contrast, authoritarian regimes based on non-democratic value systems use soft coercion, sharp power, mimetic power and dark power with the intent to mislead and confuse democratic nations and their leadership, hence the influence emanating from these approaches is inevitably negative in the normative sense and is termed here as malign.

We define malign influence in the European context as *a specific type of influence that directly or indirectly subverts and undermines European values and democratic institutions*. We follow the Treaty on European Union in understanding European values that are the following:

- human dignity
- freedom
- democracy

---

12   Nye, *Soft Power*, p. 11.

- equality
- the rule of law
- respect for human rights, including the rights of persons belonging to minorities.[13]

Democratic institutions are guardians of European values, and among them we highlight:

- representative political parties that aggregate, organise and articulate citizens' political demands, translate these demands into policy proposals, engage citizens in the democratic process, provide the basis for coordinated legislative activity, and advance government accountability;
- free and fair elections in which voters should be able to form opinions independently and free of violence or threats of violence, compulsion, or manipulative interference of any kind;
- an impartial justice system free of discrimination or favouritism;
- free, independent and pluralistic media that provide objective and accurate reporting, guarantee access to diverse views and meaningful opinions, monitor public officials, foster democratic debate, and encourage active involvement of citizens in political and social life;
- a robust civil society that holds public institutions accountable on issues of democracy and human rights, helps preserve democratic vibrancy, presents opportunities for collective action, builds community cohesion, and helps citizens articulate their interests and demands.

The main effect of malign influence is erosion and decline of European values, as well as deepening distrust of democratic institutions.

Before discussing motifs, agents, and instruments of malign influence of Putin's Russia in Europe, one caveat is in order. The fact that this authoritarian regime wields malign influence does not

---

13   "Consolidated Version of the Treaty on European Union", *EUR-Lex*, https://eur-lex.europa.eu/legal-content/EN/TXT/?uri=celex%3A12012M%2FTXT.

mean that Russia cannot produce soft power in Europe. Russia's major source of soft power is its high culture that comprises of literature (especially humanist writings), classical music, ballet, etc., and Russia has doubtlessly made an important historical contribution to world culture. The problem for Putin's regime is that it has only limited access to this source, because the Kremlin's activities and behaviour in the international arena compromise the positive effects of Russia's traditional soft power. One dramatic example here is the sharp decline of Russia as a sport superpower after the disclosure of the massive state-sponsored doping program that led to several temporary bans from the most important international sport events.

Malign influence as an effect of political warfare

It seems appropriate to discuss Russian malign influence in Europe in the framework of a political war that Putin's regime wages against Europe. Although the term "political warfare" was first introduced by the British forces during the Second World War, it was George F. Kennan, a leading American diplomat during the Cold War, who elaborated on the concept of political warfare in 1948: "political warfare is the employment of all means at a nation's command, short of war, to achieve its national objectives. Such operations are both overt and covert. They range from such overt actions as political alliances, economic measures (as ERP [i.e. Economic Recovery Plan, better known as The Marshall Plan]), and 'white' propaganda to such covert operations as clandestine support of 'friendly' foreign elements, 'black' psychological warfare and even encouragement of underground resistance in hostile states".[14] According to Paul A. Smith, "political war may be combined with violence, economic pressure, subversion, and diplomacy, but its chief aspect is the use of words, images, and ideas, commonly known,

---

14   State Department Policy Planning Staff, "The Inauguration of Organized Political Warfare", *United States Department of State*, 30 April (1948), https://hist ory.state.gov/historicaldocuments/frus1945-50Intel/d269.

according to context, as propaganda and psychological warfare".[15]
Today, political warfare is seen as a grey area between, on the one
hand, regular political, diplomatic, economic and other interac-
tions, and, on the other, high-order war, i.e. "intense, declared con-
ventional or nuclear war between the armed forces of two or more
nation-states".[16]

The framework of political warfare is useful for understanding malign influence and delineating its meaning. In times of peace,
authoritarian regimes build their relations with democratic societies predominantly on the basis of traditional and public diplomacy, trade and cultural exchange, which implies the employment
of soft power on the part of authoritarian regimes no matter how
limited their access is to it. However, in a situation of crisis, nations
tend to "deform" all areas of cooperation they enjoyed during peace
time. Traditional and public diplomacy are poisoned by the down-
grading of communications and projections of hard power, routine
trade is crippled by sanctions and trade wars, and soft power de-
generates into dark power, mimetic power and/or sharp power. If
the crisis is not resolved quickly, political warfare emerges.[17] As an
effect of political warfare, malign influence does not belong to the
areas of cooperation in times of peace, but – while it is not a reper-
cussion of high-order war – it can be observed throughout such
war. Table 1 demonstrates the forms that power and influence take
during times of peace, political warfare, and high-order war.

---

15 Paul A. Smith, *On Political War* (Washington: National Defense University
    Press, 1989), p. 3.
16 Ben Connable, Stephanie Young, Stephanie Pezard, Andrew Radin, Raphael S.
    Cohen, Katya Migacheva, James Sladden, *Russia's Hostile Measures: Combating
    Russian Gray Zone Aggression against NATO in the Contact, Blunt, and Surge Layers
    of Competition* (Santa Monica: RAND Corporation, 2020), p. 2.
17 Waller argues that political warfare is an outcome of a situation "when public
    relations statements and gentle, public diplomacy-style persuasion – the poli-
    cies of attraction that constitute 'soft power' – fail to win the needed sentiments
    and actions", see Michael Waller, "Getting Serious about Strategic Influence:
    How to Move beyond the State Department's Legacy of Failure", *The Journal of
    International Security Affairs*, No. 17 (2009), https://jmichaelwaller.com/wp-
    content/uploads/2016/08/Getting_Serious_About_Strategic_Influenc.pdf.

Table 1.   **Power and malign influence during times of peace, political warfare, and high-order war**

Peacetime	Political war	High-order war
Soft power	Projections of hard power	Hard power
	Mimetic power	
	Sharp power	
	Dark power	
Traditional influence	Malign influence	

For example, disinformation may imply different things depending on the particular context. In times of peace, disinformation may be created for profit (mercenary fake news) or for purposes of humour (satirical fake news).[18] Publishing false orders about diversionary landings or movements of troops is considered disinformation in times of war. Spreading manipulated pictures in order to confuse and disrupt a nation's opponents can be considered disinformation as part of political warfare or high-order war. In none of the cases can we talk about malign influence, unless disinformation is produced to manipulate public sentiment which leads – in the European context – to subversion of European values and/or undermining of democratic institutions. Likewise, neither corporate espionage nor money laundering necessarily produces malign influence despite the unwelcome nature of these criminal activities. Only when crime appears to be part of political warfare (for example, used to wield political influence or carry out targeted political assassinations[19]) can we talk about malign influence deriving from crime.

Furthermore, the relationship between political warfare and malign influence allows us to solve the question of whether this type of influence is an offensive or defensive measure. Any warfare implies both, so – in the context of Putin's Russia and Europe – the

---

18   On the forms of fake news see Donald A. Barclay, *Fake News, Propaganda, and Plain Old Lies: How to Find Trustworthy Information in the Digital Age* (London: Rowman & Littlefield, 2018).

19   Mark Galeotti, "Crimintern: How the Kremlin Uses Russia's Criminal Networks in Europe", *European Council on Foreign Relations*, 18 April (2017), https://www.ecfr.eu/publications/summary/crimintern_how_the_kremlin_uses_russias_criminal_networks_in_europe.

aggressive subversion and undermining of European values and democratic institutions is mirrored by the Kremlin's willingness to defend from Western influence what it considers as its own values and institutions. This echoes how some experts and practitioners understand information warfare, namely as "actions taken to *preserve the integrity of one's own information system* from exploitation, corruption, or disruption, while at the same time *exploiting, corrupting, or destroying an adversary's information system* and, [in] the process, achieving an information advantage in the application of force".[20]

Strategic and tactical goals of Russian malign influence

Elaborating on their concept of sharp power, Christopher Walker and Jessica Ludwig argue: "powerful and determined authoritarian regimes, which systematically suppress political pluralism and free expression in order to maintain power at home, are increasingly applying the same principles internationally to secure their interests".[21] This insight helps us conceptualise the major motifs of Russian state or non-state actors wielding malign influence in Europe, as it was Russian society that was the first victim of malign influence operations conducted by the Kremlin and its loyalists. In other words, before they started to wage a political war against the West in general and Europe in particular, the pro-Kremlin actors first undermined and subverted European values and democratic institutions at home.

Starting from Putin's first presidential term, the (pro-)Kremlin actors increasingly:

- took away freedoms and liberties from the Russian people;
- destroyed the rule of law replacing it with the rule of political considerations, cronyism, and nepotism;

---

20 A definition of information warfare by the US Department of Defense, cited in Edward Waltz, *Information Warfare: Principles and Operations* (Boston: Artech House, 1998), p. 20. My emphasis.
21 Walker, Ludwig, "From 'Soft Power' to 'Sharp Power,'" p. 10.

- degraded human rights and practices aimed at their defence;
- put pressure on civil society and NGOs;
- clamped down on political opposition;
- undermined the free and fair character of electoral processes.

All of these actions were needed in order to do away with democratic principles — no matter how weak they were during Boris Yeltsin's rule — to establish control over all Russian political institutions, and to enervate Russian society, thus securing the unlimited rule of Putin's authoritarian and kleptocratic regime. The Kremlin has projected its domestic agenda of subverting democratic values and institutions onto Europe in its political war against the West. From this perspective, one can concur with James Sherr who argues that the overarching aim of Putin's Russia is "the creation of an international environment conducive to the maintenance of its system of governance at home".[22]

It must be stressed, however, that there are different degrees of assertiveness in influencing the international environment, and — as argued before — it is natural that nations are, to different extents, involved in the process of influencing other states. For example, strategies of public diplomacy in times of peace can be based on engagement or shaping. In the case of engagement, nations aim to "inject new thinking and ideas", "create shared resources", "promote dialogue" and/or "fashion a common language".[23] In the case of shaping, the task is to reframe debates between nations by creating fresh perspectives, developing new concepts, changing the language of the debates, promoting rule of law and human rights.[24]

But there are disruptive and destructive public diplomacy strategies too, and nations resort to using them when engagement and shaping strategies do not seem to be effective. A disruptive

---

22   Sherr, *Hard Diplomacy and Soft Coercion*, p. 96. The original emphasis omitted.
23   Alex Evans, David Steven, "Towards a Theory of Influence for Twenty-First Century Foreign Policy: The New Public Diplomacy in a Globalized World", *Place Branding and Public Diplomacy*, Vol. 6, No. 1 (2010), pp. 18-26 (24).
24   Ibid.

strategy of public diplomacy is employed when a nation faces an unwelcome consensus. The aims of this strategy are – as Alex Evans and David Steven put it – to probe points of weakness, exploit wedge issues, redefine the terms of the debate, create a counter-narrative, galvanise allies, and divide, co-opt, or marginalise opponents.[25] A destructive strategy of public diplomacy is used when a nation does not see there to be an opportunity for further debate with what it considers its adversaries. Public diplomacy informed by this strategy aims "to sow confusion, fear and panic" through disinformation, "encourage dissention and defection" and "isolate enemies".[26] It is these strategies of public diplomacy that produce malign influence as an effect of political warfare conducted within the circumstances of a perceived crisis.

While the malign influence of Putin's Russia subverts and undermines European values and democratic institutions, these are not necessarily the primary targets of Russian influence operations. There is a difference between the effects of malign influence in our perspective and the aims of Putin's Russia.

We identify two major strategic goals of Putin's Russia when it engages in political warfare that produces malign influence.

The first goal is to protect Russian society from Western ideological, political, cultural, and other influences believed to undermine the grip on power held by Putin's regime. This goal is attained by discrediting European values and democratic institutions in the eyes of the Russian people. To this effect, Putin's regime pushes the idea that Europe is only interested in promoting European values in order to acquire advantage in geopolitical competition with Russia: narratives about democracy and rule of law are needed to denigrate the Russian authorities and pit Russian citizens against the regime; narratives about equality and human rights are directed at subverting Russian traditional, conservative values. The bottom line here is that European nations themselves care neither about democracy nor freedom nor human rights – they only weaponise these values against Russia.

---

25   Ibid.
26   Ibid.

The second goal is to advance the political, economic and security interests of Putin's Russia on the international stage. The Kremlin and pro-Kremlin actors strive to attain this goal through shaping the international environment in the image and semblance of Putin's regime, and — to this end — seek to corrupt major democratic institutions such as political parties, elections, justice systems, media and civil society.

Putin's regime and pro-Kremlin loyalists try to achieve these two strategic goals by meeting various tactical objectives. These objectives include, but are not limited to, weakening of Europe's transatlantic contacts, poisoning of bilateral relations between European states, spreading disorder on the international stage, retaining former Soviet states in the Russian sphere of influence, hindering modernisation of democratising European states, undermining trust in the EU and NATO, etc.

Areas, tools, and operators of Russian malign influence

It is important to distinguish between tools of political warfare (and malign influence) and areas of their application, although at times the difference between them is vague. An analysis of existing literature on Russian foreign policy and political warfare[27] helps us identify thirteen sometimes overlapping major areas in which actors of Putin's Russia conduct political warfare and, thus, produce malign influence:

---

27   Sherr, *Hard Diplomacy and Soft Coercion*; Keir Giles, Philip Hanson, Roderic Lyne, James Nixey, James Sherr, Andrew Wood, *The Russian Challenge* (London: Chatham House, 2015), https://www.chathamhouse.org/sites/default/files/field/field_document/20150605RussianChallengeGilesHansonLyneNixeySherrWoodUpdate.pdf; Mark Galeotti, "Controlling Chaos: How Russia Manages Its Political War in Europe", *European Council on Foreign Relations* (2017), https://www.ecfr.eu/page/-/ECFR228_-_CONTROLLING_CHAOS1.pdf; Linda Robinson, Todd C. Helmus, Raphael S. Cohen, Alireza Nader, Andrew Radin, Madeline Magnuson, Katya Migacheva, *Modern Political Warfare: Current Practices and Possible Responses* (Santa Monica: RAND Corporation, 2018), https://www.rand.org/content/dam/rand/pubs/research_reports/RR1700/RR1772/RAND_RR1772.pdf; Andrei P. Tsygankov (ed.), *Routledge Handbook of Russian Foreign Policy* (Abingdon: Routledge, 2018); Alexander Etkind, *Russia against Modernity* (Cambridge: Polity Press, 2023).

- politics
- diplomacy
- military domain
- business
- media
- cyber domain
- civil society
- academia
- religion
- crime
- law
- health
- environment

At the same time, we identify the following tools of Russian malign influence (the list, however, is far from exhaustive):

- political alliances
- interference in elections
- agents of influence
- front organisations
- international organisations
- public relations and lobbying
- energy politics
- economic subversion and sanctions
- shell companies
- intelligence operations
- cyber warfare
- cyber crime
- lawfare, or corrupt misuse of the legal system
- public diplomacy
- think-tanks
- diaspora groups
- propaganda and disinformation
- corruption
- conditional military aid
- paramilitary groups
- organised crime

- religious politics
- historical revisionism

Thus, techniques and combinations of techniques used by state and pro-Kremlin non-state actors in the framework of political warfare thus producing malign influence are innumerable. For example, the Kremlin may interfere in elections in Western nations by building alliances with particular political forces, providing funding through shell companies, and supporting them with the help of disinformation and cyber-attacks against their opponents. Or Russian pro-Kremlin actors may attempt to drive wedges between social and cultural groups in European nations through simulated "civil society" groups funded through organised crime. Or those actors may hack European think-tanks that aim to counter the Kremlin's malign influence operations, and discredit them by publishing sensitive, non-public information. Or Russian intelligence services may provide training for paramilitary groups in European societies that could later be used for radicalising peaceful democratic protests.

There are eight major categories of Russian state and non-state operators that are engaged in political warfare in Europe and thus are exercising malign influence: *siloviki* (institutions of force), official structures, political forces, business community, state-sponsored media, social media propaganda networks, think-tanks/foundations, and the traditionalist bloc. Table 2 provides non-exhaustive examples of operators belonging to these categories.

Table 2.   Russian state and non-state operators of political warfare

Siloviki	Defence Ministry, Main Directorate of the General Staff of the Armed Forces, Foreign Intelligence Service, Federal Security Service, Wagner Group
Official structures	Presidential Administration, Foreign Ministry, Committee on International Affairs of the State Duma
Political forces	"United Russia", Liberal-Democratic Party of Russia, Communist Party

Business community	Gazprom, Rosneft
State-sponsored media	RT, Sputnik
Social media propaganda networks	Internet Research Agency, Russian web brigades
Think-tanks/foundations	Rossotrudnichestvo, Valdai Discussion Club, Dialogue of Civilisations, Katehon
Traditionalist bloc	Russian Orthodox Church, anti-LGBT organisations

Although these operators of malign influence can be broken down into categories, it is important to stress that at the time of a particularly acute crisis in the relations between Putin's regime and the West, all these operators can be momentarily mobilised and function as a single unit, no matter whether they are state or non-state entities.

Russian operators of malign influence do not function in a vacuum: in the majority of cases, they are linked to Western and, in particular, European facilitators of the Kremlin's political warfare. The concept of facilitators is close to what the authors of one insightful work call "enablers", defined as entities (sometimes even countries) that "allow the Kremlin to achieve its end [...] and avoid some of the consequences of its behavior. [...] Crucially, by allowing Russian economic influence to cycle through their systems, enablers actively participate in the weakening and discrediting of their own democratic structures".[28] However, while the concept of enablers — at least as defined above — is economical in nature, facilitators operate in any area identified above thus helping Russian state and nonstate operators (see Table 2) achieve objectives that lead to the implementation of the Kremlin's strategic goals. Table 3 gives examples of facilitators of pro-Kremlin malign influence in Europe.

---

28 Heather A. Conley, Donatienne Ruy, Ruslan Stefanov, Martin Vladimirov, *The Kremlin Playbook 2: The Enablers* (Washington: Center for Strategic and International Studies, 2019), p. 12. The original emphasis omitted.

Table 3.   Facilitators of the Kremlin's political warfare in Europe

Siloviki	Transnational organised crime, paramilitary groups, biker gangs
Official structures	Agents of influence, friendly academics, experts and journalists, consulting firms, celebrities, producers
Political forces	Friendly foreign political actors, front organisations
Business community	Business partners of Russian companies
State-sponsored media	Websites amplifying Russian pro-Kremlin narratives
Social media propaganda networks	Far-right, far-left and conspiracy theory Internet activists
Think-tanks/foundations	Friendly academics, experts and journalists
Traditionalist bloc	National Orthodox churches, ultraconservative and anti-LGBT organisations

Investigating Russian malign influence

When investigating Russian malign influence, one needs, first of all, to establish the context. Malign influence emerges during a crisis between nations, which is perceived to move them into a situation inconsistent with peacetime relations when they would try to change other nations' behaviour or opinions by employing engagement or shaping strategies, rather than disruptive or destructive ones. In other words, malign influence is a product of the grey area of political warfare and cannot emerge during peacetime (see Table 1).

Understanding the context of malign influence is helpful to understand why the Kremlin and pro-Kremlin actors are strategically engaged in political warfare against the West in general and Europe in particular. These actors seek to minimise Western influences perceived as threats to Putin's regime and, at the same time, to advance various interests of the regime in the Western environment considered as unfavourable due to a crisis in relations between Putin's Russia and the West.

It is also important to assess vulnerabilities of European states because the Kremlin and pro-Kremlin actors are most likely to exploit those. Major vulnerabilities to Russian malign influence are shown in Table 4.

Table 4.   Major vulnerabilities to Russian malign influence

Corruption	Pro-Kremlin actors use corruption as a lubricant for malign influence operations
Anti-system parties	Anti-system parties, whether of far-right or far-left conviction, amplify societal divisions and make societies more vulnerable
Economic dependence	A country's economic dependence on Russia is yet another lubricant for malign influence operations
Social inequality	High levels of social inequality make European societies more vulnerable
Historical links	Religious and cultural connections to Russia may make countries less resilient to pro-Kremlin propaganda
Weak democracy	Weak or defective democratic institutions facilitate Russian malign influence operations
Weak media	Weak independent media imply weak social control over state officials and a distorted picture of developments in a country

Next, we need to identify the operators of malign influence, i.e. Russian state and non-state pro-Kremlin actors, that are engaged in political warfare in Europe and thus produce malign influence (Table 2). Furthermore, with regard to operators, we also need to identify the area(s) of their operation, the tools these operators use, and whether they also use any facilitators in Europe (Table 3).

After identifying operators, their tools and, possibly, their facilitators, as well as establishing the areas affected, we need to consider whether the malign influence operations helped the Kremlin achieve any tactical objectives that help the Kremlin achieve its strategic goals.

Finally, we need to discuss how the existing malign influence subverts European values and/or democratic institutions – it is this very effect that determines the malign nature of the influence operations of Putin's Russia.

2. Russian Election Interference in Africa
The Case of AFRIC

Introduction

At the end of July 2018, Zimbabwe held general elections to elect the president and members of both houses of parliament. The elections were held for the first time since the *coup d'état* in November 2017 that ousted President Robert Mugabe who had headed the country for 30 years. To enhance the legitimacy of the elections, Zimbabwean authorities decided to lift all restrictions on international election observation introduced by Mugabe, so hundreds of international observers were able to monitor the elections in the country.

One of the observation missions was coordinated by a little known and shady organisation called Association for Free Research and International Cooperation (AFRIC). The mission consisted of around 40 monitors many of whom had a history of involvement in various pro-Kremlin efforts, including previous participation in politically biased and/or illegitimate electoral monitoring missions organised by Russian actors, cooperation with the Russian state-controlled instruments of disinformation and propaganda, and dissemination of pro-Kremlin narratives on social media. While AFRIC positioned itself as an African organisation, investigative journalists revealed that AFRIC was organised by the people and structures linked to a Russian businessman, Yevgeniy Prigozhin.

Dubbed "Putin's chef" for providing restaurant services to the Kremlin and various Russian government agencies, Prigozhin had been, since 2014, involved in two major international developments. First, Prigozhin funded the so-called "Wagner Group", a private military company that first participated in the Russian invasion of Ukraine, fought on the side of Bashar al-Assad in the Syrian civil war, and later became involved in different campaigns across Africa.[29] Second, Prigozhin created the Internet Research Agency (better known as the "troll factory") that made attempts to subvert American democratic processes; for these attempts, the US Treasury Department's Office of Foreign Assets Control sanctioned Prigozhin in September 2019.[30]

The employment of the "Wagner Group" in Africa was determined by the need to protect Prigozhin's and, more generally, Russian interests either literally (safeguarding operations) or indirectly (providing military support for loyal politicians).[31] The latter activity overlapped with non-military support for particular African politicians and political forces that were seen by Prigozhin and his team of political consultants as useful for his endeavours. The now defunct AFRIC was part of those endeavours, and this chapter provides insights into the creation, development, and workings of AFRIC.

---

29   Kimberly Marten, "Russia's Use of Semi-State Security Forces: The Case of the Wagner Group", *Post-Soviet Affairs*, Vol. 35, No. 3 (2019), pp. 181-204; Nathaniel Reynolds, "Putin's Not-So-Secret Mercenaries: Patronage, Geopolitics, and the Wagner Group", *Carnegie Endowment for International Peace*, 8 July (2019), https://carnegieendowment.org/2019/07/08/putin-s-not-so-secret-mercenaries-patron age-geopolitics-and-wagnergroup-pub-79442; Kimberly Marten, "Into Africa: Prigozhin, Wagner, and the Russian Military", *PONARS Eurasia*, January (2019), https://www.ponarseurasia.org/into-africa-prigozhin-wagner-and-the-russian-military/; Michael Weiss, Pierre Vaux, "Russia's Wagner Mercenaries Have Moved into Libya. Good Luck with That", *The Daily Beast*, 28 September (2019), https://www.thedailybeast.com/russias-wagner-mercenaries-have-moved-into -libya-good-luck-with-that.

30   "Treasury Targets Assets of Russian Financier Who Attempted to Influence 2018 U.S. Elections", *US Department of the Treasury*, 30 September (2019), https://home.treasury.gov/news/press-releases/sm787.

31   See, for example, Dionne Searcey, "Gems, Warlords and Mercenaries: Russia's Playbook in Central African Republic", *New York Times*, 30 September (2019), https://www.nytimes.com/2019/09/30/world/russia-diamonds-africa-prig ozhin.html; Tim Lister, Sebastian Shukla, "Russian Mercenaries Fight Shadowy Battle in Gas-Rich Mozambique", *CNN*, 29 November (2019), https://www.cnn.com/2019/11/29/africa/russian-mercenaries-mozambique-intl/index.html.

The creation of AFRIC

A Russian-language PowerPoint presentation produced in April 2018 by the Russian consultants behind the creation of AFRIC[32] imagined its nature and activities as follows: (1) "expert groups in African countries", (2) "development and promotion of expert evaluations and opinions beneficial to Russia", (3) "a source of information for the media and international organisations", (4) "an alternative to organisations controlled by the US and EU and working on the African territory". According to the organisers, AFRIC would function as a "network of agents of influence" comprised of experts from African countries, as well as an Internet platform (www.afric.online) that would publish "news and analysis produced in accordance with our assignment". AFRIC would also organise forums and seminars, and send "reports and inquiries to international organisations and the media".

The presentation also described the financial aspect of the workings of AFRIC: "The funding will be provided in the form of anonymous donations in cryptocurrencies (Monero, Zcash, DASH) — it will be impossible to know who finances AFRIC". The presentation continued: "Experts register on the website, write articles and reports, organise events in accordance with our assignments and, for this, receive money in a cryptocurrency". In conclusion, the presentation listed the advantages of AFRIC: "anonymity; no need to register as a legal entity; no need for a public leader; activities are performed under the authority of the AFRIC platform, a community of independent experts; a 'smoke screen' and a cover for events; attractive modern format".

To sum up the presentation, AFRIC was envisaged as a Russian front organisation that would pretend to be an authentic African initiative but would effectively promote Russian political and economic interests in Africa.

AFRIC's website, which was run in English and French, was registered on 13 April 2018, but it was unclear where the website

---

32   Provided to the author by the Dossier Centre, a London-based organisation funded by Russian oligarch-turned-dissident Mikhail Khodorkovsky.

was hosted or who registered it, because it was protected by Cloud-flare Inc., a US company that proxies its traffic and makes it impossible to determine the location of the webhosting company.

Officially, AFRIC described itself as "a community of independent researchers, experts and activists", and its declared goals were to create "a platform for elaboration and dissemination of objective analytical information, first-hand opinions", and to establish "direct communication and cooperation".[33] The AFRIC website also claimed to be "supported by anonymous donations" that allowed "researchers to make publications, conduct research and receive remuneration for interesting materials". Explaining its use of cryptocurrencies, the website claimed that "AFRIC demonstrate[d] its independence from outdated financial and banking systems, [and] show[ed] the real freedom of opinions and analysis on the internet".[34]

A Russian operative who seemed to be originally responsible for setting up the AFRIC project was Yulia Afanasyeva, an employee of Prigozhin's back-office dealing with Africa, a manager of the Centre for Social and Cultural Initiatives (co-founded by Petr Bychkov, who headed the back office),[35] and a project manager at the International Anticrisis Centre, yet another project of Prigozhin's team. According to Afanasyeva's documents,[36] she would order notepads and pens with the AFRIC logo, coordinate the writing of articles for the AFRIC website, and formulate assignments for AFRIC members. In one communication, she wrote to her Russian addressees that she was looking for journalists and lecturers for the AFRIC project—those who could be international observers at the general elections in Zimbabwe on 30 July 2018.

One of the AFRIC experts with whom Afanasyeva exchanged messages about contributions to the AFRIC website was Russian-

---

33   "About AFRIC", *AFRIC*, https://web.archive.org/web/20180815142259/https://afric.online/about/.
34   Ibid.
35   Ilya Rozhdestvensky, Michael Rubin, Roman Badanin, "Master and Chef. How Russia Interfered in Elections in Twenty Countries", *Proekt*, 11 April (2019), https://www.proekt.media/investigation/russia-african-elections/.
36   Provided to the author by the Dossier Centre.

born Catherine Terekhova, who was based in France. Terekhova, whose professional background is in international trade, was the first person to have registered on LinkedIn as an employee of AFRIC, indicating that she started working for the organisation as an economic analyst in January 2018. One communication between Afanasyeva and Terekhova suggests that an African coordinator of AFRIC would provide a list of topics they were interested in and Afanasyeva would forward them to Terekhova so she could write on some of those topics in French.

It is unclear what African coordinator Afanasyeva referred to in her message to Terekhova, but it was most likely the Mozambican academic José Zacarias Samuel Matemulane, who at that time worked as Assistant Professor at the Mozambique Pedagogical University in Quelimane and was a president of AFRIC. Matemulane has a long history of involvement with Russian institutions and individuals. In the period between 2002 and 2012, he studied at four Russian universities and received a doctoral degree from the St. Petersburg State University. In June 2013, Matemulane registered a company, ATV Export Ltd., two of whose other co-founders were Russian citizens, Victor Prokopenko and Vitaly Solovyev.[37] On his Facebook page, Matemulane often posted messages praising Russian President Vladimir Putin and the Russian Defence Ministry.[38] Matemulane's LinkedIn page suggested that he became AFRIC's president in November 2017,[39] but this is doubtful as AFRIC appeared only in 2018.

When asked by journalists, Matemulane was first reluctant to reveal any information about the financial aspects of AFRIC's foundation, but speaking to a Mozambican journalist Alexandre Nhampossa, he stated that "the only Russian businessman who [had] been important in giving money" was Alexander Seravin, whom Matemulane described as a "mentor and tutor" as well as a "friend and colleague" — the two met in Russia when Matemulane was

---

37   "ATV Export, Limitada", *Boletim da República*, No. 52, 2 July (2013), pp. 56-58.
38   José Matemulane's account on Facebook: https://www.facebook.com/jose. matemulane. Currently deleted.
39   José Matemulane's account on LinkedIn: https://www.linkedin.com/in/jose matemulane-90002623/. Currently deleted.

doing his postgraduate study work in psychology at the Saint Petersburg State University.[40]

Alexander Seravin is a director of the research programmes of
the St. Petersburg-based expert group "PiteR", which provides political consultancy and public relations services and is headed by
Polina Sharonova. Seravin is an influential figure in the world of
Russian political consultancy. During the 2018 presidential campaign, he was Vladimir Putin's chief political strategist in St. Petersburg.[41] The Russian Presidential Administration engaged with him
several times over the years and seems to be pleased with his services. In 2019, Seravin was one of the chief political strategists of
Alexander Beglov, a member of the High Council of the ruling
"United Russia" party, who was running for (and eventually won)
the position of the Governor of Saint Petersburg.[42]

After the publication of the investigations into Prigozhin's activities in Africa, most notably two investigations by the *Proekt* website,[43] Seravin wrote a post on Facebook in which he essentially confirmed the involvement of Prigozhin's teams in African countries.
Moreover, Seravin praised Prigozhin for this involvement:

> One of the strongest modern centres of applied geopolitics is currently based
> in St. Petersburg and is related to Prigozhin. And, by the way, he is the only
> actor of this calibre in Russia. [He deals with] more than 30 countries simul-
> taneously, including Africa, CIS countries, Asia, Latin America, and the
> Arab world, as well as European countries — he is the largest employer for
> practitioners in [Russia], more than 300 specialists are working outside of
> the country in one capacity or another, and even more people are supporting
> this activity here [in Russia]. [...] Prigozhin is already a brand, both inside
> the country and across the world. [...] Some country leaders are afraid of him

---

40   "Afric Ran Mozambique Election Poll, but Denies Interference in Elections",
      Zitamar, 12 November (2019), https://zitamar.com/russia-backed-think-tank-
      admits-illegal-poll-denies-prigozhin-connection/.
41   Mariya Karpenko, Maksim Ivanov, Natalya Korchenkova, "Shtaby idut po
      shtatnomu raspisaniyu", *Kommersant*, 20 November (2017), https://www.kom
      mersant.ru/doc/3472992.
42   "Reyting vliyatel'nosti Sankt-Peterburga—2019", *Fontanka*, https://www.font
      anka.ru/longreads/reyting_best_people_2019/.
43   Ilya Rozhdestvensky, Roman Badanin, "Master and Chef. How Evgeny
      Prigozhin Led the Russian Offensive in Africa", *Proekt*, 14 March (2019),
      https://www.proekt.media/investigation/evgeny-prigozhin-africa/;   Rozh-
      destvensky, Rubin, Badanin, "Master and Chef".

and consider him an enemy, others are already dreaming of working with him. Prigozhin's technologists [i.e. consultants] have a number of convincing victories over American, Chinese, and French specialists to their names.[44]

Key figures of AFRIC

Apart from Afanasyeva, Matemulane, and Terekhova, AFRIC was represented by a number of people, many of whom, to various extents, have had relations with Russian individuals and institutions.

Mikael Cheuwa is the co-founder of AFRIC and its project coordinator. He was born in Cameroon and graduated from the University of Technology of Douala. He later studied at the Belgorod State Technological University (Russia), which he finished in 2015. An investigation by *Proekt* refers to Chewa as Afanasyeva's friend.[45]

Clifton Ellis is AFRIC's strategist and one of its project coordinators. He is based in the UK and founded, in 2018, the International Sustainable Energy Organisation, which claimed to work in Botswana, Central African Republic, Kenya, Republic of South Africa, and Tanzania.[46] However, after joining AFRIC in 2019, Ellis' organisation became inactive.

Vaiva Adomaityte joined AFRIC's administration in 2019. She is a Lithuanian citizen residing in the UK, where she founded, in 2017, ADMIS Consultancy Limited.

Volker Tschapke is the founder of the far-right Germany-based "Prussian Society". He began his career in AFRIC as an ordinary member of AFRIC's "observation" mission in Zimbabwe, but would later start coordinating its projects.

---

44   Seravin Aleks, "V otvet na mnogochislennye publikatsii...", *Facebook*, 17 May (2019), https://www.facebook.com/seravin.aleks/posts/1848198441946429.
45   Rozhdestvensky, Rubin, Badanin, "Master and Chef".
46   "Clifton Ellis", *Roscongress*, https://roscongress.org/en/speakers/ellis-klifton /biography/.

Figure 1.   AFRIC and its place in the structure of Yevgeniy Prigozhin's main "foreign policy" projects (2019)

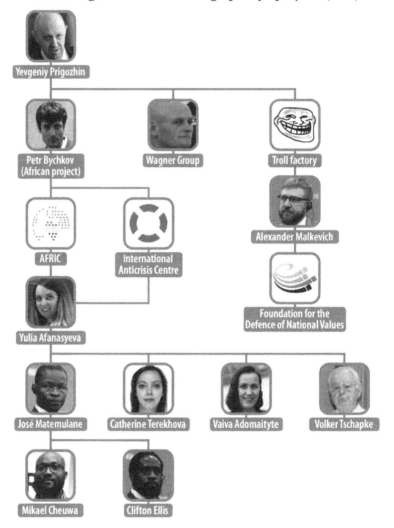

AFRIC's election observation missions

As demonstrated earlier, AFRIC was originally imagined as a network of agents of influence and a platform that would disseminate Africa-related narratives beneficial to the interests of the Russian state. However, in the period between 2018 and 2019, AFRIC

became engaged in yet another activity that did not seem to be originally projected, namely politically biased, or fake, observation of
elections in Africa. Fake observation is a form of political activity
performed by international actors with the aim of advancing interests of certain politicians and political forces by imitating credible
election monitoring during electoral processes. Aims of domestic
and third-party organisers of politically biased election observation
include, but are not limited to:

- whitewashing electoral fraud for domestic and international audiences;
- legitimising electoral processes considered illegitimate or
  illegal by the international community;
- delegitimising and weakening the institution of free and
  fair elections;
- subverting and/or relativising findings of credible election
  observation;
- weakening political rivals;
- building networks of influence not necessarily related to
  electoral processes.

AFRIC's function as a fake election observation organisation is re-
flected in its description on the list of Prigozhin's "global projects":
"AFRIC is a controlled community of loyal authors and public figures from African and European countries who produce analytical
materials and observation missions".[47]

In 2018-2019, AFRIC's loyal monitors "observed" the following elections, discussed in this section:

- Zimbabwean general election held on 30 July 2018
- Malagasy presidential election (first round) held on 7 No-
  vember 2018
- Democratic Republic of the Congo general election held on
  30 December 2018
- South African general election held on 8 May 2019

---

47   "Iz Rossii s lyubovyu: kak MID RF pomogaet 'chestnym' vyboram i kiber-
     bezopasnosti v Evrope i Afrike", *Dossier*, https://dossier.center/from-russia-
     with-love/.

- Mozambican general election held on 15 October 2019

Although the Malagasy presidential election took place later than the Zimbabwean general election, Madagascar became the first African country where Prigozhin's structures became involved in the electoral process. As the Malagasy case is also the most indicative in terms of interference in African elections by Prigozhin's structures, this example will be discussed first.

2018 Malagasy presidential election

According to an investigation by *Proekt*, Prigozhin became interested in Africa around the end of 2017. At that time, he presented to Putin an idea of strengthening Russian influence in the world and finding opportunities to push China aside in the Third World countries.[48] In January 2018, two political consultants from St. Petersburg, namely Oleg Zakhariyash and Valeriy Porubov, wrote a report—apparently commissioned by Prigozhin's structures—on the "political and socio-economic situation in the Republic of Madagascar".[49] However, the report not only covered political history and developments in Madagascar, but also projected the "structure of a technological [i.e. political consultancy] group" that would work in the country in order to advance their Russian patron's interests during the 2018 presidential election. The group would feature 31 people, including a head of the team, analysts, a lawyer, media monitors, coordinators of a "troll factory" and a "call-centre", and interpreters. It is not clear whether this proposed framework was approved, but the "Malagasy project" was apparently set in action.

In March 2018, Hery Rajaonarimampianina, who was Malagasy President at that time, visited Russia and met with Putin and Prigozhin. According to one report, Harison E. Randriarimanana, a former agriculture minister who accompanied Rajaonarimampianina to Moscow, "said that after the meeting his boss proudly

---

48   Rozhdestvensky, Badanin, "Master and Chef".
49   Provided to the author by the Dossier Centre.

announced that Mr. Putin had agreed to assist with his re-election campaign".[50]

The same month, 15-20 Russian political consultants headed by Zakhariyash arrived in Madagascar.[51] However, instead of directly supporting Rajaonarimampianina, Russian consultants split into several teams that aimed at assisting several presidential candidates in their campaigns. This can be explained by tactical considerations of supporting spoiler candidates who would be dropped at a later stage to channel all electoral support to one particular candidate. Yet another viable explanation is that Russian consultants and the Kremlin simply did not want to put all their eggs in one basket, especially against the background of poor understanding of the Malagasy politics on the part of the Russian operatives.

One Russian team, consisting of Andrey Kramar, Roman Pozdnyakov, and Vladimir Boyarishev, approached pastor André Christian Dieu Donné Mailhol, the leader of the Apocalypse Church, and offered to fully fund his presidential campaign. Mailhol accepted the offer and the Russian team brought him around €5,000 in cash and paid around €12,000 for the deposit for the presidential campaign,[52] as well as wrote some of his speeches and paid for campaign posters and television advertising.[53] Mailhol knew that the Russian operatives supported several candidates, and even signed a contract with the Russian team promising to support one of those "Russian candidates" who would turn out to be more popular than others.[54]

Yet another Russian team, which included political consultant Maxim Shugaley, approached former Prime Minister Jean Omer

50   Michael Schwirtz, Gaelle Borgia, "How Russia Meddles abroad for Profit: Cash, Trolls and a Cult Leader", *New York Times*, 11 November (2019), https://www.nytimes.com/2019/11/11/world/africa/russia-madagascar-election.html.
51   Rozhdestvensky, Badanin, "Master and Chef".
52   "Russia's Madagascar Election Gamble — Full documentary — BBC Africa Eye", *BBC News Africa*, 8 April (2019), https://www.youtube.com/watch?v=6wH6 4iztZM0.
53   Schwirtz, Borgia, "How Russia Meddles abroad for Profit".
54   "Russia's Madagascar Election Gamble — Full documentary — BBC Africa Eye".

Beriziky and offered him just under $2 million, but eventually paid less than $500 thousand.[55]

Two Russian operatives approached Zafimahaleo Dit Dama Mahaleo Rasolofondraosolo and "tried to pressure him to support a delay in the election so that the incumbent [i.e. Rajaonarimampianina] had more time to campaign". According to Rasolofondraosolo, he refused to cooperate with the Russian consultants.[56]

Rajaonarimampianina himself denied that he took money from Russian consultants but he wrote a letter addressed to the leader of the Russian group in Madagascar, Oleg Zakhariyash, requesting Russian help to "to resist attempts by international institutions to interfere" in Madagascar's election.[57] Rajaonarimampianina also argued that the Kremlin might have "worked to assist him without his knowledge", which is difficult to believe given the outcomes of his meeting with Putin in March 2018 and the fact that Rajaonarimampianina's campaign cooperated with the Russian consultants.[58]

An investigation by *Proekt* argues that Russian consultants tried to help four more presidential candidates: Jean Ravelonarivo, Saraha Rabeharisoa, Olivier Mahafaly Solonandrasana, and Andry Rajoelina.[59]

AFRIC appeared in Madagascar in August 2018, i.e. shortly after its "election observation mission" in Zimbabwe in July that year. Its first official activity was the International Economic Forum "Madagascar 2018" that took place in Antananarivo. According to AFRIC's report—which read as a bad translation from Russian—the forum discussed "the position of Madagascar in the context of African countries" and assessed "the current situation through the prism of post-colonial experience of the country", as well as considered options of "overcoming the infrastructure crisis" and

---

55   Ibid.
56   Schwirtz, Borgia, "How Russia Meddles abroad for Profit".
57   Ibid.
58   Rozhdestvensky, Badanin, "Master and Chef".
59   Ibid.

"attracting investment".[60] The true objectives of the forum, however, were different. First, AFRIC—in cooperation with the Russian
political consultants—gave a platform to several presidential candidates supported by the Russian operatives, including Beriziky,
Rasolofondraosolo, Mailhol, and Rabeharisoa. Second, the leadership of AFRIC used the forum to push its anti-Western narrative:
they invited French-Beninese far-right activist Kémi Séba (real
name: Stellio Gilles Robert Capo Chichi) to speak about the "harmful consequences of French colonialism" and "French financiers"
who allegedly retained "influence on the economy" of Madagascar.[61] Russian operatives and AFRIC needed the anti-Western spin
in order to discourage the Malagasy public from supporting pro-
Western presidential candidates.

Anti-Western and anti-French messages were central to yet
another conference, organised by AFRIC in cooperation with the
pan-African TV channel Afrique Media and called "The Islands of
Hope". The conference hosted Mailhol and Séba, and urged France
to return the Scattered Islands in the Indian Ocean "to their rightful
owners".[62] These islands constitute the 5th district of the French
Southern and Antarctic Lands, but France's sovereignty over them
is disputed by Madagascar, Mauritius, and the Comoros. During
his emotional speech, Séba, in particular, said:

> France, get out of our territories, you have no right to be there! [...] Africans
> have more trust in Russia than in the US or France. [...] We don't need to ask
> the permission of the West to regain the lands that are our right. We just
> need to ally ourselves with good geostrategic and geopolitical forces. [...]
> The 21st century will be one of African independence. Free Africa or death.
> We will be victorious.

---

60   "International Economic Forum 'Madagascar 2018'", *AFRIC*, 27 August (2018),
      https://web.archive.org/web/20190426104348/https://afric.online/projects
      /embassy-of-transparency-and-legitimacy/.
61   Ibid.
62   "The Resolutions of the International Conference 'The Islands of Hope' (The
      Territorial Dispute of the Scattered Islands)", *AFRIC*, 28 September (2018),
      https://afric.online/projects/outcomes-of-the-international-conferences-the-
      islands-of-hope-the-territorial-dispute-of-the-scattered-islands/.

The day after the conference, Séba participated in an anti-French protest in front of the French Embassy. Addressing the Embassy and his alleged supporters, Séba shouted: "Madagascar has the right to own the Scattered Isles! France must stop giving the world lessons when they are colonisers! [...] France must leave Madagascar alone! France must allow Madagascar to have its own wealth! Down with colonialism! Down with imperialism!". After the protest, it was revealed that the Russian consultants paid money to demonstrators for their participation in the protest. Moreover, because the protest was illegal (the organisers had not secured an official permit), police arrested Séba and the Russian operatives who worked with Mailhol, namely Kramar, Pozdnyakov, and Boyarishev, and later banned them from entering Madagascar.[63]

The presence of Séba at the events organised by the Russian consultants in support of particular presidential candidates was hardly accidental. A convicted anti-Semite and Black racist, Séba had been for years promoting pan-Africanism and cooperating with various European far-right organisations with the aim of amplifying their anti-immigrant and anti-multiculturalist messages to persuade Black people to return to African countries.[64] On 13 September 2017, Séba met with Russian fascist Alexander Dugin in Moscow to exchange ideas about their struggle against the West. Séba referred to Dugin as "the most important theoretician and political adviser in Russia",[65] while Dugin would write a preface to Séba's book *L'Afrique libre ou la mort* [Free Africa or Death], in which he praised Séba for his opposition to Western "mental colonialism" and for being "not just a chance for Africa" but also "a hope for all the forces of multipolar resistance".[66]

---

63   "Russia's Madagascar Election Gamble – Full documentary – BBC Africa Eye".
64   Cristiano Lanzano, "Why Are Italian Fascists Approvingly Quoting Samora Machel and Sankara?", *Africa Is Our Country*, 9 September (2018), https://africasacountry.com/2018/09/twisting-pan-africanism-to-promote-anti-africanism.
65   Ignace Sossou, "Russie: Kemi Seba reçu par Alexandre Douguine, l'idéologue de Vladimir Poutine", *Benin Web TV*, 13 December (2017), https://web.archive.org/web/20190420051539/https://beninwebtv.com/2017/12/russie-kemi-seba-recu-alexandre-douguine-lideologue-de-vladimir-poutine/.
66   Alexander Dugin, "Free Africa or Death!", *Geopolitica*, https://www.geopolitica.ru/en/article/free-africa-or-death.

In recent years, Dugin has been working for a Russian ultra-nationalist businessman, Konstantin Malofeev, who has been sanctioned by the EU and US for his material and financial support of violent pro-Russian separatists in Eastern Ukraine. Malofeev expressed his interest in investing in African countries, and in July 2018 began pushing a narrative about Russia and Africa that was very similar to the ideas that Séba promoted in Madagascar:

> Africa is a very important issue of the 21st century. Africa got liberated from the colonial rule 40-50 years ago, but it still suffers from economic colonial dependence on former metropoles and the West in general. It is very important for Russia not to blunder Africa away. [...] Africa possesses natural resources, and the West and the Chinese will all be out for them, so we need to be present there for the balance and because the Africans trust us most of all.[67]

According to *Proekt*'s investigation, it was around this time that the Russian consultants working in Madagascar started to cooperate with Séba and amplify his anti-Western and anti-French narratives with the aim of undermining pro-Western presidential candidates.

In the beginning of November 2018, just a few days before the first round of the presidential election, it emerged that AFRIC partnered up with yet another controversial election observation mission, namely CIS-EMO, which is arguably the oldest Russian organisation that has been involved in international politically biased election observation since 2003-2004.[68] AFRIC claimed that it sent 36 international observers from Benin, Cameroon, Chad, France, Gabon, Germany, Mongolia, Mozambique, Portugal, Russia, Senegal, and South Africa.[69] In its turn, CIS-EMO's representatives

---

67 "Malofeev: Afrika—eto pole dlya geopoliticheskikh bitv XXI veka", *Tsargrad TV*, 1 August (2018), https://www.youtube.com/watch?v=-IgW95LVsVs.

68 See more on CIS-EMO in Anton Shekhovtsov, "Far-Right Election Observation Monitors in the Service of the Kremlin's Foreign Policy", in Marlène Laruelle (ed.), *Eurasianism and the European Far Right: Reshaping the Europe-Russia Relationship* (Lanham: Lexington Books, 2017), pp. 223-243.

69 "Presidential Election in Madagascar: AFRIC Observers in the Field", *AFRIC*, 6 November (2018), https://afric.online/projects/presidential-election-in-madagascar-afric-observersin-the-field/; Catherine T. [Terekhova], "Presidential Elections-2018 in Madagascar: A Diary of Monitoring Mission", *AFRIC*, 12 November (2018), https://afric.online/projects/presidential-elections-2018-in-madagascar-a-diary-of-monitoring-mission/.

reported that they deployed a team of 55 international observers from Bulgaria, Poland, Nigeria, and Russia to monitor the presidential election in Madagascar.[70]

CIS-EMO and Prigozhin's team are connected to each other through the background of some of its members. Executive director of CIS-EMO Stanislav Byshok is a former activist of the Russian neo-Nazi group "Russian Image", the leader of which was given a life sentence for a number of serious crimes, including ordering assassinations. At the same time, several members of Prigozhin's structures were members of the "Russian Image". For example, Anna Bogacheva, a former member of this neo-Nazi group, was even sanctioned by the US for "material and technological support" to the Internet Research Agency.[71] Moreover, Mikhail Potepkin, one of the key figures in Prigozhin's team dealing with Africa, has extensive social contacts among former members of the "Russian Image".[72]

On 5 November, AFRIC and CIS-EMO held a joint press conference. At this event, the two organisations revealed that they were going to conduct an exit-poll on the voting day with the help of a local company called Safidiko Madagasikara.[73] This revelation drew questions from Malagasy journalists and criticism from the Independent National Election Commission (Commission Electorale Nationale Indépendante, CENI), because not only is the Malagasy population unaccustomed to exit-polls, but the latter are also illegal in Madagascar. AFRIC and CIS-EMO requested an authorisation from the CENI to conduct an exit-poll. Having received no such authorisation, and despite having been warned by the CENI

---

70   "Mezhdunarodnye nablyudateli obsudili predstoyashchie vybory prezidenta Madagaskara", CIS-EMO, 6 November (2018), http://www.cis-emo.net/ru/news/mezhdunarodnyenablyudateli-obsudili-predstoyashchie-vybory-prezidenta-madagaskara.
71   "Treasury Sanctions Russian Cyber Actors for Interference with the 2016 U.S. Elections and Malicious Cyber-Attacks", *US Department of the Treasury*, 15 March (2018), https://home.treasury.gov/news/press-releases/sm0312.
72   Mark Krutov, Sergey Dobrynin, Aleksandr Litoy, "'Russkiy obraz' Prigozhina", *Radio Svoboda*, 2 October (2019), https://www.svoboda.org/a/30195584.html.
73   "Revue de presse du 8 novembre 2018", *PEV Madagascar*, 8 November (2018), https://www.pevmadagascar.eu/main/post/article/1235.

about the illegality of the exit-poll, they forged the documents allegedly issued by the Malagasy electoral office allowing them to proceed.[74] The forgery was revealed when the pollsters hired by AFRIC and CIS-EMO were met with protests from the Malagasy voters who were shocked by the fact that the pollsters asked them about their voting preferences. After these protests drew attention of the public, a representative of the CENI went on air urging the pollsters to immediately stop their activity and requesting the police to take necessary actions against the pollsters.[75] As a result, AFRIC and CIS-EMO did not see their accreditation renewed by the CENI,[76] and — since the vote on 7 November could not establish a winner of the presidential election — they were forbidden to observe the second round of the election on 27 December, and left Madagascar.

This fiasco did not affect the activities of the Russian consultants who were working with several presidential candidates. They had a different problem, however: none of "their candidates" made it to the second round of the presidential election. In anticipation of this failure, Russian operatives decided to support a presidential hopeful, Andry Rajoelina, apparently even without his consent, just to create the impression that Russia was helping him. Russian consultants asked "their candidates" to drop out of the race and support Rajoelina, but none of them agreed.[77] Eventually, Rajoelina won the second round and Russian operatives brazenly took credit for his victory. For example, Alexander Seravin complimented Prigozhin's political consultants on not letting "the pro-American candidate Marc Ravalomanana with unlimited funding" win the election.[78]

---

74 "Sondages: des enquêteurs sement le trouble", *NewsMada*, 8 November (2018), https://www.newsmada.com/2018/11/08/sondages-des-enqueteurs-sement
    -le-trouble/.
75 "Revue de presse du 8 novembre 2018".
76 "Madagascar 2018", *European Union External Action*, 7 November (2018), https://eeas.europa.eu/sites/eeas/files/moeuemada18_rapport_final_fr_0.pdf.
77 Schwirtz, Borgia, "How Russia Meddles abroad for Profit"; "Russia's Madagascar Election Gamble — Full documentary — BBC Africa Eye".
78 Seravin, "V otvet na mnogochislennye publikatsii...".

2018 Zimbabwean general election

In Yulia Afanasyeva's above-mentioned letter, in which she wrote that she was looking for international observers for the general election in Zimbabwe, she also mentioned that she would be travelling to the Republic of South Africa and Zimbabwe in June-July 2018. Indeed, Zimbabwe was one of the African countries where political consultants connected to Prigozhin's structures interfered in elections.[79]

Prigozhin's involvement in the Zimbabwean general election was preceded by a number of high-profile contacts between Russian and Zimbabwean officials. For example, in March 2018, Russia's Foreign Minister Sergey Lavrov visited Zimbabwe's capital Harare and met with President Emmerson Mnangagwa, who led a coup d'état in November 2017 that ousted President Robert Mugabe, who had headed the country for 30 years. During his visit, Lavrov passed on a message from Putin, who "expressed his support for Mnangagwa's efforts to stabilise domestic developments, consolidate the society, and develop international cooperation".[80] Already then, it was evident that the Kremlin supported the re-election of Mnangagwa in the general election. Later that same month, the head of the Zimbabwe Electoral Commission Priscilla Chigumba and Mnangagwa's special advisor Christopher Mutsvangwa visited Moscow. Chigumba met with a member of Russia's Central Election Commission, Nikolay Levichev, and "discussed issues of electoral sovereignty [and] technological instruments used to conduct elections in different countries".[81]

Around the beginning of June 2018, a St. Petersburg-based political consultant, Valentin Bianki, who was connected to

---

79   Henry Meyer, Ilya Arkhipov, Aina Rahagalala, "Putin's Notorious 'Chef' Is Now Meddling across Africa", *Bloomberg*, 20 November (2018), https://www.bloomberg.com/news/features/2018-11-20/putin-chef-yevgeny-prigozhin-is-now-meddling-in-africa.

80   "Lavrov provyol peregovory s zimbabviyskim kollegoy Moyo", *RIA Novosti*, 29 June (2018), https://ria.ru/20180629/1523690145.html.

81   "Chlen TsIK Rossii Nikolay Levichev provyol vstrechu s glavoy izbirkoma Zimbabve Pristsilloy Chigumba", *TsIK Rossii*, 22 March (2018), http://www.cikrf.ru/news/cec/39421/.

Prigozhin's African projects,[82] presented a report on the upcoming election in Zimbabwe.[83] The report was based on research apparently conducted in the period between 25 May and 8 June 2018, and analysed the political landscape in the country. In particular, the report identified two main presidential candidates, namely Mnangagwa and the leader of the opposition Nelson Chamisa. Bianki noted that Zimbabwean users of social networks largely supported Chamisa, who had managed to unite the opposition was indirectly supported by the ousted Mugabe. The report also suggested that the legitimacy of the election was low and projected that — were Mnangagwa's victory to be announced already in the first round — the opposition would organise a continuous protest in Harare.[84] In order to secure Mnangagwa's re-election, Bianki proposed, in particular, the following: to employ an anti-Western narrative in an appeal to the nation: "Let us not allow the US and UK to colonise us again, to bleed our resources dry"; to disclose "a connection between Chamisa and Mugabe [...], and declare it illegal", which is to be followed by criminal prosecution or Chamisa's withdrawal from the elections"; and to introduce "spoiler candidates in order to undermine support for Chamisa".

In order to enhance "the external legitimacy of the elections", Bianki's report suggested to involve "observers from Russia, and countries from Africa and Europe". Bianki could not have been unaware of the fact that already in April 2018, Zimbabwe's Ministry for Foreign Affairs declared that it would invite international observers from the EU, Commonwealth of Nations, United States, and Australia, among other countries, ending the ban on Western

---

82   Olga Churakova, "V stranakh Afriki rabotayut do 200 polittekhnologov, svyazannykh s Prigozhinym", *TV Rain*, 20 March (2019), https://tvrain.ru/news/v_stranah_afriki_rabotajut_do_200_polittehnologov_svjazannyh_s_prig ozhinym-482346/.
83   Provided to the author by the Dossier Centre.
84   Indeed, Mnangagwa's victory was announced already after the first round. The opposition started a protest, but the Zimbabwean army loyal to Mnangagwa violently cracked down on the protests killing six demonstrators, arresting and beating up dozens of others. See Krista Mahr, "Zimbabwe Politics Is Still in Turmoil as Opposition Challenges Election Results", *Los Angeles Times*, 21 August (2018), https://www.latimes.com/world/la-fg-zimbabwe-election20180821-st ory.html.

observation of Zimbabwean elections introduced by Mugabe in 2002, as he believed that Western observers favoured his opponents. What Bianki's report implied was that it would be difficult to legitimise Mnangagwa's victory already in the first round of the presidential election, and it was the legitimacy of that particular outcome that needed enhancing with the help of loyal observers.

To "observe" the election in Zimbabwe, AFRIC dispatched – as it claimed – 43 monitors from Cape Verde, Germany, Mongolia, Mozambique, Republic of South Africa, Russia, Sweden, Switzerland, and Ukraine. Even before the election took place, it became clear that AFRIC directly supported Mnangagwa. For example, two days before the election, Matemulane declared that Mnangagwa "was sticking to his promises of a free, fair and credible election", and stressed that AFRIC's presence in Zimbabwe aimed "to fulfil the goals of acting as the real embassy of transparency and legitimacy of the upcoming election process". Moreover, Matemulane also played an anti-Western card – fully in accordance with Bianki's suggestions – when he indirectly attacked the US and EU: "We fully share and strongly embrace the belief that African problems require African solutions on the contrary to 'Euro or Amero-Africanised' solutions which are brought and implemented by Western States financing organisations and are used to get incredible profits for themselves".[85]

On the eve of the election, Chamisa claimed that Mnangagwa was working with Russia to win the election, but the authorities naturally dismissed Chamisa's claims.[86] Mnangagwa won the election with 50.8% of the vote, while Chamisa obtained 44.3%. In its statement on the Zimbabwean election, the EU Election Observation Mission concluded that "the elections were competitive, the campaign was largely peaceful and, overall, political freedoms during the pre-election campaign, including freedom of movement, assembly and speech, were respected". At the same time, the EU

---

85   Felex Share, "ED Walks the Talk – AFRIC", *Chronicle*, 28 July (2018), https://www.chronicle.co.zw/ed-walks-the-talk-afric/.
86   Felex Share, "Chamisa Threatens Anarchy", *The Herald*, 12 July (2018), https://www.herald.co.zw/chamisa-threatens-anarchy/.

Mission noted that "the misuse of state resources, instances of coercion and intimidation, partisan behaviour by traditional leaders and overt bias in state media, all in favour of the ruling party, meant that a truly level playing field was not achieved, which negatively impacted on the democratic character of the pre-electoral environment".[87]

As one might expect, AFRIC praised the Zimbabwean election. For example, Mirjam Katharina Zwingli "was positively impressed by the organisation [of] the presidential election".[88] In her opinion, the election was "a symbolic gesture that Zimbabwe ha[d] come to international standards in terms of holding democratic processes". Another AFRIC "observer", Rishabh Sethi, thanked the Zimbabwe Electoral Commission "for conducting elections in a very successful manner". In his comment, Russian political consultant from Prigozhin's team Fedor Turygin stated that Mnangagwa had "kept his word" to hold transparent, competitive, and legitimate elections.[89] In its joint statement, AFRIC declared that its "observers" had noticed "no signs of electoral fraud, voter intimidation or external interference in the process".[90] It is hardly surprising that comments from AFRIC were actively disseminated by state-owned, pro-Mnangagwa media such as *The Herald* or *The Chronicle*.

2018 Democratic Republic of the Congo general election

On 30 October 2018, the Congolese newspaper *Le Potentiel* published an article that accused Russia of meddling in the forthcoming

---

87   "EUEOM Zimbabwe Final Report on the 2018 Harmonised Elections", *European Union External Action*, 9 October (2018), https://eeas.europa.eu/topics/scie nce-diplomacy/51896/eueom-zimbabwe-final-report-2018-harmonised-electi ons_en.

88   Tendai Mugabe, Muchaneta Chimuka, "Observer Teams Give Polls Thumbs up", *The Herald*, 1 August (2018), https://www.herald.co.zw/observer-teams-give-polls-thumbs-up/.

89   Fedor Turygin, "As a Part of AFRIC Team, Our Group of International Observers Went to Matabeleland", *Zimbabwe Today*, 1 August (2018), https://www.fa cebook.com/ZimbabweTodayLive/posts/2139352939654144.

90   "AFRIC Observers Mission Statement", *AFRIC*, 1 August (2018), https://af ric.online/607afric-observers-mission-statement/.

general election in the Democratic Republic of the Congo (DRC) by supplying military equipment to the DRC's Independent National Electoral Commission.[91] The 2018 election in the DRC was the first election since 2011, when Joseph Kabila won the presidency. Kabila's second and last presidential term expired in 2016, but for two years he was unwilling to leave his post and hold a new election, and only due to domestic and international pressure he was eventually forced to schedule the election for the end of 2018.

After the publication of the article in *Le Potentiel*, Russia denied any interference or supply of military equipment, but acknowledged that it had delivered trucks to meet the logistical needs of the election.[92] However, Russian meddling was one of the talking points for the opposition to Kabila and the presidential candidates he presumably supported. One of the opposition leaders, Martin Fayulu, said that Kabila was "desperate for outside help", adding that it was not surprising that Russia was "moving into the Congo, given our vast mineral wealth".[93]

While the full extent of Russian interference in the 2018 DRC election is yet be uncovered, it has been established that AFRIC sent its monitors to "observe" the Congolese election, which took place on 30 December, after its fiasco in Madagascar, when the authorities had forbidden AFRIC and another Russian organisation, CIS-EMO, to observe the second round of the presidential election. According to AFRIC, it deployed to the DRC 35 monitors from Belarus, Benin, Burkina Faso, Cameroon, Chad, Gabon, Germany, India, Malaysia, Mongolia, Mozambique, Republic of South Africa, Russia, Senegal, Serbia, Sweden, Turkey, and UK.[94]

---

91   "Processus électoral en RDC: l'ingérence russe se manifeste", *Le Potentiel*, 30 October (2018), https://web.archive.org/web/20190301085834/https://lepo tentielonline.net/2018/10/30/processus-electoral-en-rdc-lingerence-russe-se-manifeste/.

92   "O statye v kongolezskoy gazete 'Le Potentiel' na temu yakoby rossiyskogo vmeshatel'stva v vybory v DR Kongo", *Posol'stvo Rosskiyskoy Federatsii v Demokraticheskoy Respublike Kongo*, https://drc.mid.ru/home/-/asset_publisher/l9b1R1GqnEb5/content/o-fejkovoj-novosti-vgazete-le-potentiel-.

93   Meyer, Arkhipov, Rahagalala, "Putin's Notorious 'Chef' Is Now Meddling across Africa".

94   "Report of the International Observation Mission of the Presidential Elections in DR Congo of December 30th, 2018", *AFRIC*, 11 January (2019),

According to official results, Félix Tshisekedi won the election by securing 38.57% of the vote, while his nearest competitor Martin Fayulu obtained 34.83%. However, Fayulu challenged the election results claiming that outgoing President Kabila had made a deal with the President-elect Tshisekidi and that the results of the election had been "rigged, fabricated and invented" and did "not reflect the truth of the ballots".[95] Fayulu's claims were supported by several institutions and countries. A joint investigation by *The Financial Times* and France 24 revealed as massive electoral fraud: an analysis of "a trove of election data [...] representing 86 per cent of total votes cast across the country" showed that "Mr Fayulu won 59.4 per cent of the vote. Rival opposition candidate Mr Tshisekedi, who was declared the surprise winner last week, finished second with 19 per cent".[96] The Catholic Church, which posted 40 thousand election observers, also said that the official results did not match its findings.[97] Furthermore, France and Belgium challenged the results,[98] while the Southern African Development Community (SADC) called for a recount of the votes, hoping that it "would provide the necessary reassurance to both winners and losers".[99]

As one might have expected, while the AFRIC mission did notice "a number of irregularities" during the voting process, it stated that "overall, the elections was [sic] organized in accordance with

---

https://afric.online/projects/international-election-observation-mission-repo rt-in-dr-congo-of-december-30th/.

95   "The Latest: Opposition Candidate Fayulu Denounces Results", *AP*, 10 January (2019), https://apnews.com/64b3de3ee8e1482682d16654b20f517e.

96   Tom Wilson, David Blood, David Pilling, "Congo Voting Data Reveal Huge Fraud in Poll to Replace Kabila", *Financial Times*, 15 January (2019), https:// www.ft.com/content/2b97f6e6189d-11e9-b93e-f4351a53f1c3. See also "DR Congo Presidential Vote Plagued by Fraud, Media Investigation Finds", *France 24*, 17 January (2019), https://www.france24.com/en/20190117-dr-congo-elec tion-fraud-kabila-fayula-tshisekedi.

97   "DR Congo Presidential Election: Church Questions Results", *BBC*, 10 January (2019), https://www.bbc.com/news/world-africa-46827760.

98   "France, Belgium Cast Doubt on DR Congo Election Result", *Al Jazeera*, 10 January (2019), https://www.aljazeera.com/news/2019/01/france-belgium-cast-doubt-dr-congo-electionresult-190110091040088.html.

99   "Regional Body SADC Calls for DR Congo Election Vote Recount", *Al Jazeera*, 14 January (2019), https://www.aljazeera.com/news/2019/1/14/regional-body-sadc-calls-for-dr-congo-election-vote-recount.

the electoral law of the country".[100] Equally unsurprising was that Russia hailed Tshisekedi's alleged victory,[101] and – together with China – "led calls at the United Nations Security Council [...] for world powers to stay out of an election dispute in the Democratic Republic of Congo".[102]

On 12 January 2019, Fayulu filed a court appeal disputing the official results of the election, but the Constitutional Court rejected his appeal on 20 January.

2019 South African general election

The contents of Afanasyeva's letter cited above make it clear that Prigozhin's team started working on the 2019 South African general election already in 2018. Documents produced by Prigozhin's team with regard to South African election[103] reveal that Russian political consultants supported the governing African National Congress (ANC) and attacked the opposition, namely the Democratic Alliance and Economic Freedom Fighters. The documents also show that Russian operatives started passing their recommendations to the representatives of the ANC on how to advance their party and damage the opposition as early as autumn 2018. These recommendations included, in particular, talking points to be used by the ANC, descriptions of methods of discrediting the opposition, as well as explanations of how to approach different social and age groups.

---

100 "Report of the International Observation Mission of the Presidential Elections in DR Congo".
101 Henry Foy, "Russia Hails Tshisekedi as Congo Election Winner", *Financial Times*, 21 January (2019), https://www.ft.com/content/a503cbe8-1d81-11e9-b2f7-97e4dbd3580d.
102 "Russia, China Push UN to Stay out of DR Congo Poll Dispute", *France 24*, 11 January (2019), https://www.france24.com/en/20190111-russia-china-push-u n-stay-out-dr-congopoll-dispute.
103 Roman Popkov, "Yuzhnaya Afrika: kak polittekhnologi Prigozhina pomogayut na vyborakh pravyashchey partii", *MBKh Media*, 7 May (2019), https://www. mbk.news/suzhet/yuzhnaya-afrika-polittexnologi-prigozhina/; Ferial Haffajee, "Exclusive: Did Putin's 'Chef' Attempt to Interfere in South African Election?", *Daily Maverick*, 7 May (2019), https://www.dailymaverick.co.za/arti cle/2019-05-07-exclusive-did-putins-chef-attempt-to-interfere-in-south-african -election/.

In early April 2019, i.e. about a month before the election that took place on 8 May, Afanasyeva wrote a brief summarising the activities of Prigozhin's team in South Africa.[104] The brief, among other matters, stated: "A group of Russian specialists renders continuous consultancy services providing recommendations and cases for the campaign and public speeches, supporting the ANC and discrediting the DA [Democratic Alliance] and EFF [Economic Freedom Fighters], as well as analysis of the ways to undermine the growth of support for smaller parties". In Afanasyeva's words, the consultancy services were underpinned by loyalty to Russia and aimed at developing two projects of Prigozhin's team – namely the International Anticrisis Centre and AFRIC – that conducted research and provided recommendations to the ANC. The same brief mentioned that 25 AFRIC monitors would observe the election in South Africa.

However, other documents – including AFRIC's website[105] – suggest that AFRIC deployed 20 monitors. A cost sheet covering AFRIC's "observation" mission in South Africa and presumably approved by Petr Bychkov, the head Prigozhin's back office in St. Petersburg, indicated that AFRIC's monitors travelled from Benin, Germany, India, Mongolia, Mozambique, Serbia, Sweden, and Switzerland.[106] The cost sheet also provided information on the financial aspect of AFRIC's monitors: they received $800 (around €715) for six days of their activities in South Africa and $40 (around €36) for subsistence per day. Interestingly, the same document specified the costs for notepads, pens, vests, and memory sticks – all featuring AFRIC's logo – in Russian roubles, in contrast to all the other costs indicated in US dollars, which implies that these accessories were purchased most likely in Russia.

Established international missions representing the African Union, Electoral Institute for Sustainable Democracy in Africa, and

---

104 Provided to the author by the Dossier Centre.
105 "South Africa: AFRIC Association Deploys Observers for Coming Elections", *AFRIC*, 4 May (2019), https://web.archive.org/web/20191027162127/https://afric.online/projects/south-africa-afric-association-deploys-election-observers-for-coming-elections/.
106 Provided to the author by the Dossier Centre.

SADC generally commended South Africa for the conduct of the election.[107] AFRIC's statement was no different, as it considered the election "largely transparent, free and fair".[108] The ANC, which Prigozhin's team supported, won the election by obtaining 57.50% of the vote. This was the lowest result for the ANC since 1994, when the first election after the end of apartheid took place, but it was still higher than what Afanasyeva expected in her above-mentioned brief: she wrote that it would be difficult for the ANC to obtain more than 50% of the vote. On the other hand, she mentioned in the same brief that the ANC was polling between 55% and 59%; therefore, it is possible that she deliberately underpredicted the ANC's prospective election results in order to attribute its eventual electoral performance to her team of political consultants. However, an investigation by the South African newspaper *The Daily Maverick* seemed to be doubtful of AFRIC's activities: "The Russian-owned Afric Centre appears to have gotten out of the blocks too late, as there is no evidence of meaningful or organised disinformation in the South African 2019 election campaign".[109]

2019 Mozambican general election

On 20 August 2019, Mozambican President Filipe Nyusi arrived in Moscow. Nyusi would participate in a business forum featuring, among others, Mozambican businessmen, and eventually meet

---

107 "African Union Election Observation Mission (AUEOM) to the Republic of South Africa 8 May 2019 National and Provincial Legislative Elections Preliminary Statement", *African Union*, 10 May (2019), https://au.int/en/pressreleases/20190510/african-union-election-observation-mission-aueom-republic-south-africa-8-may; "EISA Election Observer Mission to the 2019 National and Provincial Elections in South Africa", *Electoral Institute for Sustainable Democracy in Africa*, https://www.eisa.org.za/pdf/sou2019eom0.pdf; "The SADC Election Observation Mission Releases its Preliminary Statement on the 2019 National and Provincial Elections in the Republic of South Africa", *South African Development Community*, 12 May (2019), https://www.sadc.int/latest-news/sadc-election-observation-mission-releases-its-preliminary-statement-2019-national-and.

108 "2019 South African General Election: IEC Commends the Role of AFRIC as an Observer", *AFRIC*, 12 May (2019), https://web.archive.org/web/20191102162247/https://afric.online/projects/2019south-africa-general-election-iec-commends-the-role-of-afric-as-an-observer/.

109 Haffajee, "Exclusive".

with Putin. At that time, Russian authorities were preparing for the first Russia-Africa Summit, planned for 23-24 October 2019, and as the Mozambican election was to be held on 15 October, Putin thought that Nyusi would not be able to take part in it. However, Putin expressed his hope that "Mozambique [would] be represented at a good level at the forum" and wished Nyusi good luck in the election.[110]

In the beginning of October, it became evident that Prigozhin's team was involved in the Mozambican election. First, AFRIC announced that it deployed approximately 62 monitors from Belarus, Benin, Burkina Faso, Cameroon, Democratic Republic of the Congo, Estonia, Germany, Hungary, India, Israel, Italy, Ivory Coast, Jamaica, Japan, Madagascar, Malaysia, Mongolia, Republic of South Africa, Russia, Senegal, Serbia, United Kingdom, and Zimbabwe to observe the election in Mozambique.[111] Second, already in second half of September, AFRIC conducted a public opinion poll ahead of the election, but since polls are illegal in Mozambique during the campaign period,[112] the results of the poll were published on 4 October on the website of the International Anticrisis Centre, run by Prigozhin's team.[113] The poll predicted that Nyusi would win the election with 62.3% of the vote, while his party Mozambique Liberation Front (Frente de Libertação de Moçambique, FRELIMO) would obtain 60.5% of the vote. The analysis accompanying the results of the poll made AFRIC's agenda clear, as it stated: "Russia officially supports the legitimately elected President Filipe Nyusi and FRELIMO party and seeks to maintain peace, sustainable development, sovereignty, and political stability of the Republic of

---

110 "Russia-Mozambique Talks", *President of Russia*, 22 August (2019), http://en.kremlin.ru/events/president/news/61352.

111 "AFRIC—Mozambique Observation Mission Press Release", *AFRIC*, 1 October (2019), https://afric.online/projects/afric-mozambique-observation-mission-press-rel/.

112 "Russian Think Tank Publishes Illegal Pro-Frelimo Opinion Poll", *Zitamar*, 10 October (2019), https://zitamar.com/russian-think-tank-publishes-illegal-pro-frelimo-opinion-poll/.

113 The poll was later deleted from the website, but can still be found here: https://web.archive.org/web/20200108211745/http://anticrisis.cc/2019/10/04/forecast-for-general-election-results-in-the-republic-of-mozambique/.

Mozambique". The same analysis also tried to discredit the opposition to Nyussi with the help of anti-Western narratives: "representatives of Western countries, including the U.S., actively support MDM [Democratic Movement of Mozambique] candidate Daviz Simango, using their standard set of support-the-opposition technologies, by radicalizing society, organizing protests, primarily in the capital, spreading false information via media outlets, as well as using social networks to instigate conflicts between different population groups". According to the Mozambique Political Process Bulletin, the link to AFRIC's poll was widely (and illegally, according to the Mozambican law) shared by supporters of FRELIMO.[114]

The actual results of the election once again proved that Prigozhin's team underpredicted Nyusi's and FRELIMO's results: President Nyusi was re-elected with 73.46% of the vote, while FRELIMO obtained 71.28%. Russia was the first country to congratulate Mozambique on the election, even before the official publication of the results.[115] A press release by Russia's Foreign Ministry stated that "no serious violations were detected" during the election and that it welcomed "the success of such an important event in Mozambique's domestic political life", adding that the election was yet "another significant step in the advance of Mozambican society along the road of political stability and socio-economic development".[116]

African Union and SADC observers praised the election "for being peaceful and well organised",[117] while AFRIC, too, said that

---

114 "Mozambique Political Process Bulletin 70: Administrator Car Burned; No Plans to Shut Internet", *Zitamar*, 10 October (2019), https://zitamar.com/mozambique-political-process-bulletin-70-administrator-car-burned-no-plans-shut-internet/.

115 Communication with a Mozambican investigative journalist Alexandre Nhampossa.

116 "O vseobshchikh vyborakh v Mozambike", *Ministerstvo inostrannykh del Rossiyskoy Federatsii*, 21 October (2019), https://www.mid.ru/ru/foreign_policy/news/-/asset_publisher/cKNonkJE02Bw/content/id/3858655.

117 Manuel Mucari, "EU Blows Whistle on Mozambique's Election, but African Observers Disagree", *Business Day*, 17 October (2019), https://www.businesslive.co.za/bd/world/africa/2019-10-17-eu-blows-whistle-on-mozambiques-election-but-african-observers-disagree/.

the election complied with "the international standards for democratic elections" and that, "despite minor violations of the electoral law, the electoral campaign process was generally peaceful and transparent".[118] This praise for the 2019 Mozambican election was in stark contrast to the evaluations of the EU Election Observation Mission. In its final report on the Mozambican election, the Mission stated: "The electoral process took place in a polarised and challenging environment where inter-party violence was prevalent. Constant features throughout the process included high levels of mistrust between the main political parties, and a lack of confidence that the electoral administration (the National Election Commission — CNE and the Technical Secretariat for Electoral Administration — STAE) and the judiciary were independent and free from political influence".[119]

Shortly after the election, newly re-elected President Filipe Nyusi — despite earlier reservations — travelled to Russia to take part in the Russia-Africa Summit. AFRIC's president José Matemulane, a Mozambican citizen, was reportedly a member of Nyusi's official delegation.

AFRIC beyond fake election observation

Conceived as a Russian network of agents of influence, AFRIC's activities — apart from its website — were mostly limited to promoting African politicians apparently useful for Moscow under the veneer of election observation. However, starting from summer 2019, AFRIC became involved in other influence operations.

On 29-30 July 2019, AFRIC held a conference titled "Africa 2040: Vision of the Future" at the Hilton Hotel in Berlin. As AFRIC stated, the conference brought "experts, NGO leaders, influencers and diplomats from all walks of life to deliberate on the following

---

118 "The International Election Monitoring Mission Statement and Preliminary Conclusions of Mozambique Elections 2019", *AFRIC*, 18 October (2019), https://afric.online/projects/the-international-election-monitoring-mission-statement-and-preliminary-conclusions-of-mozambique-elections-2019/.

119 European Union Election Observation Mission, "Final Report. General and Provincial Assembly Elections 15 October 2019", *European Union External Action*, https://eeas.europa.eu/sites/eeas/files/eueom_moz2019_final_report_en.pdf.

issues: Africa's economic development, governance, energy security, infrastructural development and investment, agriculture, social policies and culture and education".[120] AFRIC claims that the
event was attended by representatives and ambassadors of Benin,
Botswana, Burkina Faso, Cameroon, Chad, Democratic Republic of
Congo, Egypt, Ethiopia, Ivory Coast, Liberia, Madagascar, Mauritius, Morocco, Namibia, Niger, Republic of South Africa, Senegal,
and Uganda.[121] As internal communications between members of
AFRIC suggest,[122] the conference was hosted by Volker Tschapke.

The conference "Africa 2040: Vision of the Future" featured
Yulia Afanasyeva, AFRIC's strategist Clifton Ellis, AFRIC's administrator Vaiva Adomaityte, Purnima Anand (president of the BRICS
International Forum), Stefan Keuter (a German MP from the far-
right party Alternative for Germany, AfD),[123] Nathalie Yamb (a
member of the liberal LIDER party in the Ivory Coast), and two
journalists: Eric Topona and Urs Unkauf. The agenda behind the
conference was to promote the idea that African countries should
align with Russia rather than with "colonial powers that today still
violate African countries' sovereignty with impunity".[124]

Furthermore, AFRIC's apparent rising prominence in the relations between Putin's regime and African countries led to the participation of AFRIC's members in the Russia-Africa Summit that
took place in Sochi on 23-24 October 2019. AFRIC's team featured,
among others, Afanasyeva, Matemulane, Cheuwa, Ellis, Adomaityte, and Séba.

---

120 "Africa Vision-2040: AFRIC Discusses Africa's Emergence in Berlin", *AFRIC*, 13
July (2019), https://afric.online/projects/africa-vision-2040-afric-discusses-af
ricas-emergence-in-berlin/.
121 "AFRIC – Berlin Foresight Session on Africa's Transformation", *AFRIC*, 30 July
(2019), https://afric.online/projects/afric-berlin-foresight-session-on-africas-
transformation/.
122 Provided to the author by the Dossier Centre.
123 On the relations between the European far right and Russian state and non-
state actors see Anton Shekhovtsov, *Russia and the Western Far Right: Tango Noir*
(Abingdon: Routledge, 2018).
124 Clifton Ellis, Vaiva Adomaityte, Dolicia Ratovonkery, Julia Houlimi, "Africa
2040: Vision of the Future", *AFRIC*, https://web.archive.org/web/20200518
075123/https://afric.online/wp-content/uploads/2019/11/AFRICA-2040-Fu
ll-version-ENG.pdf.

On the first day of the summit, Matemulane signed a memorandum on cooperation and coordination between AFRIC and the
Foundation for the Defence of National Values (FDNV). The latter
is headed by Alexander Malkevich, a member of the Civic Chamber
of the Russian Federation. In December 2018, Malkevich was sanctioned by the US for his attempts at targeting Americans with
online disinformation through the website *USA Really*, linked to
Prigozhin.[125] In July 2019, Russian political consultant Maxim
Shugaley, who used to work with Prigozhin's team in Madagascar,
was arrested in Libya as a member of Malkevich's FDNV.[126] In
Libya, Shugaley, as well as his partner Alexander Prokofiev (who
escaped arrest), were accused of being "involved in 'securing a
meeting' with Saif al-Islam al-Qaddafi, the fugitive son of the
ousted dictator and a potential presidential candidate who enjoys
the backing of some officials in Moscow".[127]

Officially, the memorandum between AFRIC and FDNV provides a framework for the exchange of information between the two
organisations and "allows for the development of cooperation in
the area of conducting independent research on the African continent and developing strategies and propositions based on traditional values and people's interests".[128] In other words, the signing
of the memorandum formalised cooperation between two organisations related to the activities of Prigozhin's team in Africa.

---

125 "Treasury Targets Russian Operatives over Election Interference, World Anti-
     Doping Agency Hacking, and Other Malign Activities", *US Department of the
     Treasury*, 19 December (2018), https://home.treasury.gov/news/press-release
     s/sm577.
126 Samer Al-Atrush, Ilya Arkhipov, Henry Meyer, "Libya Uncovers Alleged Rus-
     sian Plot to Meddle in African Votes", *Bloomberg*, 5 July (2019), https://
     www.bloomberg.com/news/articles/2019-07-05/libya-arrests-two-russians-
     accused-of-trying-to-influence-vote.
127 Ibid.
128 "Fond zashchity natsional'nykh tsennostey zaklyuchil soglashenie o sotrud-
     nichestve s Association for Free Research and International Cooperation (AF-
     RIC)", *Fond zashchity natsional'nykh tsennostey*, 23 October (2019), https://web.
     archive.org/web/20191027145808/https://fznc.world/zayavleniya-fonda/
     fond-zashhity-nacionalnyh-czennostej-zaklyuchil-soglashenie-o-sotrudnich-
     estve-s-association-for-free-research-and-international-cooperation-afric/.

On the second day of the summit, AFRIC's leadership participated in the panel discussion "The Future of the African Continent:
Sovereignty and Traditional Values as Crucial Elements of a Development Strategy". The panel was moderated by Malkevich and,
apart from several members of AFRIC, featured Abdelrahman
Noureldayem Saeed Abdelwahab, a member of the Sudanese Econ-
omists Association; Marie Noelle Koyara, Minister of National Defense and Army Reconstruction of the Central African Republic;
Laurence Ndong, Vice-President of the International "Let's Turn
the Page" Campaign; and Anton Morozov, Member of the Russian
Parliament. The narrative of the panel was similar to the "Africa
2040" conference: unlike Western countries, Russia has never been
a colonial power and respects the sovereignty of African countries;
thus, cooperation with Russia is beneficial to African nations.[129]

Following its performance at the Russia-Africa Summit, representatives of AFRIC also participated in the conferences "Made
in Russia" (14 November 2019)[130] and "From Inequality to Justice:
World Experience and Solutions for Russia" (10 December 2019).[131]

African activities of Prigozhin's team in general and of AFRIC
in particular did not escape the attention of international researchers and experts. As early as November 2018, the European Platform
for Democratic Elections published a report titled "The Globalisation of Pro-Kremlin Networks of Politically Biased Election Observation", which analysed dubious activities of AFRIC during the

---

129 "The Future of the African Continent: Sovereignty and Traditional Values as
      Crucial Elements of a Development Strategy", *Roscongress*, 24 October (2019),
      https://roscongress.org/en/sessions/africa-2019-obraz-budushchego-afrikan
      skogo-kontinenta-suverenitet-i-traditsionnye-tsennosti-kak-vazhnye-elementy
      /discussion/.
130 "AFRIC Make Strides towards Establishing a Reputation as a Business Match-
      maker to Fuel African Development", *AFRIC*, 15 November (2019), https://af
      ric.online/projects/afric-make-strides-towards-establishing-a-reputation-as-a-
      business-matchmaker-to-fuel-african-development/.
131 "AFRIC, Honorable Guest of the International Conference from Inequality to
      Justice", *AFRIC*, 13 December (2019), https://afric.online/projects/afric-hon
      orable-guest-of-the-international-conference-from-inequality-to-justice-world-
      experience-and-solutions-for-russia/.

2018 Zimbabwean general election.[132] At the end of October 2019, the Stanford Internet Observatory published a report titled "Evidence of Russia-Linked Influence Operations in Africa", which linked AFRIC to Prigozhin's structures.[133]

On 30 October 2019, Facebook removed "35 Facebook accounts, 53 Pages, seven Groups and five Instagram accounts that originated in Russia and focused on Madagascar, the Central African Republic, Mozambique, Democratic Republic of the Congo, Côte d'Ivoire and Cameroon".[134] Nathaniel Gleicher, Head of Facebook's Cybersecurity Policy, explained:

> Although the people behind these networks attempted to conceal their identities and coordination, our investigation connected these campaigns to entities associated with Russian financier Yevgeniy Prigozhin, who was previously indicted by the US Justice Department. [...] The individuals behind this activity used a combination of fake accounts and authentic accounts of local nationals in Madagascar and Mozambique to manage Pages and Groups, and post their content. They typically posted about global and local political news including topics like Russian policies in Africa, elections in Madagascar and Mozambique, election monitoring by a local non-governmental organization and criticism of French and US policies.[135]

AFRIC's official Facebook account was one of those pages removed by Facebook. On 9 November 2019, AFRIC registered a second account, but Facebook deleted it on 9 January 2020. Confused by Facebook's actions, AFRIC and Malkevich's FDNV held a roundtable discussion called "Freedom of Speech in Social Networks" at the Hilton Hotel in Berlin on 20 January 2020. The roundtable featured Afanasyeva, Malkevich, Ellis, Tschapke, Eric Topona, Nathalie Yamb (who by that time had already become an AFRIC-affiliated expert), Qemal Affagnon (the head of the West Africa division of Internet Without Borders), AfD's Stefan Keuter, German filmmaker

---

132 Shekhovtsov, "The Globalisation of Pro-Kremlin Networks of Politically Biased Election Observation".

133 Shelby Grossman, Daniel Bush, Renée DiResta, "Evidence of Russia-Linked Influence Operations in Africa", *Stanford University*, 30 October (2019), https://fsi.stanford.edu/news/prigozhin-africa.

134 Nathaniel Gleicher, "Removing More Coordinated Inauthentic Behavior from Russia", *Facebook*, 30 October (2019), https://about.fb.com/news/2019/10/removing-more-coordinated-inauthentic-behavior-from-russia/.

135 Ibid.

Wilhelm Domke-Schulz (known for anti-Ukrainian propaganda), and a Latvian pro-Russian activist Jānis Kuzins.

The aim of the discussion was to portray AFRIC as a victim of censorship. Ellis used populist rhetoric to argue that the interests of the political establishment were diametrically opposed to the interests of "the citizens of many countries resulting in a zero-sum situation culminating in the establishment doubling down on support for their agenda by demanding that extra judicial measures be implemented by social media companies to silent 'unfavourable' political speech".[136] It is interesting to note that yet another member of AfD, namely a member of the Berlin state parliament, Gunnar Lindemann, was present in the audience, which may mean that AFRIC has established contacts with this far-right German party.

However, if Facebook and international experts have been critical of the activities of Prigozhin's team in Africa, Russian elites, by contrast, appear to highly appreciate its work. AFRIC's participation in the Russia-Africa Summit, which the Russian authorities took very seriously, corroborates this assumption. Moreover, one Russian report suggests that people who worked on Prigozhin's African projects were issued state awards.[137] For example, Russian political consultant Valentin Bianki, who wrote the analysis of the election in Zimbabwe, was apparently decorated with the "Order of Friendship",[138] which is awarded, in particular, "for special merit in strengthening peace, friendship, cooperation and understanding between nations", "for fruitful work on the convergence and mutual enrichment of cultures of nations and peoples", and "for great contribution to the implementation of joint ventures with the Russian Federation".[139] Petr Bychkov, head of Prigozhin's back-office dealing with Africa, and Fedor Turygin were presumably awarded

---

136 Clifton Ellis, "Freedom of Speech in Social Networks", *AFRIC*, 22 January (2020), https://afric.online/projects/freedom-of-speech-in-social-networks/.
137 Churakova, "V stranakh Afriki rabotayut do 200 polittekhnologov, svyazannykh s Prigozhinym".
138 Ibid.
139 "O vnesenii izmeneniy v Statut ordena Druzhby i opisanie ordena Druzhby, utverzhdyonnye Ukazom Prezidenta Rossiyskoy Federatsii ot 7 sentyabrya 2010 g. N. 1099", *Ofitsial'ny internet-portal pravovoy informatsii*, 7 September (2010), http://pravo.gov.ru/proxy/ips/?docbody=&nd=102154588.

with promotions. In November 2019, Bychkov was appointed a deputy head of the Office of Internal Politics of the Administration of the Pskov oblast, while Turygin was appointed an acting head of the public communications policy of the same Administration. It is highly likely that Seravin was instrumental in this promotion: he was the chief political strategist of the election campaign of Mikhail Vedernikov, who was elected the Governor of the Pskov oblast in 2018.[140]

Conclusion

AFRIC was created in 2018 by Russian political consultants working for Yevgeniy Prigozhin, a Russian businessman close to Vladimir Putin. At the end of 2017, Prigozhin took interest in developing business relations with African countries. While his activities were underpinned, first and foremost, by self-interest, Prigozhin managed to convince Putin that Russia benefited from his work in Africa, as it allegedly contributed to Russia's pride and prestige on that continent, as well as strengthening Russia's global standing against the background of its conflict with the West.

Prigozhin's activities in Africa can be broken down into three categories:

- concluding and executing business contracts with state and non-state entities;
- providing private military contractors to secure Prigozhin's business interests;
- providing different types of support for African politicians and political forces seen as useful for Prigozhin's endeavours.

AFRIC, as a network of agents of influence and loyal election "observers", belongs to the third category, as its activities aim at advancing political interests of particular African politicians and can be qualified as interference in electoral processes.

---

140 Mariya Karpenko, "Tochno v yabloko. Gubernatoru Pskovskoy oblasti porazhat' politicheskie tseli pomozhet peterburgskiy polittekhnolog", *Fontanka*, 19 November (2019), https://www.fontanka.ru/2019/11/19/084/.

In the period between 2018 and 2019, AFRIC interfered in elections in five African countries: Zimbabwe, Madagascar, Democratic Republic of the Congo, South African Republic, and Mozambique. In these countries, AFRIC closely coordinated its work with Russian political consultants from Prigozhin's team that had its back office in St. Petersburg, as well as with another Prigozhin's structure, International Anticrisis Centre, and loyal media. AFRIC's election "observers" received remuneration for the services they provided and had all their expenses covered by Prigozhin's team.

AFRIC and its monitors have been involved in the following activities in the five above-mentioned African countries:

- organising conferences and other events with an objective of promoting particular candidates;
- organising anti-Western protests to discredit and undermine perceived pro-Western politicians;
- publishing public opinion polls with an aim to influence voters' preferences;
- whitewashing unfair and unfree elections for domestic and international audiences;
- subverting and/or relativising findings of credible election observation.

Despite the Russian authorities' apparently high appreciation of the work performed by Prigozhin's operatives in general and AFRIC in particular, the results of this work do not seem to be meaningful. In the majority of cases, Russian consultants supported candidates who were expected to win (or "win" with the help of electoral fraud) anyway, without any assistance from Prigozhin's team. To justify its helpfulness and usefulness, Russian operatives apparently underpredicted prospective election results of candidates and political forces they supported in order to attribute their eventual electoral performances to the work of Prigozhin's team. In other cases, they would simply take credit for politicians' victories or, at very least, try to create an impression that Russian operatives were somehow involved in the electoral success.

3. Russian Malign Influence Operations in Coronavirus-Hit Italy

Introduction

Pandemics always provided fertile soil for conspiracy theories, as facing global disasters often disempowers people and makes them susceptible to conspiratorial explanations of the sources of calamities. Global disasters are also often used by world powers to advance political objectives either domestically or vis-à-vis other nations.

In the 1980s, when AIDS started to spread across the globe and became the "the first postmodern pandemic",[141] the Soviet Union ran a covert international campaign to convince the world that AIDS was a result of the Pentagon's experiments aimed at creating new biological weapons.[142] At that time, while the Soviet leadership was convinced that the US was preparing a nuclear strike against the country, the Soviets realised that they could not compete with the West in the technological and military spheres. However, political warfare was a much cheaper means of competition with the West, and the Soviet Union became especially active in this particular area.

Today, observing the confrontation between Russia and the West, one can see similarities and dissimilarities with the Cold War, but one analogy with the later period of the Cold War is obvious: due to its economic weakness, Russia is unable to match Western technological advances and increasingly relies on various instruments of political warfare in order to damage the West by subverting transatlantic relations, undermining trust in the EU and NATO, and sowing discord between Western nations.

---

141 Lars O. Kallings, "The First Postmodern Pandemic: 25 Years of HIV/AIDS", *Journal of Internal Medicine*, Vol. 263, No. 3 (2008), pp. 218-243.
142 Thomas Boghardt, "Operation INFEKTION: Soviet Bloc Intelligence and Its AIDS Disinformation Campaign", *Studies in Intelligence*, Vol. 53, No. 4 (2009), pp. 1-24.

As COVID-19 spread from China to the rest of the world and became a pandemic, Moscow used the disaster to intensify its political war against the West. Despite the fact that the pandemic hit Russia too, Vladimir Putin's regime seems to have refused an opportunity to scale down political confrontation with the West by ending aggression against Ukraine and discontinuing attempts to destabilise Europe. On the contrary, the Kremlin decided to exploit the pandemic and target European countries that suffered the most from the deadly virus. Italy became one of these countries.

"From Russia with Love"

On March 21, 2020, Putin spoke with Italian Prime Minister Giuseppe Conte,[143] and the same day Putin ordered the Russian Ministry of Defence to form "an air grouping for a prompt delivery to Italy of help for fighting Coronavirus".[144] The help, as the press release of the Ministry of Defence read, would consist of "eight mobile brigades of expert virologists and military medics, automobile systems for aerosol disinfection of transport and territories, as well as medical equipment".[145]

At that time, there were over 42 thousand active cases of COVID-19 in Italy and almost 5 thousand people had died of the virus.[146] Of all European states, Italy was hit the hardest, and, already on 10 March, Maurizio Massari, Italy's permanent representative to the EU, made an appeal for help and European solidarity.[147] According to Massari, in February Italy asked the European Commission to activate the EU Mechanism of Civil Protection "for

---

143 "Telephone Conversation with Italian Prime Minister Giuseppe Conte", *President of Russia*, 21 March (2020), http://en.kremlin.ru/events/president/news/63048.
144 "Minoborony Rossii sozdaet aviatsionnuyu gruppirovku dlya operativnoy dostavki pomoshchi Ital'yanskoy respiblike v bor'be s koronavirusom", *Ministerstvo oborony Rossiyskoy Federatsii*, 22 March (2020), https://function.mil.ru/news_page/country/more.htm?id=12283218@egNews.
145 Ibid.
146 "Italy", *Worldometer*, https://www.worldometers.info/coronavirus/country/italy/.
147 Maurizio Massari, "Italian Ambassador to the EU: Italy Needs Europe's Help", *Politico*, 10 March (2020), https://www.politico.eu/article/coronavirus-italy-needs-europe-help/.

the supply of medical equipment for individual protection"; the Commission forwarded the request to the EU Member States but by the time Massari wrote his article, no EU nation had responded to the Commission's call.[148]

At the same time, China had responded bilaterally and on 12 March, a Chinese aircraft brought to Italy nine medical experts and unloaded "31 tons of medical supplies including intensive care unit equipment, medical protective equipment, and antiviral drugs" – they were sent by the Chinese Red Cross.[149] For the Chinese Communist Party, which had been accused by some Western experts, journalists and politicians, for mishandling of the COVID-19 outbreak,[150] the help to Italy was clearly an attempt to shift the international focus from blame to humanitarian response.

With Putin's offer of help, the Kremlin apparently did not want to miss out on demonstrating its seeming goodwill against the background of the allegedly selfish EU countries. In the period

---

148 Elisabeth Braw, "The EU is Abandoning Italy in its Hour of Need", *Foreign Policy*, 14 March (2020), https://foreignpolicy.com/2020/03/14/coronavirus-eu-abandoning-italy-china-aid/. Following Massari's criticism, Germany suspended the controversial decree that had prohibited the export of masks, protective suits, etc. abroad, and declared that it would supply one million masks to Italy, see Tonia Mastrobuoni, "Coronavirus, la Germania invierà un milione di mascherine all'Italia", *La Repubblica*, 13 March (2020), https://www.repubblica.it/esteri/2020/03/13/news/coronavirus_la_germania_invia_un_milione_di_mascherine_all_italia-251219227/. Later, Germany was joined by France in providing one million masks to Italy, see Michel Rose, "Europe Failing to Communicate Its Response to Coronavirus Crisis, France Says", *Reuters*, 25 March (2020), https://www.reuters.com/article/us-health-coronavirus-europe-france/europe-failing-to-communicate-its-response-to-coronavirus-crisis-france-says-idUSKBN21C3DT. On the European solidarity in action see Coronavirus: "European Solidarity in Action", *European Commission*, https://ec.europa.eu/info/live-work-travel-eu/health/coronavirus-response/coronavirus-european-solidarity-action_en.

149 Braw, "EU is Abandoning Italy"; "Coronavirus, Di Maio: 'Se sei solidale, ricevi solidarietà,'" *ANSA*, 13 March (2020), https://www.ansa.it/lazio/notizie/2020/03/12/coronavirus-arrivati-gli-aiuti-dalla-cina-anche-9-medici-specializzati_1a56ddbc-7bae-4f5a-8353-f0d15ba3a465.html.

150 Paul D. Miller, "Yes, Blame China for the Virus", *Foreign Policy*, 25 March (2020), https://foreignpolicy.com/2020/03/25/blame-china-and-xi-jinping-for-coronavirus-pandemic/; David Gitter, Sandy Lu, and Brock Erdahl, "China Will Do Anything to Deflect Coronavirus Blame", *Foreign Policy*, 30 March (2020), https://foreignpolicy.com/2020/03/30/beijing-coronavirus-response-see-what-sticks-propaganda-blame-ccp-xi-jinping/.

between 23 and 25 March, fifteen Russian aircrafts landed on the Pratica di Mare military airbase delivering military experts and special equipment.[151] At the same time, Russian Defence Ministry "made an extraordinary effort to communicate the mission": it sent 18 press releases on the subject between 21 and 24 March.[152] On 25 March, the Russian military formed a convoy consisting of 22 military vehicles—carrying stickers saying "From Russia with love" in Russian, English, and Italian—as well as buses with military experts.[153] The convoy travelled 600 kilometres to the Orio al Serio airport in Bergamo, "where the joint Italian-Russian headquarters for the fight against coronavirus infection will be stationed".[154]

For Russian state-controlled international media such as RT and Sputnik, Moscow's help to Rome was the beginning of a long anti-EU campaign. With headlines saying "Italians praise Russia, deride EU after Vladimir Putin sends in coronavirus aid",[155] or "EU left Italy 'practically alone' to fight coronavirus, so Rome looked for help elsewhere, incl Russia",[156] "With united Europe MIA in its Covid-19 response, worst-hit nations turn to 'evil' Russia & China

151 "Pyatnadtsaty Il-76 VKS RF dostavil v Italiyu sredstva dlya bor'by s korona-virusom", *Ministerstvo oborony Rossiyskoy Federatsii*, 25 March (2020), https://function.mil.ru/news_page/country/more.htm?id=12283692@egNews.
152 "Coronavirus—Russische Hilfsoperation in Italien bisher vor allem PR", *Austria Presse Agentur*, 24 March (2020).
153 "Spetsialisty Minoborony Rossii pristupili k soversheniyu marsha s aviabazy VVS Italii v g. Bergamo dlya okazaniya pomoshchi v bor'be s rasprostraneniem koronavirusnoy infektsii", *Ministerstvo oborony Rossiyskoy Federatsii*, 25 March (2020), https://function.mil.ru/news_page/country/more.htm?id=12283714 @egNews.
154 "Voennye spetsialisty Minoborony Rossii pribyli na aerodrom Orio-al'-Serio v gorode Bergamo", Ministerstvo oborony Rossiyskoy Federatsii, 26 March (2020), https://function.mil.ru/news_page/country/more.htm?id=12283835 @egNews.
155 "Watch: Italians Praise Russia, Deride EU After Vladimir Putin Sends in Coronavirus Aid", *Sputnik*, 24 March (2020), https://sputniknews.com/europe/202003241078693863-watch-italians-praise-russia-deride-eu-after-vladimir-putin-sends-in-coronavirus-aid/.
156 "EU left Italy 'practically alone' to fight coronavirus, so Rome looked for help elsewhere, incl Russia—ex-FM Frattini to RT", *RT*, 24 March (2020), https://www.rt.com/news/483897-italy-eu-coronavirus-solidarity-russia/.

for help",[157] the message was clear: the EU showed no solidarity with Italy, while Putin's Russia demonstrated its goodwill despite the fact that Italy — along with the other EU nations — imposed economic and political sanctions on Russia. In the eyes of the Western audience, videos and pictures showing Russian military vehicles flying Russian flags and driving through Italy apparently had to project an image of Russia as a self-avowed saviour of Italy and a mighty military force rushing to the rescue where NATO was feeble. And there were other Russian specialists who were in charge of promoting such an image: Russian journalists from the Zvezda TV network run by the Russian Defence Ministry who arrived in Italy together with the Russian military.[158]

The entire operation appeared to be a successful publicity coup for the Kremlin. Italy's Foreign Minister Luigi Di Maio personally welcomed the Russian aid at the Pratica di Mare airbase. Italian Chief of the Defence Staff General Enzo Vecciarelli was present at the airbase too and "thanked the Russian people for lending a helping hand".[159] Former Prime Minister Silvio Berlusconi sent a letter to his personal friend Vladimir Putin saying that the Russian aid was "a real sacrifice made for friendship and love for Italy and the Italians", adding that Italians would "not forget it".[160]

The visuals were important too. Russia's Ministry of Defence published a photo, which was later republished by dozens of media outlets across the world, in which Russian General Sergey Kikot, who led the Italian operation, showed something on the map of Italy to the representatives of the Italian military thus creating an impression that Russians had command power in a NATO member

---

157 Damian Wilson, "With United Europe MIA in Its Covid-19 Response, Worst-hit Nations Turn to 'Evil' Russia & China for Help", *RT*, 23 March (2020), https://www.rt.com/op-ed/483865-europe-coronavirus-russia-china/.

158 Konstantin Khudoleyev, "Iz Rossii s lyubov'yu: kak okhvachennaya korona-virusom Italiya vstretila rossiyskikh spetsialistov", *Zvezda*, 23 March (2020), https://tvzvezda.ru/news/vstrane_i_mire/content/20203231327-JqrfK.html.

159 "Russian Military Planes with Medics & Supplies Land in Coronavirus-Hit Italy (VIDEO)", *RT*, 22 March (2020), https://www.rt.com/russia/483796-russian-military-coronavirus-aid-italy/.

160 Giorgia Baroncini, "Coronavirus, Putin invia aiuti all'Italia. Il Cav: 'Non lo dimenticheremo,'" *Il Giornale*, 23 March (2020), https://www.ilgiornale.it/news/politica/coronavirus-putin-invia-aiuti-allitalia-cav-non-1845152.html.

state.[161] Russian media resources also talked about ordinary Italians replacing EU flags with Russian ones and showed a video of an Italian engineer who did this while showing a piece of paper thanking Putin and Russia.[162]

However, soon after the arrival of the Russian aid, details started to emerge suggesting that the operation "From Russia with love" had much more to do with political theatrics rather than with Moscow's philanthropy.

The darker side of Russian gifts

The logistics of the delivery of the Russian aid alone pointed to a hidden agenda of the operation: why had the aid been delivered first to the Pratica di Mare airbase and then driven 600 kilometres to the Orio al Serio airport if the Russian airplanes could have delivered the aid directly to any of the four airports around Bergamo capable of receiving Russian military cargo airplanes? There are two possible explanations for this. First, the Russian military wanted to impress the public and the media with a long convoy of over 20 military vehicles symbolically conquering a NATO member state. Moscow would not have achieved such an effect had the aid been delivered straight to the destination point. Alexander Sladkov, a Russian military journalist working for the All-Russia State Television and Radio Broadcasting Company, called the operation "'a humanitarian axe' run into NATO's chest".[163] He also likened the Russian operation in Italy with the forced march of Russian forces to the Pristina International Airport in the aftermath of the Kosovo War in June 1999: the Russian military arrived in the airport ahead

161 "The Use of Russian Military Specialists in the Fight against the Coronavirus Pandemic Was Discussed in Rome", *Ministry of Defence of the Russian Federation*, 24 March (2020), https://eng.mil.ru/en/news_page/country/more.htm?id=12283590@egNews.

162 It later turned out that the person was "personally fond of Russia and of President Putin" and had "done some business with Russian companies", see "Coronavirus: What Does 'from Russia with Love' Really Mean?" *BBC*, 3 April (2020), https://www.bbc.com/news/world-europe-52137908.

163 Alexander Sladkov, "Kuzhugetych Zhzhet!", *Sladkov +*, 22 March (2020), https://t.me/Sladkov_plus/1916.

of the NATO forces and occupied it.[164] Yet another possible explanation for the apparently unreasonable 600-kilometre drive from the Pratica di Mare airbase to Bergamo is that the Russian mission to Italy was "a front for intelligence gathering", so the trip could, indeed, be used by the Russian military to collect intelligence "at the heart of NATO".[165] Of course, one can argue that it was cheaper for the Russian military to deliver the aid to the Pratica di Mare airbase than all the way to the Orio al Serio airport. However, the distance between the two airports is insignificant in comparison to the distance between Russia and Italy, and, furthermore, the Russian military anyway charged the Italians for the fuel and the flights of their cargo airplanes.[166]

Furthermore, Italian expert Massimiliano Di Pasquale argued—with a reference to Italian specialists—that "there was no need at all in the disinfection of the streets" in Bergamo.[167] Andrea Armaro, a former spokesperson for Italy's Defence Ministry, also "questioned the need for Russian military medics to disinfect areas when there were already nuclear, biological and chemical military teams in Italy capable of doing the job".[168]

According to the investigation by Italian investigative journalist Jacopo Iacoboni, high-level political sources told *La Stampa* that 80% of the Russian aid was either useless or of little use to Italy, as the Russian delivery mostly consisted of disinfection and sterilisation equipment. The same sources argued that Putin was pursuing

164 Ibid.
165 Natalia Antelava, Jacopo Iacoboni, "The Influence Operation behind Russia's Coronavirus Aid to Italy", *Coda*, 2 April (2020), https://www.codastory. com/disinformation/soft-power/russia-coronavirus-aid-italy/.
166 Jacopo Iacoboni, Paolo Mastrolilli, "Nella spedizione dei russi in Italia il generale che negò i gas in Siria", *La Stampa*, 16 April (2020), https://www.lastampa.it /topnews/primo-piano/2020/04/16/news/nella-spedizione-dei-russi-in-itali a-il-generale-che-nego-i-gas-in-siria-1.38722110.
167 Natal'ya Kudrik, "Ital'yanskiy obozrevatel': rossiyskaya 'pomoshch'—eto operatsiya propagandy", *Krym.Realii*, 4 April (2020), https://ru.krymr.com/a/ italianskiy-obozrevtel-rossiyskaya-pomoshch-operaciya-propagandy/3052976 5.html.
168 Angela Giuffrida, Andrew Roth, "Moscow's Motives Questioned over Coronavirus Aid Shipment to Italy", *Guardian*, 27 April (2020), https://www.thegua rdian.com/world/2020/apr/27/moscow-motives-questioned-over-coronavir us-aid-shipment-to-italy.

"geopolitical and diplomatic" interests, while Conte had to play along as he needed any help in the situation of the severe crisis.[169]

Moscow immediately and angrily responded to Iacoboni's article. Russia's Ambassador to Italy Sergey Razov called the Russian aid "a selfless desire to help a friendly people in trouble" and slammed the assertions made in the article as "the product of a perverse mind".[170]

The Russian Defence Ministry joined the campaign too. Its spokesman Major General Igor Konashenkov called Iacoboni's article in *La Stampa* an attempt "to discredit the Russian mission" and added, in awkward English:

> Hiding behind the ideals of freedom of speech and pluralism of opinions, *La Stampa* manipulates in its materials the most low-grade Russophobic fakes of the Cold War, referring to so called certain "opinions" of anonymous "high-ranking sources. At the same time, '*La Stampa*' does not disdain to use literally everything that the authors manage to invent on the basis of recommendations from apparently not decayed textbooks on anti-Soviet propaganda. [...] As for the attitude to the real customers of the Russophobian media campaign in *La Stampa*, which we know — we recommend that you learn the ancient wisdom — Qui fodit foveam, incidet in eam (He that diggeth a pit, shall fall into it). And to make it clearer: Bad penny always comes back.[171]

Reacting to Konashenkov's "ancient wisdom", Iacoboni said: "It is a threatening and intimidating phrase [...] not only towards me but also towards my newspaper. In Italy we do not let ourselves be intimidated; freedom of criticism exists here. We are not Chechnya".[172] In their turn, the editorial board of *La Stampa* expressed its

---

169 Jacopo Iacoboni, "Coronavirus, la telefonata Conte-Putin agita il governo: 'Più che aiuti arrivano militari russi in Italia,'" *La Stampa*, 25 March (2020), https://www.lastampa.it/topnews/primo-piano/2020/03/25/news/corona-virus-la-telefonata-conte-putin-agita-il-governo-piu-che-aiuti-arrivano-militari-russi-in-italia-1.38633327.

170 "Posol v Italii otsenil soobshcheniya o 'vystavlenii scheta' za pomoshch,'" *RIA Novosti*, 25 March (2020), https://ria.ru/20200325/1569157787.html.

171 "Statement by the Spokesman of the Ministry of Defence of the Russian Federation Major General Igor Konashenkov", *Facebook*, 2 April (2020), https://www.facebook.com/mod.mil.rus/posts/2608652339377506. Italics added.

172 Monica Rubino, Concetto Vecchio, "Russia contro il giornalista de 'La Stampa' Jacopo Iacoboni. Esteri e Difesa: 'Grazie per aiuti ma rispettare libertà di stampa,'" *La Repubblica*, 3 April (2020), https://www.repubblica.it/politica/2020/04/03/news/iacoboni_la_stampa_russia-253020378/.

"outrage upon the serious attack" of the Russian Defence Ministry on the newspaper and Iacoboni.[173]

What Moscow did not realise was that its vicious attacks against Italian journalism ruined much of the positive effect of the Russian mission in Italy. In their joint notice, Italy's Defence Ministry and Foreign Ministry declared that Italy was grateful for the Russian aid, but, at the same time, they could not "help but blame the inappropriate tone of certain expressions used by the spokesman of the Ministry of Russian Defence against some articles published the Italian press. Freedom of speech and the right to criticise are fundamental values for Italy, as well as the right to reply, both characterised by formality and substantial fairness. In this moment of global emergency, the control and analysis task of the free press is more essential than ever".[174] Mayor of Bergamo Giorgio Gori tweeted: "Solidarity with @jacopo_iacoboni and *La Stampa* subjected to the intimidation from a Russian defence spokesman. We are grateful to have Russian doctors and nurses in #Bergamo who help us treat our patients, but no threat to free information is acceptable".[175] Many other politicians and journalists expressed their solidarity with Iacoboni too.[176]

However, Russian officials and state-controlled international media continued their attack on *La Stampa* and Iacoboni.

Russian Foreign Ministry Spokeswoman Maria Zakharova declared that a company registered in London was behind Iacoboni's article in *La Stampa*. She did not provide either the name of the company or any other details, but vaguely noted: "When we began to study it [the article], it turned out that this is a purely commercial

---

173 "Le accuse di Mosca e la nostra risposta", *La Stampa*, 3 April (2020), https://www.lastampa.it/lettere/2020/04/03/news/le-accuse-di-mosca-e-la-nostra-risposta-1.38672825.

174 "Nota congiunta del Ministero della Difesa e del Ministero degli Affari Esteri e della Cooperazione Internazionale", *Ministero degli Affari Esteri e della Cooperazione Internazionale*, 3 April (2020), https://www.esteri.it/it/sala_stampa/arc hivionotizie/comunicati/2020/04/nota-congiunta-del-ministero-della-difesa-e-del-ministero-degli-affari-esteri-e-della-cooperazione-internazionale/.

175 Giorgio Gori, "Solidarietà a @jacopo_iacoboni e alla Stampa per le intimidazioni ricevute da portavoce della Difesa russo", *Twitter*, 3 April (2020), https://twitter.com/giorgio_gori/status/1246008841755668480. Italics added.

176 Rubino, Vecchio, "Russia contro il giornalista de 'La Stampa' Jacopo Iacoboni".

operation that some foreign structures attempted to stage using non-transparent methods".[177] While it is unclear what British "commercial operation" Zakharova had in mind, a fringe Russian-language website, Foundation for Strategic Culture, ran a story that claimed that "Anglo-Saxons" were behind *La Stampa*'s "provocative attack" referring to the incorrect information that the newspaper was owned by Chrysler whose chairman John Elkann was from New York and CEO Michael Manley was from Britain.[178]

The Italian edition of Sputnik published an article written by now late Giulietto Chiesa, a long-time pro-Kremlin activist and associate of Russian fascist Alexander Dugin,[179] who claimed that *La Stampa* was a "notoriously Russophobic newspaper" (ironically, Chiesa wrote for *La Stampa* in 1991-2000), while Iacoboni allegedly "specialised in spreading the germs of an apparently very infectious disease of Russophobia".[180]

Chiesa was not the only Italian "friend of Russia" who was directly or indirectly mobilised by the Russian state and non-state actors in Moscow's attempts to generate "hype" around the Russian aid to Italy. On April 14, 2020, the Russian Defence Ministry issued a press release stating that Professor Maria Chiara Pesenti from the University of Bergamo sent a letter of appreciation to the Russian military. Pesenti, due to her specialisation in Russian language and literature, is a frequent visitor of Russia, and, in November 2019, Putin awarded her with a Medal of Pushkin.[181] And

---

177 "UK Company behind La Stampa's Article Claiming Russian Aid to Italy Useless – Diplomat", *TASS*, 2 April (2020), https://tass.com/politics/1139323.

178 Vladimir Malyshev, "Uchebniki po antisovetskoy propagande eshche ne sgnili", *Fond strategicheskoy kul'tury*, 9 April (2020), https://www.fondsk.ru/news/2020/04/09/uchebniki-po-antisovetskoj-propagande-esche-ne-sgnili-50575.html.

179 Andreas Umland, "Aleksandr Dugin's Transformation from a Lunatic Fringe Figure into a Mainstream Political Publicist, 1980-1998: A Case Study in the Rise of Late and Post-Soviet Russian Fascism", *Journal of Eurasian Studies*, Vol. 1, No. 2 (2010), pp. 144-152.

180 Giulietto Chiesa, "Quelli che sparano sulla Croce Rossa", Sputnik, April 7, 2020, https://it.sputniknews.com/opinioni/202004078943748-quelli-che-sparano-sulla-croce-rossa/.

181 "Putin v Den' narodnogo edinstva vruchil nagrady v Kremle", *RIA Novosti*, 4 November (2019), https://ria.ru/20191104/1560560522.html.

already in March 2020, Italian far-right activist Gian Luigi Ferretti, who was part of the politically biased election observation mission at the Russian 2018 presidential election,[182] uploaded a video on YouTube on which a recording of the Russian anthem was played from the headquarters of the Italian fascist organisation Casa-Pound.[183] (Uninitiated viewers would, however, hardly recognise the headquarters of CasaPound and just see Italian flags and hear the Russian anthem.)

Furthermore, Italian newspaper *La Repubblica* reported that Russian citizens were sending requests to their Italian friends and acquaintances offering €200 for thank-you videos on Facebook, Instagram or Twitter. The requests allegedly came from the Russian media, but no name was given. In order to earn money, Italians were supposed "to say something good" about the Russian aid offered to Italy: "better videos or texts with photos, but for videos they pay 200 euros, for text they give less".[184] However, La Repubblica was cautious about linking these practices to the activities of the Russian state actors.

Far-right freeloading

The Russian aid to Italy offered an opportunity to a number of pro-Kremlin actors to pursue their own political and personal interests. On 23 March, Alexey Pushkov, a Russian senator who is prone to self-promotion through provocative tweets related to foreign policy, tweeted that Poland had "not let Russian aircraft carrying aid

---

182   See Anton Shekhovtsov, "Politically Biased International Election Observation at the 2018 Regional Elections in Russia", *European Platform for Democratic Elections*, 5 October (2018), https://www.epde.org/en/documents/details/politically-biased-international-election-observation-at-the-2018-regional-elections-in-russia.html.

183   Gian Luigi Ferretti, "25 marzo 2020: Inno russo da CasaPound a Roma", *YouTube*, 25 March (2020), https://www.youtube.com/watch?v=rlOK4gQKtxc.

184   Fabio Tonacci, "'200 euro se ringrazi la Russia per gli aiuti': quello strano arruolamento su WhatsApp", *La Repubblica*, 12 April (2020), https://www.repubblica.it/esteri/2020/04/12/news/russia_propaganda_a_pagamento-25379426 4/.

to Italy pass through its airspace".[185] Pushkov is also one of the most cited politicians in the Russian media space, and several Russian media outlets – including various editions of Sputnik – quickly picked up Pushkov's message that generally fed into the Kremlin's animosity towards Poland.[186] However, Poland's Foreign Ministry promptly refuted Pushkov's claim, and Sputnik had to amend its reports on the issue,[187] while Pushkov deleted his tweet. Nevertheless, his claim permeated into the milieu of Italian conspiracy theorists and anti-EU activists.[188]

While Pushkov's tweet was hardly underpinned by any other reason apart from the Russian senator's proclivity for provocative political utterances, some other developments around the Russian aid to Italy had complex agendas behind them.

On 20 March, Ulrich Oehme, a member of the German parliament from the far-right party Alternative for Germany (Alternative für Deutschland, AfD), sent letters to two Russian contacts. One letter was addressed to the Chairman of the State Duma Committee on International Affairs Leonid Slutsky and the other – to a member of the Moscow City Duma, Roman Babayan. The letters seem to be practically identical and, in particular, read: "Today, Mr. Paolo Grimoldi, a member of the Council of Europe from the Northern League (Lombardy), turned to us with a desperate cry for help via the WhatsApp group of European Conservatives. The situation

---

185 Alexey Pushkov, "Pol'sha ne propustila rossiyskie samolety s pomoshch'yu dlya Italii cherez svoe vozdushnoe prostranstvo", *Twitter*, 23 March (2020), https://web.archive.org/web/20200323232823/https://twitter.com/Alexey_Pushkov/status/1242166190711111683. Archived here: http://archive.is/fdk6R.

186 See, for example, "Russian Planes Carrying Aid to Italy Blocked from Using Poland Airspace – Russian Lawmaker", *Sputnik*, 23 March (2020), https://web.archive.org/web/20200324003727/https://sputniknews.com/world/2020032 31078687190-russian-planes-carrying-aid-to-italy-blocked-from-using-poland-airspace---russian-lawmaker/.

187 See "Poland Says Its Airspace Open for Russian Planes Carrying Aid to Italy", *Sputnik*, 23 March (2020), https://sputniknews.com/world/202003231078687 190-russian-planes-carrying-aid-to-italy-blocked-from-using-poland-airspace---russian-lawmaker/.

188 "Russia Exploits Italian Coronavirus Outbreak to Expand Its Influence", *Medium*, 30 March (2020), https://medium.com/dfrlab/russia-exploits-italian-coronavirus-outbreak-to-expand-its-influence-6453090d3a98.

with the hospitals in Lombardy is extremely critical. They urgently need doctors. For this reason, I ask you to see whether the Russian Federation can help people of Lombardy with doctors and ventilators. I have just talked with Mr. Grimoldi on the phone and he is excited about my idea to talk to you about help".[189] When the media reported about Putin's decision to provide aid to Italy, the AfD claimed that "the Russian leadership responded to a request from the Bundestag member Ulrich Oehme concerning Northern Italy severely affected by the coronavirus".[190]

The background of the above-mentioned figures suggests that Oehme's letters were most likely part of an elaborate influence operation.

The AfD's foreign policy positions very often coincide with those of the Kremlin, and this far-right party is extremely critical of the EU's sanctions imposed on Putin's Russia. The AfD's members often pay visits to Moscow to meet Russian officials, and, in February 2017, the AfD's leadership discussed cross-party cooperation with a number of Russian politicians including Leonid Slutsky, one of the two Russian politicians to whom Oehme addressed his letters. Oehme himself was involved in pro-Kremlin activities. In March 2018, he illegally visited Russia-annexed Crimea where he "observed" the illegitimate Russian presidential election.[191] Furthermore, he tried to promote the interests of the Russia-controlled

---

189 "Oehme: Europaratsmitglieder bilden Phalanx zur Bewältigung der Corona-Krise in Italien", *Fraktion der AfD im Deutschen Bundestag*, 23 March (2020), https://www.afdbundestag.de/mdb-ulrich-oehme-europaratsmitglieder-bil den-phalanx-zur-bewaeltigung-der-corona-krise-in-italien/; "Deputat Bundes-taga obratilsya k Rossii za pomoshch'yu okhvachennoy koronavirusom Italii", *Govorit Moskva*, 21 March (2020), https://govoritmoskva.ru/news/228659/.

190 "Oehme: Europaratsmitglieder bilden Phalanx zur Bewältigung der Corona-Krise in Italien".

191 See Anton Shekhovtsov, "Foreign Observation of the Illegitimate Presidential Election in Crimea in March 2018", *European Platform for Democratic Elections*, 3 April (2018), https://www.epde.org/en/news/details/foreign-observation-of -the-illegitimate-presidential-election-in-crimea-in-march-2018-1375.html.

"Donetsk People's Republic" and "Lugansk People's Republic" in the Council of Europe in 2019.[192]

Paolo Grimoldi's party Northern League (Lega Nord, LN) is known for its pro-Kremlin foreign policy positions too, and signed, in March 2017, a coordination and cooperation agreement with the ruling United Russia party. Grimoldi himself contributed to the development of the relations between his party and Russian state and non-state actors. In October 2014, he announced the creation of the cross-party group, Friends of Putin, in the Italian parliament.[193] Although there is no evidence that this group eventually took off or was successful in promoting rapprochement between Italy and Russia, the Russian media widely reported on this initiative attempting to show — against the backdrop of the Western sanctions against Putin's Russia — the alleged growth of pro-Kremlin sentiments in the West.

In his turn, Slutsky — as chairman of the parliamentary committee on international affairs — coordinated several important contacts between the European far right and Russian state actors. For example, it was Slutsky who officially invited Marine Le Pen, the leader of the French far-right National Front (Front National) to meet Putin in March 2017, a month before the first round of the French presidential election.[194] Slutsky also supervised several politically biased international election observation missions that included many European far-right politicians.[195]

According to the German media outlet *Bild*, in parallel to Oehme's efforts, the LN essentially forced a difficult choice on Conte: either accept aid from Moscow and grant Russia a publicity

---

192 "Predstaviteli ORDLO vstretilis' v Minske s deputatom PASE", *Naviny*, 16 December (2019), https://naviny.by/new/20191216/1576476063-predstaviteli-ordlo-vstretilis-v-minske-s-deputatom-pase.

193 Shekhovtsov, *Russia and the Western Far Right*, pp. 185-186.

194 "France's Le Pen, on Russia Visit, Heads to Kremlin for Exhibition", *Reuters*, 24 March (2017), https://www.reuters.com/article/us-russia-france-lepen-idU SKBN16V12E.

195 Anton Shekhovtsov, "Politically Biased Foreign Electoral Observation at the Russian 2018 Presidential Election", *European Platform for Democratic Elections*, 16 April (2018), https://www.epde.org/en/documents/details/politically-bi ased-foreign-electoral-observation-at-the-russian-2018-presidential-election-14 23.html.

stunt, or reject it and suffer an outrage from the suffering Italian population.[196] From this perspective, Oehme's letters to Russian politicians seem to be not only an attempt to advance political interests of the AfD and LN, but also an endeavour to put additional pressure on Conte.

Like Slutsky, Grimoldi and Oehme are members of the Council of Europe, and—given this fact, as well as Grimoldi's engagement with the pro-Kremlin activities—he did not really need Oehme to be an intermediary between him and Slutsky. The involvement of Oehme can be simply explained by his desire to secure Russian favours not only for the LN, but also for the AfD—by displaying servility before Russia. Slutsky was an obvious choice as the first addressee of the letter coordinated by Grimoldi and Oehme, due to his membership in the Council of Europe and coordination of the relations between European politicians and Russian state actors. Unlike Slutsky, however, Roman Babayan has little in common with European politicians or Russian malign influence operations in Europe, but he seemed to be a good choice as a second addressee of the letter because of his connections with the Russian media. Babayan is a chief editor of the "Govorit Moskva" radio station and cooperates with the functionally state-controlled NTV television channel, so his task was to spread the word about Italy's "cry for Russian help" in the media, and so he did.[197] The outcome of the operation was obvious: Oehme and Grimoldi strengthened pro-Kremlin foreign policy positions of their parties in order to seek further favours from Moscow, while contributing to the domestic pressure on Conte and consolidating the international image of Putin's Russia as the true friend of Italian people.

---

196 Julian Röpcke, "Wie die AfD Putins Militär in Italien einschleuste", *Bild*, 26 March (2020), https://www.bild.de/politik/ausland/politik-ausland/corona-krise-wie-die-afd-putins-militaer-in-italien-einschleuste-69638656.bild.html.

197 "Deputat Bundestaga obratilsya k Rossii za pomoshch'yu okhvachennoy koronavirusom Italii".

Conclusion

It would be wrong to argue that the Russian aid delivered to Italy was completely useless. However, it would be equally wrong to assume that this aid was primarily driven by humanitarian considerations, because the main objective of the "From Russia with love" operation was to demonstrate to the Italian people that it was Russia, rather than the EU or NATO, that was the true friend of Italy.

The relevance of such an operation could only become possible due to the initial confusion in European capitals in the face of the unfolding crisis. As President of the European Commission Ursula von der Leyen said in the middle of April 2020, "too many were not there on time when Italy needed a helping hand at the very beginning".[198] Von der Leyen offered "a heartfelt apology" for the lack of European solidarity with Italy at the start of the crisis,[199] but neither her apology nor the fact that EU states eventually rendered much greater assistance to Italy than China or Russia could undo what had been done: the erosion of Italians' trust towards the EU.

The Kremlin readily helped to erode this trust as Italy was "perceived by Moscow as the weak link in the EU".[200] By launching its malign influence operation, Putin's regime hoped that—by undermining Italy's trust in the EU—the Kremlin contributed to strengthening Italy's opposition to the EU's sanctions policy on Russia. At the end of April 2020, Moscow decided to covertly test the efficiency of its tactics in Italy. On 27 April, Russian Ambassador Sergey Razov forwarded to Vito Rosario Petrocelli, chairman of the Italian Senate's Foreign Affairs Committee, an appeal by Slutsky, and asked his addressee to inform Italian senators of its

---

198 "Speech by President Von der Leyen at the European Parliament Plenary on the EU Coordinated Action to Combat the Coronavirus Pandemic and Its Consequences", *European Commission*, 16 April (2020), https://ec.europa.eu/commiss ion/presscorner/detail/en/speech_20_675.
199 Ibid.
200 Luigi Sergio Germani, "The Coronavirus Pandemic and Russian Information Warfare Activities in Italy", *Centre for Democratic Integrity*, 28 April (2020), https://democratic-integrity.eu/the-coronavirus-pandemic-and-russian-info rmation-warfare-activities-in-italy/.

contents.[201] In his appeal, Slutsky called upon the international community — without singling out any particular nation — to support Russia's resolution at the United Nations that would make it easier to lift sanctions imposed on Russia.[202] Razov forwarded Slutsky's appeal in two versions: an original Russian version and a translation into Italian. Curiously, Razov specified in his cover letter that the Italian version was an unofficial translation which implies that his efforts took place behind closed doors and was yet another malign influence operation.

Russia was not the only beneficiary of its influence operations in Italy: representatives of German and Italian far-right parties, known for their pro-Kremlin foreign policy attitudes, had an opportunity to showcase their allegiance to Russia by reinforcing its self-imposed image of a well-meaning global power, and, therefore, seek support from Moscow in the future.

---

201 Razov's cover letter and Slutsky's appeal can be found here: https://www.linkiesta.it/wp-content/uploads/2020/05/Lettera-nr.1072-del-27.04.2020.pdf.

202 The appeal appeared on several websites of Russian diplomatic institutions, see, for example: Leonid Slutsky, "An Appeal by Mr L. Slutsky, MP, to Abandon the Sanction Policy in the Face of COVID-19 Pandemia", *The Embassy of the Russian Federation in the Republic of India*, 24 April (2020), https://india.mid.ru/en/press-office/news/an_appeal_by_mr_slutsky/.

4. How to Fail a Malign Influence Operation
The Case of Russian Aid to Serbia

Introduction

"The great international solidarity does not exist. European solidarity does not exist. That was a fairy tale on paper".[203] These words were spoken by Serbian President Aleksandar Vučić as he was making — on 15 March 2020 — an announcement about the introduction of a state of emergency related to the COVID-19 pandemic. By the time of the announcement, Serbia had registered 48 active cases of the virus in the country.

These emotional words contrasted with the confidence that the Serbian authorities demonstrated at the end of February. On 25 February, Serbian Health Minister Zlatibor Lončar stated that there was "no reason for panic over coronavirus" adding that, while it was "realistic to expect this virus to appear in Serbia", the country's health system was ready and that all recommendations of the World Health Organisation (WHO) had been implemented.[204] The following day, Vučić himself reiterated the same message saying that Serbia's health system was "fully prepared" for the virus.[205] At the same time, one expert from the government's Crisis Center dismissed the seriousness of COVID-19 calling it the "most laughable virus in the history of humanity".[206] And on 11 March, Vučić said that Serbia was "keeping things under control", adding that "a

---

203 CGTN, "Serbia's State of Emergency: 'China Is the Only Country that Can Help,'" *YouTube*, 16 March (2020), https://www.youtube.com/watch?v=P4 2OrsA045M.

204 "Serbia Ready for Possible Coronavirus Outbreak", *The Government of the Republic of Serbia*, 25 February (2020), https://www.srbija.gov.rs/vest/en/150594/serbia-ready-for-possible-coronavirusoutbreak.php.

205 "Serbia Fully Prepared for Possible Emergence of Coronavirus", *The Government of the Republic of Serbia*, 26 February (2020), https://www.srbija.gov.rs/vest/en/150669/serbia-fully-prepared-forpossible-emergence-of-coronavirus.php.

206 Ivan Vejvoda, "Coronavirus in Serbia — from Bad to Better to Much Worse", *European Forum Alpbach*, 13 July (2020), https://www.alpbach.org/en/efa-guest-commentary-coronavirus-in-serbia/.

meeting of top state officials and representatives of all relevant institutions" decided to ban indoor gatherings of more than 100 people, but saw "no reason to suspend classes in schools".[207] Just a few
days later, Vučić's rhetoric dramatically changed.

Vučić's anti-EU messaging on 15 March seemed to have been
driven by two main considerations. First, he needed to shift the
blame for the outbreak of the pandemic from the authorities, who
seemed to be content with the handling of the pandemic up until
very recently, to an external scapegoat. Second, Vučić's anti-EU
messaging was praise towards Serbia's authoritarian ally, China.
The Serbian president used the same announcement of the state of
emergency to inform the public of his plea for help from the country
where COVID-19 had originated: "Today I sent a special paper, because we expect a lot and we have highest hopes in the only ones
who can help us in this difficult situation, and that is the People's
Republic of China".[208]

The state-controlled China Global Television Network
(CGTN) widely circulated the video of Vučić insulting the EU and
presenting China as Serbia's last hope. The CGTN even subtitled
the video for the English-speaking audience and uploaded it to the
CGTN's channel on YouTube, which had been, ironically, blocked
in mainland China since 2009. The agenda behind the CGTN and
similar channels of Chinese propaganda was clear: as China was
suffering reputational losses in Europe and elsewhere for the failure to contain the spread of COVID-19, the country needed to show
to the world that it was helping other nations in their struggle
against the pandemic, especially in those places where it had — or
hoped to have — significant investments. Serbia is currently "Europe's fourth-biggest recipient of Chinese foreign direct

---

207 "Serbia Fighting Coronavirus in a Good Way", *The Government of the Republic of
     Serbia*, 11 March (2020), https://www.srbija.gov.rs/vest/en/151176/serbia-
     fighting-coronavirus-in-a-good-way.php.
208 CGTN, "Serbia's State of Emergency".

investment",[209] and China "has gradually become one of the most important foreign policy partners of Serbia".[210]

But Chinese propaganda was not only about words — it was about deeds too, as it did deliver aid. The first Chinese aid, namely one thousand rapid test kits, came already on 15 March — a donation from the Shenzhen Mammoth Public Welfare Foundation.[211] Yet following Beijing's official approval on 17 March to help Belgrade combat the pandemic,[212] more aid started to arrive in Serbia later the same month. The first Chinese airplane carrying medical experts and equipment landed in Serbia on 21 March and was welcomed by Vučić and the Chinese Ambassador to Serbia, Chen Bo. As the Serbian government said, "medical packages sent from China ha[d] an inscription written in Chinese and in Cyrillic: 'Steel friendship, we share good and bad,' with a heart whose one side ha[d] the flag of Serbia and the other the flag of China".[213]

Perhaps coincidentally, a similar symbol was featured on the airplanes that brought Russian aid to Serbia on 4 April — Russian and Serbian flags in the form of two hearts with an inscription in Russian and Serbian: "From Russia with love".[214] Even if Moscow was not directly inspired by Beijing's visual symbolism, it was obvious that Russia was following China in its attempts to exploit the

---

209 Majda Ruge, Janka Oertel, "Serbia's Coronavirus Diplomacy Unmasked", *European Council on Foreign Relations*, 26 March (2020), https://www.ecfr.eu/article/commentary_serbias_coronavirus_diplomacy_unmasked.

210 Stefan Vladisavljev, "A Friend in Need Is a Friend Indeed — Belgrade Leans Closer to Beijing in the Fight against the COVID-19 Epidemic", *Choice*, 19 March (2020), https://chinaobservers.eu/the-friend-in-needis-a-friend-indeed-belgrade-leans-closer-to-beijing-in-the-fight-against-the-covid-19-epidemic/.

211 Mu Xuequan, "China Sends First Batch of Medical Aid to Serbia to Help Fight COVID-19", *Xinhua*, 17 March (2020), http://www.xinhuanet.com/english/2020-03/17/c_138884776.htm.

212 "Chinese Ambassador Tells Vucic: Aid to Battle Coronavirus Coming", *N1*, 17 March (2020), https://n1info.rs/english/news/a578849-chinese-ambassador-tells-vucic-aid-to-battle-coronavirus-coming/.

213 "Another 90 Tons of Medical Equipment Arrive at Belgrade Airport", *The Government of the Republic of Serbia*, 29 March (2020), https://www.srbija.gov.rs/vest/en/152805/another-90-tons-of-medical-equipment-arrive-at-belgrade-airport.php.

214 This image was first used in the case of Russian malign influence operation in Italy in March 2020, see the chapter "Russian Malign Influence Operation in Coronavirus-hit Italy" in this book.

pandemic for its own benefit. Unlike China, however, that seemed to be driven predominantly by economic interests; evidence suggests that Russia's COVID-related operations in Serbia were underpinned by the Kremlin's geopolitical interests and its political warfare against the West.

A window of opportunity

Before discussing Russian information operations in Serbia, it is important to understand the context in which Moscow (and, earlier, Beijing) operated — a context that was alleged to by Vučić in his anti-EU messaging.

Vučić's sweeping statement that "European solidarity" was "a fairy tale" was naturally an obvious insult to the EU. In the period between 2000 and 2018, the EU provided Serbia "with grants worth around €3.6 billion", while Chinese grants to Serbia amounted to an estimated €30 million (and "no Russian financial aid to Serbia was publicly registered" in the same period).[215] Moreover, in the past 20 years, "the EU donated above 200 Million euros and loaned 250 million others to make the health system in Serbia stronger".[216] As Majda Ruge and Janka Oertel rightly note, "without the EU, Serbia's health system would be much less capable of handling the coronavirus outbreak in the first place".[217]

Clearly, neither China nor Russia can effectively compete with the EU in terms of the size of financial aid provided to Serbia. But where they can compete is the sphere of decision-making time, and both Beijing and Moscow are superior to Brussels as they are able to make decisions instantly — an ability intrinsic to authoritarian

---

215 Majda Ruge, Nicu Popescu, "Serbia and Coronavirus Propaganda: High Time for a Transactional EU", *European Council on Foreign Relations*, 4 June (2020), https://www.ecfr.eu/article/commentary_serbia_and_coronavirus_propaganda_high_time_for_a_transactional.

216 "EU Assistance to Health Sector in Serbia — a Fundamental Effort that Modernised the Whole Serbian Health System", *The Delegation of the European Union to the Republic of Serbia*, 23 March (2020), http://europa.rs/eu-assistance-to-health-sector-in-serbia-a-fundamental-effort-that-modernised-the-whole-serbian-health-system/?lang=en.

217 Ruge, Oertel, "Serbia's Coronavirus Diplomacy Unmasked".

regimes that avoid and despise debate in the decision-making process.

A day before Vučić complained about the alleged lack of European solidarity in the fight against the pandemic, the EU adopted the "Commission Implementing Regulation (EU) 2020/402" that temporarily restricted export of "personal protective equipment" to countries outside of the EU "in order to ensure adequacy of supply in the Union in order to meet the vital demand".[218] As the regulation entered into force, it made void national restrictions on export of protective medical equipment that had been placed by several EU member states, including the Czech Republic, France, and Germany.[219] Those national restrictions were clearly harmful for the EU's struggle against the pandemic, because production of personal protective equipment was, at that time, mostly concentrated in the Czech Republic, France, Germany, and Poland.

The entry of "Commission Implementing Regulation (EU) 2020/402" into force largely solved the problem of distribution and trade of protective and other medical equipment inside the EU, but left all the other countries out. However, as the EU grew more confident of its resources and capabilities, it started to exempt third countries from the export restrictions. On 19 March, the EU adopted the "Commission Implementing Regulation (EU) 2020/426" that excluded Andorra, the Faeroe Islands, Iceland, Liechtenstein, Norway, San Marino, Switzerland, the Vatican City, as well as some overseas territories, from the scope of application of "Commission

---

218 "Commission Implementing Regulation (EU) 2020/402 of 14 March 2020 Making the Exportation of Certain Products Subject to the Production of an Export Authorisation", *Official Journal of the European Union*, 15 March (2020), https://eur-lex.europa.eu/legal-content/EN/TXT/?uri=uriserv:OJ.LI.2020.077.01.00 01.01.ENG.

219 Amie Tsang, "E.U. Seeks Solidarity as Nations Restrict Medical Exports", *New York Times*, 7 March (2020), https://www.nytimes.com/2020/03/07/busin ess/eu-exports-medical-equipment.html. It must be stressed that Germany had suspended those restrictions a few days before the adoption of "Commission Implementing Regulation (EU) 2020/402", see Tonia Mastrobuoni, "Coronavirus, la Germania invierà un milione di mascherine all'Italia", *La Repubblica*, 13 March (2020), https://www.repubblica.it/esteri/2020/03/13/news/coronavirus_la_germania_invia_un_milione_di_mascherine_all_italia-251219227/.

Implementing Regulation (EU) 2020/402".[220] The same day, the EU's High Representative Josep Borrell called Vučić to inform him that the EU was "looking at how to associate the Western Balkans to the initiatives" the EU was taking with regard to the pandemic and "how to best offer support in mitigating the socio-economic impact of the coronavirus" in the Western Balkans.[221] Although the Western Balkans (Albania, Bosnia and Herzegovina, Kosovo, Montenegro, North Macedonia, and Serbia) were excluded from the export restrictions by the adoption of "Commission Implementing Regulation (EU) 2020/568" only on 23 April,[222] the EU started providing aid to Serbia much earlier.

On 20 March, the EU decided to grant Serbia €7.5 million to strengthen the country's capacities and support its fight against the pandemic.[223] Out of that amount, €2 million would be used to cover the costs of transportation of medical supplies from China and India. Moreover, on 25 March, the European Commissioner for Neighbourhood and Enlargement Olivér Várhelyi instructed his office to release €93.4 million from the funds of Instrument for Pre-Accession that is intended to help Serbia prepare for its future membership in the EU: €15 million for immediate needs of the

---

220 "Commission Implementing Regulation (EU) 2020/426 of 19 March 2020 Amending Implementing Regulation (EU) 2020/402 Making the Exportation of Certain Products Subject to the Production of an Export Authorisation", *Official Journal of the European Union*, 20 March (2020), https://trade.ec.europa.eu/do clib/docs/2020/march/tradoc_158671.pdf.

221 "Serbia: Phone Call between High Representative Borrell President Vučić", *European Commission*, 20 March (2020), https://ec.europa.eu/neighbourhood-en-largement/news_corner/news/serbiaphone-call-between-high-representati ve-borrell-president-vučić_en.

222 "Commission Implementing Regulation (EU) 2020/568 of 23 April 2020 Making the Exportation of Certain Products Subject to the Production of an Export Authorisation", *Official Journal of the European Union*, 23 April (2020), https://eur-lex.europa.eu/legal-content/EN/ALL/?uri=uriserv:OJ.L_.2020.129.01.0007.01 .ENG. The regulation also exempted Gibraltar and territories of EU Member States excluded from the EU Customs Union.

223 "EU to Assist Serbia with €7.5m to Curb Coronavirus", *The Government of the Republic of Serbia*, 20 March (2020), https://www.srbija.gov.rs/vest/en/ 151944/eu-to-assist-serbia-with75m-to-curb-coronavirus.php.

health sector and €78.4 million for short- and medium-term needs (social and economic recovery).[224]

This aid from the EU notwithstanding, there was — as the timeline discussed above suggests — a short period in March 2020 when the EU was absent from the unfolding epidemiological drama in Serbia. Beijing and Moscow, as well as Belgrade itself, seized this opportunity to criticise and attack Brussels and other European capitals for the "lack of European solidarity" while advancing their own interests in Serbia.

From pro-Chinese and anti-EU messaging to silence

Moscow began its Serbian influence operation by echoing Chinese and Vučić's anti-EU messaging in the Russian state-controlled media. RT uncritically reported on Vučić's rant about European solidarity as "a fairy tale on paper",[225] without providing the context and failing to acknowledge that the EU remained by far the biggest donor of non-refundable assistance to Serbia, in particular to the country's health sector. For RT's senior writer Nebojša Malić, "the incompetence and hypocrisy of the European Union in dealing with the Covid-19 outbreak seem[ed] to have sobered up Serbia, a country that [had] previously slavishly committed itself to following orders from Brussels".[226] Another RT writer, Damian Wilson, contrasted the EU's "feebleness" with China's "soft-power offensive", against the background of "European nations outside the bloc, such

---

224 "€94m Redeployed from IPA Funds for Serbia", *The Government of the Republic of Serbia*, 25 March (2020), https://www.srbija.gov.rs/vest/en/152322/94m-redeployed-from-ipa-funds-for-serbia. php; "EU Response to the Coronavirus Pandemic in the Western Balkans", *European Commission*, April (2020), https://ec.europa.eu/neighbourhood-enlargement/sites/near/files/corona-virus_support_wb.pdf; "EU Response to the Coronavirus Pandemic", *European Commission*, https://www.europarl.europa.eu/doceo/document/E-9-2020-00 2307-ASW_EN.html.

225 "European Solidarity Doesn't Exist, Only China Can Help Us: Serbia Goes Full Emergency over Coronavirus", *RT*, 16 March (2020), https://www.rt.com/news/483239-serbia-eu-china-coronavirus/.

226 Nebojsa Malic, "Goodbye, Globalism? Coronavirus Sobers up Serbia to EU Hypocrisy", *RT*, 17 March (2020), https://www.rt.com/oped/483335-corona-virus-pandemic-serbia-border/.

as Serbia, hav[ing] been left to fend for themselves".[227] Arguing that the EU was "left looking poorly-prepared and slow to act" in the response to the pandemic,[228] Wilson cynically ignored a simple fact that when China started its charm offensive in March 2020, it had already managed to contain the spread of the virus in its own country, while the pandemic only started gaining momentum in Europe. Even when mentioning the EU's aid for Serbia, RT could not but question the raison d'être of Serbia's rapprochement with the EU: "Serbia has subordinated much of its domestic, foreign and economic policy to Brussels in an effort to eventually be considered for admission to the bloc, but the decades-long pro-EU narrative took a massive hit from the Covid-19 crisis".[229]

Yet as the Kremlin propaganda was trying – following Serbian President Vučić – to denigrate Brussels and European capitals, the only positive message it pushed was praise of Beijing while keeping silent on Moscow.

Ironically, against the background of the dominant anti-EU narrative being "feeble" and "slow" in its response to the spread of COVID-19 in Serbia, Russia – by its own standards – was even slower than the EU in providing any aid to Serbia. The latter did not seem to be of tactical importance to Russia, which predominantly focused on its influence operation in Italy in the course of March 2020.[230] Moreover, Serbian Foreign Minister Ivica Dačić, in a phone conversation with his Russian counterpart Sergey Lavrov on 16 March 2020, explicitly asked Russia "for assistance in the procurement of additional medical equipment, which would be necessary in case of a sudden increase in the number of patients".[231]

---

227 Damian Wilson, "From Villain to Hero? After Its Badly Botched Response to the Covid-19 Outbreak, China Now Seeks to Be the World's Savior", *RT*, 20 March (2020), https://www.rt.com/op-ed/483673china-coronavirus-europe-doctors-aid/.

228 Ibid.

229 "Serbian PM: 'Fake News' that We Don't Appreciate EU Help, but Covid-19 Aid Came from China", *RT*, 27 March (2020), https://www.rt.com/news/484322-serbia-coronavirus-eu-fake-news/.

230 See the chapter "Russian Malign Influence Operation in Coronavirus-hit Italy" in this book.

231 "Mutual Support, Assistance from Russia in Fight against Coronavirus", *The Government of the Republic of Serbia*, 16 March (2020), https://www.srbija.

Russian state-controlled media widely reported Serbia's plea for Russian help, as well as the words of Lavrov who promised that his country, "as always, would help Serbia", and wished "the brotherly Serbian people and its leadership to defeat this vicious virus as quickly as possible".[232]

Between 16 March, when the phone conversation between Dačić and Lavrov took place, and the end of the month, the number of active cases of COVID-19 registered in Serbia went up from 56 to 835,[233] but no aid from the Russian state was coming. As demonstrated above, at that time, the EU was already making important decisions on providing dozens of millions of euros to help Serbia fight the pandemic, but the Kremlin was still bashing the EU for being "slow", while, in its own turn, not sending any aid to "the brotherly Serbian people".

Leading Serbian independent newspapers wondered about the inaction of the Russian authorities. The left-leaning newspaper *Danas* wrote that there was "no point in expecting any significant help from Russia, because it had no considerable experience in fighting the virus, but also because of its weak economy".[234] The liberal *Blic* noted that Russia's Foreign Minister Lavrov offered Serbia words of support, but was disappointed by the lack of later developments:

> There is no doubt about the verbal support, but it was followed by silence from the Russian side. Meanwhile, the Chinese came to Serbia, flights with medical equipment were announced, money from the European Union, donations from Norway and aid from the United Arab Emirates. And then from those, who the majority of Serbian citizens consider their only true friends always and selflessly helping in time of need, although the evidence

---

gov.rs/vest/en/151491/mutual-support-assistance-from-russia-in-fight-against-coronavirus.php.

232 "Vizit lavrova v Serbiyu otlozhili iz-za koronavirusa", *RIA Novosti*, 16 March (2020), https://ria.ru/20200316/1568690255.html; "Serbiya obratilas' k Rossii za pomoshch'yu v bor'be s koronavirusom", *TASS*, 16 March (2020), https://tass.ru/mezhdunarodnayapanorama/7996439.

233 "Serbia", *Worldometer*, https://www.worldometers.info/coronavirus/country/serbia/.

234 Lidija Valtner, "Izostanak pomoći Moskve ne treba da čudi", *Danas*, 20 March (2020), https://www.danas.rs/politika/izostanak-pomocimoskve-ne-treba-da-cudi/.

suggests the opposite, we get only a slap on the shoulder. Is it surprising or not?[235]

Replying to the to the question about the absence of Russian aid, Suzana Vasiljević, an advisor to President Vučić, asserted that it could be explained by the problems that Russia experienced and the "paramount need to provide everything for its citizens".[236] But as Russia provided aid to Italy—in the period between 23 and 25 March, fifteen Russian aircrafts delivered experts and equipment to Italy[237]—Vasiljević's argument was disputable. Serbian political scientist Igor Novaković, director of research at the International and Security Affairs Centre, agreed that Russia had its own problems but—with perhaps with an implicit reference to the Russian aid to Italy –made an insightful point: "So if they [Russia] decide to help, then they think it is beneficial to use this help for foreign policy objectives. They probably choose [a country] where [the help] can be most noticeable".[238] Vasiljević's point implies that, for Moscow, providing of aid to Rome was more politically urgent than providing aid to Belgrade. Italy, in contrast to Serbia, is a member of the EU and NATO, so the Kremlin's influence operations in Italy could potentially have impact on decision-making inside these alliances, while little could be gained in Serbia where the socio-political climate is friendly for Russia anyway. A public opinion poll conducted in February-March 2020 demonstrated that 87% of Serbs viewed Russia favourably.[239] Moreover, contrary to all the publicly available statistics, Serbs put Russia second on the list of the biggest foreign donors to the country: 27% of respondents think Russia is

---

235 Lana Gedošević, "A od Putina, tapšanje po ramenu: Srbiji su u pomoć pritekle Kina, EU i Norveška, ali na tom spisku Rusije nema", *Blic*, 28 March (2020), https://www.blic.rs/vesti/drustvo/a-od-putinatapsanje-po-ramenu-srbiji-su -u-pomoc-pritekle-kina-eu-i-norveska-ali-na/qbv4ls7.
236 Ibid.
237 See the chapter "Russian Malign Influence Operation in Coronavirus-hit Italy" in this book.
238 Gedošević, "A od Putina, tapšanje po ramenu".
239 "Western Balkans Regional Poll. February 2, 2020—March 6, 2020", *International Republican Institute*, March (2020), https://www.iri.org/sites/default/files/fin al_wb_poll_for_publishing_6.9.2020.pdf.

the biggest donor and 28% believe it is the EU; China comes third with 20%.[240]

On 26 March, the Serbian government directly asked Russia to provide help to Serbia.[241] And eventually, Vučić had to call Russia's President Vladimir Putin on 2 April, and the two finally "agreed on the provision of humanitarian aid to Serbia in order to fight the spread of the infection in the spirit of traditional friendly bilateral relations".[242] As in the case of Italy, Putin assigned the task of delivering the aid to Serbia to Defence Minister Sergey Shoigu. On 3 April, Shoigu "ordered to create the aviation group for operational delivery of Russian military specialists to support the Republic of Serbia in the fight against coronavirus".[243] Russian airplanes started delivering aid the same day, and the first flight to the Batajnica Air Base was personally greeted by Serbian Prime Minister Ana Brnabić, Defence Minister Aleksandar Vulin, and Russian Ambassador to Serbia Aleksandr Botsan-Kharchenko.[244] Brnabić "expressed her gratitude to the Russian Federation for the assistance it provided to Serbia in the fight against coronavirus" noting that the Russian aid was "a partnership assistance that the Russian Federation sends to other countries too".[245] By the morning of 4 April, eleven Russian airplanes had delivered, according to the Russian government sources, "87 servicemen of the Russian Ministry of Defence, including military physicians, specialist virologists of the NBC protection

---

240   Ibid.
241   "Dačić: Srbija tražila pomoć Rusije", *Danas*, 28 March (2020), https://www.danas.rs/politika/dacic-srbija-trazila-pomoc-rusije/.
242   "Telephone Conversation with President of Serbia Aleksandar Vucic", *President of Russia*, April 2, 2020, http://en.kremlin.ru/events/president/news/63137.
243   "Russian Defence Minister Gives Instructions on Creation of Air Group for the Prompt Delivery of Assistance to Serbia", *Ministry of Defence of the Russian Federation*, http://eng.mil.ru/en/news_page/country/more.htm?id=12284998@egNews.
244   "Eleven Airplanes Delivered Medical Aid from the Russian Federation", *Ministry of Defence Republic of Serbia*, 4 April (2020), http://www.mod.gov.rs/eng/15843/jedanaest-avionadopremilo-medicinsku-pomoc-iz-ruske-federacije-15843.
245   "Plane from Russia Arrives with Doctors, Medical Equipment", *The Government of the Republic of Serbia*, 3 April (2020), https://www.srbija.gov.rs/vest/en/153281/plane-from-russia-arrives-withdoctors-medical-equipment.php.

troops, special medical equipment, protective equipment and 16 pieces of military equipment".[246]

Curiously, the Russian international media such as RT or Sputnik — with very few exceptions[247] — reported on the Russian aid to Serbia in a neutral way. That was in contrast to the reporting on the Russian aid to Italy, where facts about the aid were mixed with political messaging about the alleged failures of the EU and NATO to help Italy. As Moscow started delivering aid to Belgrade, narratives about the EU predominantly disappeared from RT's and Sputnik's coverage of the coronavirus-related developments in Serbia. It is unclear why this happened, but it is viable to suggest that Moscow realised that it could no longer afford pushing those narratives. If the EU was late with its assistance to Serbia, then Russia was behind not only China but even the EU it attacked, and Serbian society was aware of the situation, so praising Russia while criticising the EU could potentially do more harm to public perceptions of Russia than good.

Russian aid to Serbia in the international context

As Serbia was waiting for Russian aid for "the brotherly Serbian people" in the second half of March, the Kremlin was engaged in an international campaign aimed at convincing the West to lift sanctions against Putin's Russia that were imposed for its war against Ukraine and other aggressive actions. On 26 March, Russia submitted to the UN General Assembly (UNGA) an initiative to adopt its version of a Declaration of solidarity of the United Nations in the face of the challenges posed by the coronavirus disease 2019. Russia's draft declaration suggested "recognizing the leading role of the WHO in combating the pandemic", urged "states to

---

246 "Russian Aerospace Forces Complete Transferring Russian Military Specialists, Necessary Equipment and Machinery to the Republic of Serbia", *Ministry of Defence of the Russian Federation*, 4 April (2020), http://eng.mil.ru/en/news_page /country/more.htm?id=12285128@egNews.
247 For one prominent exception, see "Russian Aid to Help Serbia Avoid Italian Scenario Amid Pandemic — Lawmaker", *Sputnik*, 3 April (2020), https://sputniknews.com/analysis/202004031078825909-russian-aidto-help-serbia-avoid-italian-scenario-amid-pandemic---lawmaker/.

cooperate with each other and with the WHO" and made some other sensible propositions related to the pandemic.[248] However, the same draft also appealed to "abandon trade wars and unilateral sanctions adopted in circumvention of the UN Security Council"[249] — an appeal which the EU, UK, US, Ukraine, and Georgia perceived as Moscow's ill-concealed attempt to do away with the sanctions and, for this reason, eventually blocked what Russia's Foreign Ministry called an "absolutely humanistic document".[250] At the same time, the UNGA unanimously adopted a resolution on global solidarity to fight COVID-19 spearheaded by Ghana, Indonesia, Liechtenstein, Norway, Singapore, and Switzerland.

Russia's version of the declaration was killed in the UN on 2 April, and it was exactly on that day that Putin agreed to deliver aid to Serbia in a phone conversation with Vučić.

One of the Russian officials who was especially vocal in condemning Western countries and its East European allies for blocking the Russian draft declaration was Leonid Slutsky, the chair of the Committee on International Affairs and president of the Russian Peace Foundation (RPF). In recent years, Slutsky, who became one of the first Russian officials sanctioned by the West for his involvement in the Russian war on Ukraine, has been engaged in various malign influence operations aimed at advancing Russia's foreign policy interests ranging from organising fake election observation missions to cooperating with anti-EU far-right forces inside the EU.[251] Following the refusal to include Russia's proposal to ease

---

248 "Initiative to Adopt a UN General Assembly Declaration on Solidarity in Countering COVID-19", *Permanent Mission of the Russian Federation to the United Nations*, 27 March (2020), https://russiaun.ru/en/news/covid19_270320.

249 Ibid.

250 "Comment by the Information and Press Department on the UN General Assembly Reviewing the Declaration of Solidarity on Combating the Coronavirus Pandemic", *The Ministry of Foreign Affairs of the Russian Federation*, 4 April (2020), https://www.mid.ru/en/foreign_policy/news/-/asset_publisher/cKNonkJ E02Bw/content/id/4094623.

251 See "Politically Biased Election Observation — a Threat to the Integrity of International Institutions", *European Platform for Democratic Elections*, 15 February (2019), https://www.epde.org/en/news/details/politically-biased-election-observation-a-threat-to-theintegrity-of-international-institutions-1774.html;

sanctions in the final draft of the UNGA declaration, Slutsky described it as a manifestation of "political coronaegoism" on the part of the US and EU, adding that "hegemonistic ambitions upset common efforts against the pandemic".[252] Moreover, on 7 March, Slutsky published an appeal, which, again, criticised the refusal to support the Russian version of the UNGA resolution—"an inhumane attitude of some states", as Slutsky put it.[253] Slutsky's appeal also called upon "all rational politicians in the leadership of the European Union, the USA, Great Britain, leading international and inter-parliamentary organizations to abandon the destructive sanctions policy".[254]

Slutsky's appeal was distributed to Russian embassies across the world in order to garner support for Moscow's attempts to push its revised version of the declaration on the pandemic through the UNGA—the revised version dropped the call to lift sanctions but still suggested to end "protectionist practices".[255] Furthermore, the RPF's website published, on 16 April, a news report saying, in particular, that the Foundation provided "humanitarian aid" to Italy, Iran, and Serbia.[256] It was unclear when exactly the RPF's aid had been sent to those three countries, but the same news report featured letters of appreciation sent to Slutsky by ambassadors of Iran and Italy dated 24 March and 6 April respectively. However, there was no proof that the RPF had delivered any aid to Serbia by the time of the publication of the report.

---

see also the chapter "Russian Malign Influence Operation in Coronavirus-hit Italy" in this book.

252 "US, EU Refusal to Block Russia's Anti-Sanctions Resolution Is 'Coronaegoism'—Lawmaker", *TASS*, 3 April (2020), https://tass.com/politics/1139745.

253 "Leonid Slutskiy Urged to Abandon the Sanctions Policy in the Light of the Coronavirus Epidemic", *The State Duma*, 7 April (2020), http://duma.gov.ru/en/news/48236/.

254 Ibid.

255 Edith M. Lederer, "Russia Tries Again to Win UN Approval for Virus Resolution", *ABC News*, 18 April (2020), https://abcnews.go.com/US/wireStory/russia-win-approval-virus-resolution-70221150.

256 "Rossiyskiy fond mira napravil gumanitarnuyu pomoshch' grazhdanam Italii, Irana i Serbii", *Rossiyskiy Fond Mira*, 16 April (2020), http://www.peacefond.ru/news/?id=1518.

The timing of the report was hardly coincidental: the UN was to consider Russian amendments to the UNGA declaration on the pandemic on 22 April, and Slutsky needed to demonstrate his active participation in the promotion of the Kremlin's foreign policy interests on the international stage. This can explain why the RPF decided to refer, rather belatedly, to the aid it apparently delivered to Iran more than three weeks earlier, and to Italy more than a week before the publication of the news report. And the RPF evidently jumped ahead in the case of Serbia: during the meeting between Serbian Foreign Minister Ivica Dačić and Russian Ambassador Aleksandr Botsan-Kharchenko, the former mentioned that the RPF's aid had arrived in Serbia in the period between 20 and 26 of April.[257]

The efforts of the Russian Foreign Ministry and Slutsky were doomed to failure. On 22 April, Western countries and their allies blocked Russian amendments to the UNGA declaration on the pandemic again.

Conclusion

When COVID-19 arrived in Europe from China, which failed to contain the virus and, as a consequence, triggered the pandemic, the EU was perplexed. The EU's confusion as to how to deal with the pandemic was felt on many levels. Brussels was late with providing assistance to Italy, which initially was hit the hardest among all the EU member States, and it was late with providing aid to the Western Balkans including Serbia.

However, it is important to stress that by using the word "late" in this context, we implicitly refer to the fact that China's aid had arrived to Italy, Serbia, and some other countries earlier than the aid from the EU. Apart from the EU's confusion at the start of the pandemic, three major factors contributed to the EU being "late". First, by that time, China had managed to stop the spread of COVID-19 inside the country and could grant medical equipment

---

257 "Exceptional Relations, Cooperation with Russia in Fight against Coronavirus", *The Government of the Republic of Serbia*, 27 April (2020), https://www.srbija. gov.rs/vest/en/155223/exceptional-relations-cooperation-with-russia-in-figh t-against-coronavirus.php.

and protective gear to other countries. Second, as China had been investing heavily in European countries, it needed to restore its reputation damaged by the failure to contain the virus. Third, as an authoritarian state, China could coordinate the delivery of aid very quickly and without the red tape that is characteristic of rule-based democratic systems.

The EU did catch up, however, and eventually delivered more aid to Serbia than that from all the third-party countries combined. Nevertheless, there was a short period of time — around one week — between Serbian President Aleksandar Vučić's plea for help from China and the EU's promises to grant millions of euros to Serbia to help it fight the pandemic that was cynically exploited by Beijing and Moscow to attack Brussels and other European capitals while advancing their own objectives. For China, those objectives were predominantly economic — China is interested in investing in Serbia. Russia, rather, was driven by its political warfare with the West in general and the EU in particular.

However, by attacking the EU, the Kremlin was mostly engaged in pro-Chinese propaganda, which could naturally be considered as indirectly pro-Kremlin, but was nevertheless primarily pro-Chinese. Russia offered Serbia words of overwhelming support but failed to quickly follow up with medical, financial, or expert assistance to "the brotherly Serbian people".

At that time, Belgrade was not important for Moscow's geopolitical game — Russia used its resources instead to woo the EU and NATO member, Italy. Yet the absence of Russian aid undermined the Kremlin's own narrative about the EU being "feeble" and "slow" in Serbia in comparison to China. And as Russia finally started sending aircrafts with humanitarian aid to Serbia after the EU had promised dozens of millions of euros to the country, the Kremlin media largely abandoned its anti-EU messaging in the context of the coronavirus-related developments in the Western Balkans.

This notwithstanding, the Russian parliament or, more specifically, its Committee on International Affairs chaired by Leonid Slutsky, tried to use Russian aid to Serbia as part of the Kremlin's campaign to convince the international community to adopt a

Russian version of the UNGA declaration on the COVID-19 pandemic that would potentially allow lifting Western sanctions imposed on Putin's Russia for the annexation of Crimea and its war on Ukraine. However, Moscow's trick did not work, and, in general, there is no evidence that Moscow has achieved any tangible result in its malign influence operations in Serbia.

5. Putin's "Foot Soldier" in the Kremlin's Political War against France

Introduction

"He's a hero for the entire Islamic world. In France and Europe, they consider faggots as heroes, but that's not the case here".[258] The "he" in question is Abdoullakh Anzorov, an 18-year-old Russian refugee of Chechen origin who murdered and then decapitated French schoolteacher Samuel Paty in a suburb of Paris on the 16th of October 2020. And the person who called Anzorov "a hero for the entire Islamic world" is Salman Magamadov, a head of the Shalazhi village in the Chechen Republic where Anzorov was buried after the French police shot him following his deadly terrorist attack. Around 200 male relatives and friends of the Anzorov family attended his funeral ceremony in Shalazhi shouting "Allahu akbar" ("God is the greatest") during the procession of his coffin.[259]

Samuel Paty was a French history teacher, and his only "crime" — in the eyes of the Islamists like Anzorov — was that he showed satirical cartoons, including some depicting Muhammad, the founder of Islam, to his class during a lesson about freedom of speech, as part of a moral and civic education course. Following the lesson, Paty was attacked on social media by Islamists, including a religious militant Abdelhakim Sefrioui and a parent of one of his pupils.[260]

---

258 "'Kakie pochesti? V Shalazhi on pervy raz pokoynikom okazalsya.' Glava sela, gde pokhoronili terrorista Abdulakha Anzorova, otritsaet, chto tseremoniya proshla v torzhestvennoy obstanovke", *Pod'yom*, 7 December (2020), https://pdmnews.ru/18328/.

259 "Chechen Who Beheaded French Teacher Buried on Home Soil — Reports", *Moscow Times*, 7 December (2020), https://www.themoscowtimes.com/2020/12/07/chechen-who-beheaded-french-teacher-buried-on-home-soil-reports-a72252.

260 "France Teacher Attack: Seven Charged over Samuel Paty's Killing", *BBC*, 22 October (2020), https://www.bbc.co.uk/news/worldeurope-54632353.

Anzorov had no direct connection either to Paty or the school where he taught;[261] most likely, he became aware of Paty's "crime" as a result of the online hate campaign against the schoolteacher orchestrated by the Islamists. Anzorov tracked Paty down on 16 October, more than a week after the freedom-of-speech lesson, and murdered him with a knife. According to witnesses, Anzorov was shouting "Allahu akbar" during the attack.[262] The killer also photographed Paty's severed head and posted the picture on Twitter, addressing French President Emmanuel Macron: "To Macron, the leader of the infidels, I executed one of your hellhounds who dared to belittle Muhammad, calm his fellow human beings before a harsh punishment is inflicted on you".[263] French police confronted Anzorov shortly after Paty's murder and, as he was offering armed resistance to the arrest, shot him dead.

President Macron called the murder an "Islamist terrorist attack", adding that Paty had been murdered because he taught "freedom of expression, the freedom to believe or not believe".[264] Macron also said that the killer sought to "attack the republic and its values" and called the battle against Islamist terrorism "existential".[265]

After yet another Islamist attack in Nice on the 29th of October, European leaders issued a joint statement saying that they were

---

261   "France Teacher Attack: Suspect 'Asked Pupils to Point Samuel Paty out'", *BBC*, 17 October (2020), https://www.bbc.co.uk/news/worldeurope-54581827.

262   "France Terror Attack: Teacher Decapitated in Paris Suburb Named as Samuel Paty", *Sky News*, 18 October (2020), https://news.sky.com/story/france-terror-attack-47-year-old-decapitated-in-paris-suburb-named-as-teacher-samuel-paty-12105885.

263   Cécile Chambraud, Elise Vincent, Nicolas Chapuis, "Attentat de Conflans: ce que l'on sait de l'enquête après le meurtre brutal de Samuel Paty", *Le Monde*, 17 October (2020), https://www.lemonde.fr/societe/article/2020/10/17/attentat-de-conflans-un-hommage-national-sera-rendu-a-l-enseignant-assassine-vendredi-annonce-lelysee_6056408_3224.html.

264   Elaine Ganley, "French Leader Decries Terrorist Beheading of Teacher", *AP*, 16 October (2020), https://apnews.com/article/france-teacher-decapitated-erag ny-f1ecd575344d171ff8fc8c33c5320f0c.

265   Kim Willsher, "Macron Speaks of 'Existential' Fight against Terrorism after Teacher Killed in France", *Guardian*, 17 October (2020), https://www.theguardian.com/world/2020/oct/16/french-police-shoot-man-dead-after-knife-attack-near-paris-school.

"shocked and saddened by the terrorist attacks in France" and condemning "in the strongest possible terms these attacks which represent attacks on our shared values".[266] The statement continued: "We stand united and firm in our solidarity with France, with the French people and the Government of France – in our common and continued fight against terrorism and violent extremism".[267]

In France itself, the overwhelming majority of Muslim communities condemned the murder of Samuel Paty. The French Council of the Muslim Faith said that the "the horrible assassination of our fellow citizen" was a reminder "of the scourges which sadly mark our reality: that of the outbreaks, in our country, of radicalism, violence and terrorism".[268] The Strasbourg-based Assembly of Chechens in Europe and Paris-based Chechen Association Bart-Marsho sent an open letter to President Macron saying that they condemned the crime and "all forms of religious extremism and all acts of violence".[269] The signatories of the letter stated that members of their organisations were grateful to the French state for allowing thousands of Chechen refugees who had fled war and persecution to stay on French territory and that they condemned extremism, calling on their compatriots "to respect the law and respect all members of the societies" in which they lived.[270]

What, then, can explain the contrasting, somewhat apologetic reactions to Paty's murder among particular circles in the Chechen Republic – reactions that went beyond praising the murderer as "a hero for the entire Islamic world" on the part of the local authorities of Shalazhi and seemed to be shared even by the political and religious leadership of Chechnya? And why did those reactions differ

266 "Joint Statement by the Members of European Council", *Council of the European Union*, 29 October (2020), https://www.consilium.europa.eu/en/press/press-releases/2020/10/29/joint-statement-by-the-members-of-european-council/.
267 Ibid.
268 "Attentat à Conflans: Le CFCM propose un prêche aux imams de France", *20 minutes*, 22 October (2020), https://www.20minutes.fr/societe/2891475-2020 1022-attentat-conflans-cfcm-propose-precheimams-france.
269 "Lettre ouverte au Président de la République Française et au Ministre de l'Interieur", *Bret Marsho*, 18 October (2020), https://bartmarsho.com/открытое-письмо-президенту-французс/.
270 Ibid.

from the Kremlin's official unambivalent condemnation of "the barbaric murder of a French teacher" by the Islamist?[271]

Macron: from Russia scepticism to Realpolitik

In order answer these questions, we first need to review, if briefly, the relations between Putin's Russia and Macron's France.

The background of these relations was problematic: Macron was not Moscow's preferred candidate in the 2017 French presidential elections.

In late autumn to early winter 2016, national public opinion polls predicted that, while no candidate would be able to secure a victory in the first round, the final stand-off would be between François Fillon, the candidate of the centre-right Republicans (Les Républicains) party, and Marine Le Pen, the leader of the far-right National Front. The Kremlin felt optimistic about both of them.

Both candidates were seen as friendly towards Putin's Russia. The likeliest winner, Fillon, a former Prime Minister of France (2007-2012) under President Nicolas Sarkozy, was "advocating a dramatic change of tack with Moscow, favouring lifting economic sanctions imposed by the EU after Russia's annexation of Crimea", and was "also pushing for a military alliance with Mr. Putin and the Syrian regime of Bashar al-Assad to combat Isis".[272] During the Russian invasion of Eastern Ukraine, Fillon "argued that it was mostly Russian-speaking and more or less belonged to Moscow".[273] In his turn, Putin called Fillon "a professional to the highest degree and an honest person".[274] And the Russian state-controlled media

---

271 "Telephone Conversation with President of France Emmanuel Macron", *President of Russia*, 20 October (2020), http://en.kremlin.ru/events/president/news/64249.

272 Anne-Sylvaine Chassany, Jack Farchy, "François Fillon's Rapprochement Plans Meet with Putin Approval", *Financial Times*, 23 November (2016), https://www.ft.com/content/554b82ea-b18a-11e6-a37c-f4a01f1b0fa1.

273 Nicholas Vinocur, "François Fillon, Thatcherite with a Thing for Russia", *Politico*, 21 November (2016), https://www.politico.eu/article/francois-fillon-that cherite-with-a-thing-for-russia-juppe-france/.

274 "Russia Ready to Work with French Leadership to Restore Relations — Putin", *Sputnik*, 23 November (2016), https://sputniknews.com/politics/20161123104 7755531-putin-work-france-president/.

hailed the candidacy of Fillon, describing him as "the most prag-
matic candidate in international politics" and suggesting that he
"lived up to the expectations of the French people".[275]

Le Pen was even friendlier towards Moscow. Already in 2011,
she said she believed that "France should stop 'bowing to America's decisions' and strengthen its ties with Russia instead",[276] and
that if she came to power, she would make Russia "a privileged
partner" of France.[277] Le Pen justified the annexation of Crimea;[278]
her advisor on international relations at that time, Aymeric
Chauprade, even "observed" the so-called "referendum" on Crimea joining Russia in March 2014—and blamed the EU for the Rus-
sia-backed separatist activities in Eastern Ukraine.[279] In 2014, her
party obtained a €9.4 million loan from the First Czech-Russian
Bank, a now defunct bank that at that time was owned by the structures of Gennadiy Timchenko, a major Russian businessman from
Putin's inner circle.[280] Since 2014, Le Pen had consistently criticised
the EU's sanctions on Russia for the annexation of Crimea and invasion of Eastern Ukraine.[281]

In the beginning of 2017, the "win-win" situation with the
French presidential elections ended for Moscow: because of a

275 "Russia Hails Francois Fillon (as a Worried Germany Looks on)", *The Local*, 28
     November (2016), https://www.thelocal.fr/20161128/russian-media-hail-fill
     on-as-a-worried-germany-looks-on.
276 "I Want to Free France from EU Straitjacket—Far-Right Party Leader", *RT*, 27
     April (2011), https://www.rt.com/news/france-eu-immigrants-pen/.
277 "Marine Le Pen veut aller en Russie", *Le Figaro*, 2 May (2011), https://www.
     lefigaro.fr/flash-actu/2011/05/02/97001-20110502FILWWW00503-marine-le-
     pen-veut-aller-en-russie.php.
278 Tom Batchelor, "Marine Le Pen Insists Russian Annexation of Crimea Is Totally
     Legitimate", *Independent*, 3 January (2017), https://www.independent.co.uk/
     news/world/europe/marine-le-pen-crimea-russia-putin-ukraine-illegal-anne
     xation-france-front-national-fn-a7507361.html.
279 Anton Dolgunov, "Marin Le Pen: Evropa neset otvetstvennost' za pro-
     iskhodyashchee na Ukraine", *ITAR-TASS*, 1 June (2014), https://tass.ru/
     mezhdunarodnaya-panorama/1230269.
280 Marine Turchi, "Le Front national décroche les millions russes", *Mediapart*, 22
     November (2014), www.mediapart.fr/journal/france/221114/le-front-nationa
     l-decroche-les-millionsrusses; Shekhovtsov, *Russia and the Western Far Right*, pp.
     197-198.
281 "France's Marine Le Pen Urges End to Russia Sanctions", *BBC*, 24 March (2017),
     https://www.bbc.com/news/world-europe-39375969.

corruption scandal, public support for Fillon dramatically de-
creased, and Emmanuel Macron replaced him as the presumptive
winner of the presidential race. Macron, when still the Minister of
Economy, Industry and Digital Affairs (2014-2016), did support the
idea of lifting the EU's sanctions on Russia, but he insisted on the
conditionality of the removal of the sanctions: "The objective we all
share is to provide the lifting of sanctions by the summer, as far as
the peace process in south-eastern Ukraine is respected", Macron
said in January 2016 during his trip to Moscow.[282] In Macron, the
Kremlin seemed to anticipate the continuation of President
François Hollande's policies towards Putin's Russia: maintaining a
polite conversation with Moscow while remaining firm on the need
for Russia to stop its aggression against Ukraine.

Before Macron's rise, the Kremlin preferred not to interfere in
the presidential elections in France, but when its preferred candidate's popularity fell, Putin's regime decided to attack Macron
through media and cyber operations. Russian state-controlled RT
and Sputnik propagated and amplified conspiracy theories about
Macron,[283] while his team complained that their website and data-
bases were subject to cyber-attacks originating from Russia.[284]
Moreover, in March 2017, just one month before the first round of
the presidential elections, the Kremlin invited Macron's closest opponent, Marine Le Pen, to visit Moscow and meet with Putin. The
political message was clear: the Kremlin had resigned itself to the
failure of Fillon and presented Le Pen as its candidate in the French
presidential elections. "We all know who Le Pen's allies are: the

---

282 "Macron in Moscow: France Wants Russia Sanctions Lifted by Mid-Year", *RFI*,
    25 January (2016), https://www.rfi.fr/en/economy/20160125-macron-mosco
    w-france-wants-russia-sanctions-lifted-mid-year.
283 "Dupont-Aignan soupçonne Macron de conflits d'intérêts et veut qu'il clarifie
    'ses financements'", *RT*, 11 February (2017), https://francais.rt.com/france/
    33829-dupontaignan-soupconne-macron-conflitinteretsclarifie-financements;
    "Ex-French Economy Minister Macron Could Be 'US Agent' Lobbying Banks'
    Interests", *Sputnik*, 4 February (2017), https://sputniknews.com/20170204/
    macron-us-agent-dhuicq-1050340451.html.
284 "France Condemns Alleged Russian Cyber Attacks Targeting Presidential Can-
    didate Macron", *France 24*, 19 February (2017), https://www.france24.com/
    en/20170219-france-condemns-cyberattacks-targeting-presidential-candidate-
    macron-points-russia.

regimes of Orban, Kaczynski, Putin. These aren't regimes with an open and free democracy. Every day they break many democratic freedoms", Macron said just days before his victory in the final stand-off between him and Le Pen.[285]

Already, at the end of the presidential campaign, Macron's team had denied press access to RT and Sputnik, "accusing them of spreading 'propaganda' and 'misleading information.'"[286] Furthermore, at a press conference with Putin, who had arrived in Paris to meet with the newly elected president of France at the end of May 2017, Macron held his ground and reiterated that RT and Sputnik had behaved during the campaign not "as media organisations and journalists" but as "agencies of influence" and "lying propaganda".[287]

At that time, the Russian attacks on Macron made him out to be "a Russia hawk".[288] In June 2018, the French edition of RT "received its first reprimand from the French regulator CSA (Conseil de Surveillance Audiovisuel) [...] for its biased coverage of the chemical attack in [Syrian] Douma in April 2018".[289] At the end of

---

285   Lidia Kelly, "Poland Outraged after Macron Comments on Le Pen and Putin", *Reuters*, 2 May (2017), https://www.reuters.com/article/us-france-election-po land-russia/poland-outraged-after-macron-comments-on-le-pen-and-putin-id USKBN17Y1IE.

286   "French Presidential Hopeful Macron Bans Russian-State Media from Campaign Trail", *France 24*, 29 April (2017), https://www.france24.com/en/ 20170429-macron-campaign-drops-accreditation-kremlin-backed-media.

287   "Video: Macron Slams RT, Sputnik News as 'Lying Propaganda' at Putin Press Conference", *France 24*, 30 May (2017), https://www.france24.com/en/2017 0530-macron-rt-sputnik-lying-propaganda-putin-versailles-russia-france-electi on. On the French edition of RT see, in particular, Hugo Littow, "Copying, Distorting and Questioning: The Mediatic Populism of RT France", in Anton Shekhovtsov (ed.), *RT in Europe and beyond: The Wannabe Elite of the Anti-Elites* (Vienna: Centre for Democratic Integrity, 2022), pp. 26-40; Élie Guckert, "Manufacturing Dissent: RT France's Challenge in a Brand-New Media Landscape", in Anton Shekhovtsov (ed.), *RT in Europe and beyond: The Wannabe Elite of the Anti-Elites* (Vienna: Centre for Democratic Integrity, 2022), pp. 42-53; Maxime Audinet, *Russia Today (RT): Un média d'influence au service de l'État russe* (Bry-sur-Marne: Éditions de l'INA, 2021).

288   Ben Judah, "Emmanuel Macron's Foreign Policy Doctrine(s)", *Politico*, 8 May (2017), https://www.politico.eu/article/emmanuel-macrons-foreign-policy-d octrines/.

289   Anastasia Kirilenko, "RT France and Sputnik's Attempts to Enhance French Society's Divisions", *The Kremlin's Influence Quarterly*, No. 2 (2020), pp. 34-45 (39).

the same year, France adopted a law on the "fight against the manipulation of information" that enabled "the transmission of foreign state controlled radio and television services that broadcast disinformation to be curtailed, or temporarily suspended, prior to key elections", and established "a new civil procedure by which a judicial order [could] be obtained requiring online communication providers to block further transmission of false information in the runup to elections and referenda".[290]

The Kremlin continued its political warfare against Macron and started building contacts with representatives of the radically anti-Macron Yellow Vest movement. The Kremlin engaged with them with the help of Leonid Slutsky, the chair of the Committee on International Affairs and president of the Russian Peace Foundation (RPF). In 2014, Slutsky had helped organise an illegitimate referendum in Ukraine's Autonomous Republic of Crimea, which was followed by its annexation by Russia, and for this he was sanctioned by Western countries. Since then, Slutsky had become one of the key operators of Russian political warfare in Europe. For example, it was Slutsky who officially invited Marine Le Pen to meet with Putin in 2017, and, in 2020, he was actively engaged in Russian malign influence operations in Italy and Serbia.[291] As revealed by *The Insider*, Slutsky's RPF issued special invitations for several French Yellow Vest members so they could visit Russia, allegedly to discuss RPF's "humanitarian and charitable programmes and projects".[292] Given the subversive nature of Slutsky's activities in Europe, it is viable to suggest that the Kremlin wanted to exert influence on the Yellow Vest movement with the aim of strengthening it and/or pushing particular narratives through its activists.

---

290 Rachael Craufurd Smith, "Fake News, French Law and Democratic Legitimacy: Lessons for the United Kingdom?", *Journal of Media Law*, Vol. 11, No. 1 (2019), pp. 52-81 (52).

291 See chapters "Russian Malign Influence Operation in Coronavirus-hit Italy" and "How to Fail a Malign Influence Operation: The Case of Russian Aid to Serbia" in this book.

292 "Khotim kak v Parizhe. Dokumenty podtverdili kontakty rossiyskhikh vlastey s 'zheltymi zhiletami' i nemetskimi natsionalistami", *The Insider*, 18 November (2019), https://theins.ru/politika/188244.

However, despite Russia's flirtations with the anti-Macron Yellow Vests and while remaining sceptical about Russian propaganda and disinformation, Macron increasingly adopted a *Realpolitik* approach towards Russia. Former Foreign Minister Hubert Védrine (1997-2002) and former Prime Minister Dominique de Villepin (2005-2007) apparently played a crucial role in Macron's transformation from a Russia-sceptic to a politician who called for deeper cooperation with Russia despite the latter's non-compliance with international norms. In the summer of 2019, Macron declared: "Pushing Russia away from Europe is a profound strategic error, because we will push Russia either into an isolation that increases tensions or into alliances with other great powers such as China".[293] He did not suggest "to forget all our disagreements and to embrace each other again", but he still held that "the European continent [would] never be stable, [would] never be in security, if we [didn't] pacify and clarify our relations with Russia".[294]

The Kremlin enthusiastically received Macron's *Realpolitik* turn towards Moscow, and, in August 2019, Putin visited Macron at the latter's summer retreat at the Brégançon Fort to discuss Ukraine and Syria. And yet, Moscow officially maintained its contacts with anti-Macron forces in France. On 11 November 2019, while in Paris, Russian Foreign Minister Sergey Lavrov and Spokesperson for the Ministry of Foreign Affairs Maria Zakharova held a meeting "with members of the French civil society", as Zakharova described them.[295] Among them one could identify, among others, Martial Bild, a co-founder of the far-right Party of France (Parti de la France) who was also involved in launching the far-right, pro-

---

293 Victor Mallet, James Shotter, Michael Peel, "Emmanuel Macron's Pivot to Russia Sparks EU Unease", *Financial Times*, 11 September (2019), https://www.ft.com/content/00ac54f4-d30f-11e9-8367-807ebd53ab77.

294 "Keeping Russia out of Western Fold a 'Strategic Error', Macron Says in Key Speech", *France 24*, 27 August (2019), https://www.france24.com/en/2019 0827-france-macron-ambassadors-speech-new-economic-order-diplomacy-for eign-policy.

295 "In Paris, FM Sergey #Lavrov Met with Members of the French Civil Society", *Facebook*, 11 November (2019), https://www.facebook.com/MIDRussia/pos ts/2090333797732717.

Kremlin TV Libertés;[296] Olivier Berruyer, a blogger and regular commentator for RT;[297] Bertrand Pillet, who runs the ThinkerView YouTube channel that regularly hosts far-right and far-left activists, as well as conspiracy theorists and Eurosceptics; and Dimitri de Kochko, a co-founder of the Union of Russophones of France and a regular commentator for the French edition of the Russian state-controlled Sputnik website.

There is naturally nothing new in the Kremlin's double game of striving to have a high-profile dialogue with the leaders of European countries and yet keeping communication lines open with anti-system actors aiming to undermine that very leadership. And this double game is exactly the background that provides insight into the Kremlin's behaviour towards Paris in the wake of Samuel Paty's brutal murder by a Russian Islamist.

The Kremlin's double game

For most of 2020, which was dramatically affected by the coronavirus pandemic, relations between Moscow and Paris remained positively neutral. However, the Kremlin disrupted the balance with the poisoning of major opposition figure Alexei Navalny on 20 August 2020. Two days later, Navalny was evacuated to Germany, where specialists established that Navalny had been poisoned by a Novichok nerve agent. Navalny survived, but the West was shocked by the attempt on his life: not only was it an outrageous act aimed at silencing the leading Russian critic of Putin's regime, but the use of the nerve agent against a political opponent was also a clear violation of the Chemical Weapons Convention signed and ratified by the overwhelming majority of the world's countries, including Russia. Because of these considerations, French Foreign Minister Jean-Yves Le Drian and German Foreign Minister Heiko Maas called on Russia to "urgently clarif[y] in full the facts and responsibilities behind this assassination attempt on a

---

296   Shekhovtsov, *Russia and the Western Far Right*, pp. 146-147.
297   Anastasia Kirilenko, "Advokaty d'yavola. Kak Kreml' zadeystvoval svoyu set' vo Frantsii, dokazyvaya v sude, chto kremlyovskoy seti vo Frantsii net", *The Insider*, 15 March (2019), https://theins.ru/antifake/147120.

member of the Russian political opposition using a military-grade nerve agent that belongs to a group of agents developed by Russia".[298]

As could have been expected, the Kremlin denied any responsibility for the poisoning of Navalny. On 6 October, the Organisation for the Prohibition of Chemical Weapons confirmed the conclusions of the German experts who said that the Russian opposition activist had been poisoned by a Novichok nerve agent.[299] The following day, Le Drian and Maas issued yet another joint statement saying that there was "no other plausible explanation for Mr. Navalny's poisoning than a Russian involvement and responsibility", adding that France and Germany would "share with European partners proposals for additional sanctions" targeting "individuals deemed responsible for this crime and breach of international norms".[300] Russian Foreign Ministry Spokesperson Maria Zakharova responded to the statement accusing France and Germany of "heading the anti-Russian coalition" allegedly taking shape in the EU "contrary to the earlier statements by Paris and Berlin on their commitment to partnership with Russia".[301] Zakharova finished her response to the statement of Le Drian and Maas by saying that Russia did not "consider it possible to conduct 'business as usual' with Berlin and Paris".[302]

---

298 "Joint Communiqué by the Foreign Ministers of France and Germany (4 Sept. 2020)", *Ministère de l'Europe et des Affaires étrangères*, 4 September (2020), https://www.diplomatie.gouv.fr/en/country-files/russia/news/article/alexei-navalny-joint-communique-by-the-foreign-ministers-of-france-and-germany.

299 "OPCW Issues Report on Technical Assistance Requested by Germany", *Organisation for the Prohibition of Chemical Weapons*, 6 October (2020), https://www.opcw.org/media-centre/news/2020/10/opcw-issues-report-technical-assista nce-requested-germany.

300 "Joint Statement by the Foreign Ministers of France and Germany Alexeï Navalny (7 October 2020)", *Ministère de l'Europe et des Affaires étrangères*, 7 September (2020), https://www.diplomatie.gouv.fr/en/country-files/russia/news/article/joint-statement-by-the-foreign-ministers-of-france-and-germany-alexei-navalny.

301 "Comment by Foreign Ministry Spokeswoman Maria Zakharova on the Joint Statement by the French and German Foreign Ministers on the Situation with Alexey Navalny", *The Ministry of Foreign Affairs of the Russian Federation*, 7 October (2020), https://www.mid.ru/en/foreign_policy/news/-/asset_publish er/cKNonkJE02Bw/content/id/4372528.

302 Ibid.

The EU and the United Kingdom imposed sanctions on top Russian officials and a number of Russian entities on 15 October 2020. The EU determined that Navalny had been poisoned with a Novichok nerve agent, and, since that toxic agent was "accessible only to State authorities in the Russian Federation", it was "reasonable to conclude that the poisoning of Alexei Navalny was only possible with the consent of the [Russian] Presidential Executive Office".[303]

The following day, Samuel Paty was murdered in an Islamist terror attack in a suburb of Paris. It would be a paranoid fantasy to suggest that there was any connection between the EU's sanctions and Paty's murder. However, the introduction of the new sanctions against Putin's regime may help explain the nature of the double game that the Kremlin started in relation to Macron.

The official Russian reaction was unambiguous. Putin called Macron on 20 October; he "expressed his condolences in connection with the terrorist act—the barbaric murder of a French teacher", and both reportedly reaffirmed "mutual interest in stepping up cooperation to combat terrorism and the spread of extremist ideology".[304] A few days earlier, the head of the Chechen Republic Ramzan Kadyrov, who calls himself Putin's "foot soldier",[305] had condemned the terrorist attack in France and offered condolences to the relatives of the murdered teacher.[306] Kadyrov also called on the French authorities "not to provoke the faithful, [and] not to hurt their religious feelings".[307] And, importantly, Kadyrov essentially disowned Abdoullakh Anzorov as a Chechen, saying that the latter had lived almost his entire life in France, spoke French, and had

303 *Official Journal of the European Union*, Vol. 63, 15 October (2020), https://eur-lex.europa.eu/legal-content/EN/TXT/PDF/?uri=OJ:L:2020:341:FULL&from =EN.

304 "Telephone Conversation with President of France Emmanuel Macron", *President of Russia*, 20 October (2020), http://en.kremlin.ru/events/president/news/64249.

305 Andrew Osborn, Dmitry Solovyov, "Chechen Leader, amid Reshuffles, Says Ready to Die for Putin", *Reuters*, 27 November (2017), https://www.reuters.com/article/us-russia-chechnya-idUSKBN1DR03I.

306 Ramzan Kadyrov, "Dorogie druz'ya!", *Telegram*, 17 October (2020), https://t.me/RKadyrov_95/1008.

307 Ibid.

visited Chechnya only once, at the age of two.[308] For a person who – since at least 2010 – had insisted that he was the national leader of all Chechens no matter whether they lived, in Chechnya or anywhere else in the world,[309] the disownment of Anzorov as a co-ethnic implied an even deeper denunciation than Kadyrov's official condemnation of the terrorist attack.

But already then, in particular Chechen circles, some were condoning Anzorov's terror attack. In his Instagram post, Chechen MMA fighter Zelim Imadaev called Anzorov "a hero of Islam" and asked Allah to approve of his jihad.[310] Yet another Chechen MMA fighter, Albert Duraev, noted in his Instagram account that "freedom of speech lost its origin in France", adding a laughing emoji to his post.[311]

By the end of October, Chechen leadership had changed its positions with regard to the terrorist attack in France. Using the Instagram account of the Spiritual Administration of the Muslims of Chechnya, Salakh-Khadzhi Mezhiev, a mufti and advisor to Kadyrov, started spreading disinformation about Macron, claiming that the French president was having Muhammad cartoons posted on all government buildings in France.[312] Reacting to this made-up story, Mezhiev called Macron "the number one terrorist in the world", "the most degraded creature", "the enemy of the human-kind", and "the enemy of all Muslims".[313] There was an ideological angle to Mezhiev's hateful attack on Macron too, as the mufti also talked about "genuine terrorism and extremism cultivated on the Western pseudo-values of multi-liberalism [sic] and all-

308 Ibid.
309 Elena Milashina, "Khozyain chechentsev", *Novaya gazeta*, 28 July (2019), https://novayagazeta.ru/articles/2019/07/28/81403-hozyain-chechentsev.
310 Karim Zidan, "Former UFC Fighter Praises Chechen Teen who Beheaded French Teacher", *Bloody Elbow*, 19 October (2020), https://www.bloodyelbow.com/2020/10/19/21523149/ufc-fighter-praises-chechen-teen-beheaded-french-teacher-decapitation-prophet-mma-news.
311 Ibid.
312 "Sovetnik Glavy ChR, Muftiy Chechenskoy Respubliki SalakhKhadzhi Mezhiev vystupil s zayavleniem", *Instagram*, 26 October (2020), https://www.instagram.com/p/CG0I-pPF4vO/.
313 Ibid.

permissiveness".[314] And by making the "insane professor" a national hero, France, Mezhiev claimed, "deliberately incited Muslims to provocative actions".[315]

Mezhiev's words were almost immediately echoed by
Kadyrov. He wrote that the murdered teacher was himself responsible for what happened, because he "provoked pupils".[316] If Anzorov was a terrorist, Kadyrov argued, then Macron was much worse:
"the leader and encourager of terrorism".[317]

The new approach to the terrorist attack offered by Mezhiev
and Kadyrov became the main narrative of the entire story in
Chechnya: Paty had it coming, his murder was not a terrorist attack
but a result of provocation, Macron is a terrorist himself.

Moreover, a similar narrative was being pushed by Dmitry
Kiselyov, a major Russian propagandist and the head the Russian
government-owned international news agency "Rossiya Segodnya". Kiseloyov had been sanctioned by the EU in 2014 for his participation in the information warfare against Ukraine. During a TV
program that he anchored (after the Islamist attack in Nice on 29
October), Kiselyov claimed that France was "descending into a religious war", and that the state itself was "pitting the majority of its
citizens and law enforcement against Muslims".[318] And while he
talked about "the soul-chilling brutality and massacre of the inno-
cent", he still referred to them as "desperate resistance of the Muslims" to the allegedly repressive state actions that he himself fabricated.[319] Kiselyov's message was clear: the West in general hated
traditional values, was on the brink of collapse, and could not serve
as an ideological inspiration for Russia.

---

314 Ibid.
315 Ibid.
316 Ramzan Kadyrov, "Frantsuzskie vlasti podderzhivayut publikatsii karikatur na
Proroka Mukhammada", *Telegram*, 27 October (2020), https://t.me/RKad
yrov_95/1010.
317 Ibid.
318 Yuriy Bershidskiy, "Feyk Dmitriya Kiselyova: Zapad provotsiruet religioznuyu
voynu protiv musul'man", *The Insider*, 3 November (2020), https://theins.
ru/antifake/236555.
319 Ibid.

Furthermore, Kadyrov made a U-turn on disownment of Anzorov as a Chechen: he allowed the body of the terrorist to be transported from France to Chechnya and buried in the Shalazhi village where his relatives lived. The clear message was that Kadyrov claimed Anzorov as one of his own: he was no longer a person who had lived his entire life in France; he was, first and foremost, a Chechen. At the same time, the re-owning of Anzorov as a Chechen through his burial in Chechnya was a violation of the Russians' own tradition with regard to the terrorists: in Russia (including Chechnya), bodies of killed terrorists are never given to their relatives.

Dozens of police officers secured Shalazhi; only residents were allowed to enter the village during the funeral and reception, and only around 200 hundred people were allowed to take part in the ceremony.[320] After the funeral, which some media described as a funeral "with honours",[321] the Chechen State Television and Radio Company "Grozny" aired a report that reiterated Kadyrov's narrative of the terrorist attack. The report, referencing his relatives, called Anzorov "a god-fearing young man who was not known for any aggressiveness" and claimed that the "incident" (i.e. the murder of Paty) would not have taken place if not for the "overt Islamophobic provocation and pressure on religious feelings".[322]

It was after the funeral that the head of the Shalazhi village called Anzorov "a hero for the entire Islamic world".[323] And on the

---

320 Benoît Vitkine, "Le terroriste qui a assassiné Samuel Paty enterré en Tchétché-
     nie", *Le Monde*, 8 December (2020), https://www.lemonde.fr/societe/artic
     le/2020/12/08/attentat-de-conflans-sainte-honorine-l-assassin-de-samuel-pa
     ty-enterre-en-tchetchenie_6062554_3224.html.
321 "Chechen Who Beheaded French Teacher Buried on Home Soil—Reports",
     Moscow Times, 7 December (2020), https://www.themoscowtimes.com/2020/
     12/07/chechen-who-beheaded-french-teacher-buried-on-home-soil-reports-a
     72252.
322 Aleksandr Baklanov, "Telekanal 'Grozny' vypustil syuzhet o pokhoronakh 18-
     letnego chechentsa, obezglavivshego uchitelya pod Parizhem. I nazval ubiytsu
     zhertvoy provokatsii", *Meduza*, 8 December (2020), https://meduza.io/fea
     ture/2020/12/08/telekanal-groznyy-vypustil-syuzhet-o-pohoronah-18-letne
     go-chechentsa-obezglavivshego-uchitelya-pod-parizhem-i-nazval-ubiytsu-zh
     ertvoy-provokatsii.
323 "'Kakie pochesti?'".

18th of December, around 50 horseback riders performed a *ziyarat* (a pilgrimage to holy sites in Islam) to Anzorov's grave. As they reached it, they said a prayer asking Allah to accept Anzorov's *ghazwa*, i.e. a military jihad against infidels.[324]

Kadyrov as an instrument of the Kremlin's political war

There is little doubt that following Kadyrov's U-turn on Anzorov and the latter's burial in Chechnya, the "Grozny" report on the funeral and the glorification of his actions was not simply tolerated but directly sanctioned by Kadyrov or his inner circle.[325] The leadership in Chechnya — described as "a black hole in the Council of Europe's human rights protection system"[326] — is even more authoritarian than Putin's regime, and no significant development in Chechnya (apart from sporadic terrorist activities) can happen without approval from Kadyrov's circles.

Kadyrov's departure from a more moderate position on Anzorov's terrorist attack, which was generally compliant with the Kremlin's official position, can be explained by a combination of several factors.

First, the praise of Anzorov was a continuation of Kadyrov's fight against Western secularism. For example, shortly after the Islamist terror attack on the office of the French satirical newspaper *Charlie Hebdo*, which left 12 people dead, Kadyrov organised a demonstration of hundreds of thousands of people against the newspaper in

---

324   "Pol'zovateli sotsseti odobrili konny pokhod k mogile Anzorova v Chechne", *Kavkazskiy Uzel*, 21 December (2020), https://www.kavkaz-uzel.eu/articles/357839/.

325   Amina Zakaeva, Semen Charny, "Opravdanie Anzorova v syuzhete ChGTRK 'Grozny' pokazalo neposledovatel'nost' Kadyrova", *Kavkazskiy Uzel*, 9 December (2020), https://www.kavkaz-uzel.eu/articles/357382/.

326   "No Justice in Sight for Grave Crimes in Chechnya", *European Center for Constitutional and Human Rights*, https://www.ecchr.eu/en/case/no-justice-in-sight-for-grave-crimes-in-chechnya/.

Chechnya's capital Grozny—a demonstration that pushed pro-Muslim and anti-Western narratives.[327]

Second, Kadyrov aspires to be recognised as a major defender of Islam, and as the leaders of important Muslim countries such as Turkey and Iran harshly attacked Macron for his intentions to combat radical Islam,[328] Kadyrov's radicalised move was about joining the front of other major self-proclaimed defenders of Islam.

Third, by sanctioning Islamist actions normalising or even glorifying Anzorov and his terror attack, Kadyrov allows Chechen Islamists "to let off steam" and express their radical sentiments in a controlled environment created by the Chechen leadership to contain Islamism.

Fourth, Kadyrov positions himself as the leader of all Chechens wherever they live, and the re-owning of Anzorov as a Chechen sent a double message to the Chechen diaspora in Europe and elsewhere: on the one hand, whatever you do, whatever crime you commit, we will always support you (unless your crime was against Russian leadership or Kadyrov); on the other hand, we own you, so you should behave and never try to undermine Kadyrov's authority.

The Kremlin never strayed from its official unambiguous condemnation of the terror attack. Putin's press secretary Dmitry Peskov even publicly distanced himself twice from Kadyrov's statements. In one instance, Peskov, commenting on Kadyrov's anti-Macron attack, said that Russian regional leaders cannot engage in or shape foreign policy, and that one should keep the line formulated by the president.[329] In another instance, Peskov, when asked about the above-mentioned report on Anzorov's funeral on the

327 "Up to 800,000 Chechens Protest over Cartoons of Prophet Muhammad", *Guardian*, 19 January (2015), https://www.theguardian.com/world/2015/jan/19/chechens-protest-cartoons-prophet-muhammad-charlie-hebdo.

328 Michael Safi, Redwan Ahmed, Akhtar Mohammad Makoii, Shah Meer Baloch, "Anger towards Emmanuel Macron Grows in Muslim World", *Guardian*, 28 October (2020), https://www.theguardian.com/world/2020/oct/28/anger-towards-emmanuel-macron-grows-in-muslim-world.

329 "Peskov predlozhil sledit' vo vneshney politike za slovami Putina, a ne Kadyrova", *Interfax*, 28 October (2020), https://www.interfax.ru/russia/734545.

Chechen "Grozny" TV channel, said that the report did not corre-
late with the Kremlin's position, while defending the alleged pluralism of the Russian state-controlled media.[330]

Nevertheless, the Kremlin, if it did not directly authorise, then,
at the very least, permitted Kadyrov and his circles, as well as propagandist Dmitry Kiselyov, to voice a radically different position on
the same case on Samuel Paty's murder. This can also be explained
by two major considerations.

First, the Kremlin, which was initially pleased with Macron's
Realpolitik turn, was deeply disaffected when France took a leading
role in the introduction of the EU sanctions in response to the poisoning of Navalny by the Russian security services. Kadyrov thus
became an element of Moscow's double game in relation to Macron.
As argued above, this game consists of maintaining a dialogue with
Western leaders while simultaneously keeping open communication lines with anti-system and anti-establishment actors. In the
case of Anzorov's Islamist terror attack, Putin's regime supported
Macron and yet empowered, through Kadyrov and others, the Islamist opposition to Macron as part of the Kremlin's political warfare against France.

Second, as Ivan Preobrazhensky insightfully noted, against
the background of the rise of anti-Macron sentiments in many Muslim countries, with Turkish President Recep Erdoğan effectively becoming the leader of the anti-French front, Putin's regime could not
afford further consolidation of Erdoğan's regional authority.[331]
Kadyrov's entry into this front erodes Erdoğan's claims to political
leadership of the Islamic world. (The Kremlin naturally does not
allow Kadyrov to criticise China for the genocide of Uyghur Muslims—and Kadyrov knows perfectly well his limits as a self-proclaimed defender of Islam—but the rhetoric aimed at radicalising
Muslims and inciting them against Macron and French liberal democracy does fit into Moscow's subversive agenda in Europe.)

---

330 "Peskov ne soglasilsya s TV Chechni v otsenke deystviy ubitsy uchitelya Pati",
    Interfax, 8 December (2020), https://www.interfax.ru/russia/740383.
331 Ivan Preobrazhensky, "Kadyrov—golos iz RF v islamskom internatsionale pro-
    tiv Makrona", *Deutsche Welle*, 28 October (2020), https://www.dw.com/ru/
    kommentarij-rossijskij-golos-v-islamistkom-internacionale/a-55420069.

Conclusion

At the moment, it seems impossible to establish whether Kadyrov's attack on Macron was authorised or simply permitted by the Kremlin. Staying on the safe side and assuming the latter is true, Kadyrov's anti-French rhetoric and apologetic stance towards the perpetrator of the terror attack seems to be shaped by political, personal, and tactical concerns. Kadyrov is illiberal and attacked French liberalism; he lays claim for leadership in the Islamic world and joined other leaders in attacking "Islamophobic" Macron; he diverts radical Islamist sentiments in Chechnya to a foreign power; and he strengthens his authority among the Chechens worldwide by defending the terrorist just because of his Chechen origin.

Regardless of which concerns are more important to Kadyrov, the Kremlin benefits from his attacks against Macron and France. On the one hand, by empowering Islamists in France, Kadyrov contributes to religious polarisation and undermines social cohesion in France, which, despite Macron's discovered *Realpolitik* approach to Putin's Russia, still takes principled stands with regard to the Kremlin and its violations of international agreements such as the Chemical Weapons Convention. On the other hand, Kadyrov helps Moscow covertly fight another political war, with Istanbul, consolidating its positions in the region and competing with Moscow in different areas.

Focusing on the Kremlin's use of Kadyrov as an instrument of its political warfare against France, it must be said that while not all Chechens living in Europe in general and France in particular are supportive of Kadyrov (and, as demonstrated earlier, official Chechen organisations in Europe unambiguously condemned the terror attack), Chechen youth in Europe is susceptible to his illiberal propaganda.[332] And as his attacks on Macron and French secularism continue, they pose a clear security threat to French society.

---

332 Anastasia Kirilenko, "Propaganda Kadyrova povliyala na radikalizatsiyu chechenskoy molodezhi v Evrope", *Kavkazskiy Uzel*, 21 October (2020), https://www.kavkaz-uzel.eu/articles/355564/.

6. The Rise and Fall of a Polish Agent of the Kremlin Influence
The Case of Janusz Niedźwiecki

Introduction

In the beginning of June 2021, the Press Department of Poland's National Public Prosecutor's Office published a press release that stated, in particular, the following:

> On 31 May 2021 in Warsaw, on the order of the prosecutor of the Mazowieckie Branch of the Department for Organised Crime and Corruption of the National Public Prosecutor's Office, officers of the Internal Security Agency arrested Janusz N. [...]

> The prosecutor [...] charged the detainee with espionage for the secret services of the Russian Federation against the interests of the Republic of Poland, qualified under Article 130, paragraph 1 of the Penal Code.

> This act is punishable by up to 10 years of imprisonment.

> During the proceedings, the places of residence of Janusz N. and the offices of related entities were searched. In the course of these activities, money in the amount of over PLN 300,000 [approximately €65,485] and a large amount of data carriers were found. [...]

> In the course of the investigation, the prosecutor found that the suspect was involved in activities in favour of the Russian Federation — activities that intensified after his associate had previously been arrested on suspicion of espionage. Janusz N., commissioned by people working for Russian intelligence, tried to establish contacts with Polish and foreign politicians, including those working in the European Parliament. The suspect carried out his activities in Poland, the European Union and other countries, and those activities were part of Russian propaganda and disinformation projects undertaken in order to weaken the position of the Republic of Poland in the EU and in the international arena.[333]

---

333 "Areszt za szpiegostwo na rzecz obcego wywiadu", *Prokuratura Krajowa*, 10 June (2021), https://pk.gov.pl/aktualnosci/aktualnosci-prokuratury-krajowej /areszt-zaszpiegostwo-na-rzecz-obcego-wywiadu/.

While the Polish National Public Prosecutor did not disclose the full name of the suspect, all the evidence suggested that it was a Polish national named Janusz Gabriel Niedźwiecki.

The Western regressive Left called Niedźwiecki a "peace activist";[334] Alexander Lukashenka's authoritarian regime in Belarus described him as a "journalist" and "civic activist";[335] and Russian pro-Kremlin media called Niedźwiecki "a renowned human rights advocate".[336]

Refuting these false portrayals, this chapter traces Niedźwiecki's development from a fringe political activist, through a coordinator of fake election observation missions and facilitator of international contacts of Ukrainian pro-Russian politicians, to an agent of malign Russian influence. Simultaneously, by focusing on the figure of Niedźwiecki, the chapter reveals a part of the vast network of Kremlin and other authoritarian influences operating in Europe and elsewhere.

Setting the scene

In late February 2014, at the height of the mass popular protests that became known as the Revolution of Dignity, Ukraine's President Viktor Yanukovych fled to Russia. Following his flight, Russia annexed Crimea and started the invasion of eastern Ukraine. Against this background, Yanukovych's Party of Regions (Partiya rehioniv, PoR), which was characterised by predominantly pro-Russian stances, dramatically lost popularity. The PoR won the 2012 parliamentary elections with 30% of the vote, but in summer 2014 it polled so poorly that it hardly had a chance to enter the parliament again.

---

334 Monika Carbowska, "Political Persecutions in Poland", *Defend Democracy Press*, 15 June (2021), https://www.defenddemocracy.press/stalinism-is-back-now-in-westerneurope/.

335 "Naibolee rezonansnye sluchai narusheniya prav cheloveka v otdel'nykh stranakh mira", *Ministry of Foreign Affairs of the Republic of Belarus*, https://www.mfa.gov.by/publication/reports/e424905d68e54d40.html.

336 Lyudmila Chertkova, "Kontrrazvedka Pol'shi arestovala izvestnogo pravozashchitnika kak 'russkogo shpiona'", Pravda, 10 June (2021), https://www.pravda.ru/news/world/1621676-polsha/.

Ukrainian businessman and one of the PoR's main sponsors Rinat Akhmetov decided to re-brand the party in order to keep his influence over Ukrainian politics. In order to re-brand the party, Akhmetov turned to American political consultant and lobbyist Paul Manafort, who had been advising the PoR and Yanukovych since 2005.[337] Manafort came up with the name of the new party, Opposition Bloc (Opozytsiyny blok), that rallied many of the PoR's former members, and was reported to have personally approved the list of the Opposition Bloc's candidates in the snap 2014 parliamentary elections. In political terms, the new party differed little from the PoR: it was still pro-Russian in foreign policy orientations and was supported and, to a certain degree, run by rich businessmen who had economic interests primarily in eastern and southern Ukraine, as well as Russia. Nevertheless, with Manafort's help, the Opposition Bloc obtained 9.43% of the vote in the snap elections and Ukrainian parliament retained a strong pro-Russian voice despite the Russian-Ukrainian war.[338]

Until 2014, all the presidential and parliamentary elections in Ukraine had been characterised by the significant presence of politically biased, or simply fake, international monitoring missions that aimed at advancing interests of corrupt pro-Russian politicians by imitating credible election monitoring. A number of fake election observation organisations had sent representatives to Ukraine, and the following organisations had been especially active in Ukraine at different times: Interparliamentary Assembly of the CIS Member Nations (Russia), British Helsinki Human Rights Group (United Kingdom), CIS-EMO (Russia), European Centre for Geopolitical Analysis (Europejskie Centrum Analiz Geopolitycznych, ECAG, Poland), Eurasian Observatory for Democracy and Elections (Belgium), International Expert Centre for Electoral Systems (ICES,

---

337 Steven Lee Myers, Andrew E. Kramer, "How Paul Manafort Wielded Power in Ukraine Before Advising Donald Trump", *New York Times*, 31 July (2016), https://www.nytimes.com/2016/08/01/us/paul-manafort-ukraine-donald-trump.html.

338 Michal Kranz, "Manafort Didn't Just Consult for Russian-Backed Politicians in Ukraine—He Also Helped Them Form a New Party", *Business Insider*, 18 November (2017), https://www.businessinsider.com/manafort-russia-backed-politicians-ukraine-opposition-bloc-yanukovych-trump-2017-11.

Israel), and European Academy for Elections Observation (Belgium). All of them had engaged in advancing political interests of pro-Russian and pro-authoritarian politicians and political forces at Ukrainian elections.

At the snap presidential and parliamentary elections in 2014, however, there was a decline in the presence of politically biased election observation in Ukraine, especially in comparison to the 2012 parliamentary elections. Only representatives of the ECAG "observed" the presidential election in May 2014, while the mission of the ICES did the same at the parliamentary elections in October 2014. The decline in fake election observation in 2014 can be explained by two major factors. First, pro-Russian forces suffered a political backlash and were apparently too confused to organise any significant operations in that area. Second, during 2014, many members of previous fake election observation missions became increasingly involved in "observing" illegitimate plebiscites in Russia-occupied Crimea and particular areas of eastern Ukraine, which resulted in travel bans to the parts of Ukraine controlled by the legitimate Kyiv government.

In 2015, Ukraine's President Petro Poroshenko sanctioned dozens of individuals, many of whom participated in "observation" missions on the Ukrainian territories occupied by Russia, and the sanctions, which included travels bans, further undermined fake observation in Ukraine. However, by the time of the regional elections in autumn 2015, the Opposition Bloc's politicians had recovered from the confusion of 2014 and made attempts to reclaim political power, especially in eastern and southern regions of Ukraine.

One of the cities contested between the representatives of the forces loyal to the post-revolutionary authorities and those who represented the "old guard" of the Yanukovych era was the city of Dnipropetrovsk (renamed into Dnipro in 2016). There, the main mayoral contest was between Borys Filatov, backed by Ukrainian businessman Ihor Kolomoyskyi, and the Opposition Bloc's Oleksandr Vilkul, backed by Akhmetov. Vilkul's party turned to friendly European "election observers" whose job would be to provide information support to his campaign.

Operation Dnipropetrovsk: Enter Janusz Niedźwiecki

Polish political activist Janusz Gabriel Niedźwiecki arrived in Dnipropetrovsk in autumn 2015 as a coordinator of the observation mission organised by the International Civic Organisation "Political Initiative". It was apparently Niedźwiecki's first participation in an international observation mission.

In 2001-2006, Niedźwiecki studied philosophy at the University of Warmia and Mazury in his native city of Olsztyn. Later, he got interested in politics and joined the youth wing of the social-liberal Palikot's Movement party (Ruch Palikota), founded by Janusz Palikot. In February 2012, at the age of 32, Niedźwiecki became the chairman of the Palikot's Movement in the Olsztyn district.[339] In 2013, the party was renamed into "Your Movement" (Twoj Ruch); Niedźwiecki remained its member but, at the end of 2013, he lost the party leadership election in the Olsztyn district.[340] Niedźwiecki's defeat presumably marked the start of his estrangement from Your Movement. In September 2014, he left the party and submitted a notification to the prosecutor's office accusing the leadership of his former party, including Janusz Palikot himself, of misappropriating a large share of state subsidies.[341]

Niedźwiecki's briefly collaborated with the agrarian Polish People's Party (Polskie Stronnictwo Ludowe, PSL), and ran, unsuccessfully, in the local elections in Olsztyn as a representative of the PSL.

---

339 "Janusz Niedźwiecki szefem Ruchu Palikota w okręgu olsztyńskim", *Gazeta Współczesna*, 14 February (2012), https://wspolczesna.pl/janusz-niedzwiecki-szefemruchu-palikota-w-okregu-olsztynskim/ar/5805191.

340 "Palikot: w gminach pracują działacze partyjni, trzeba reformy samorządu", *Money.pl*, 8 December (2013), https://www.money.pl/archiwum/wiadomosci_agencyjne/pap/artykul/palikot;w;gminach;pracuja;dzialacze;partyjni; trzeba;reformy;samorzadu,182,0,1438134.html.

341 "Odchodzi z TR. 'Palikot sprzeniewierzył wielomilionową subwencję'", *Wprost*, 16 September (2014), https://www.wprost.pl/469028/odchodzi-z-twojego-ruchu-palikot-sprzeniewierzyl-wielomilionowa.html; Malwina Gadawa, "Prokuratura sprawdzi Twój Ruch – także kandydatkę na prezydenta Wrocławia", *Gazeta Wrocławska*, 30 September (2014), https://gazetawroclawska.pl/prokuratura-sprawdzi-twoj-ruch-takze-kandydatke-na-prezydenta-wroclawia/ar/3592033.

In February 2015, Niedźwiecki found himself in another party, Change (Zmiana), the ideology of which was very different from Palikot's political project or PSL. Zmiana was formed (yet never registered) by arguably the most notorious Polish pro-Kremlin activist, Mateusz Piskorski. In the late 1990s, Piskorski was a member of the Polish neo-fascist group "Niklot", but would later join the right-wing populist Self-Defence of the Republic of Poland (Samoobrona Rzeczpospolitej Polskiej). In the beginning of the 2000s, Piskorski started visiting Russia and building networks with like-minded Russian far-right activists. In 2004-2005, Piskorski became engaged in politically biased election observation advancing the interests of authoritarian regimes in Belarus and Russia-occupied Transnistria. As he developed contacts with — at that time — the major Russian organisation involved in coordinating fake election observation, namely CIS-EMO, Piskorski founded his own organisation in 2007, the European Centre for Geopolitical Analysis (ECAG), which became a Polish "node" in a vast European pro-Kremlin network of fake election observers.[342]

The foundation of the radically anti-American, anti-NATO, anti-EU, and pro-Russian Zmiana party in 2015 was yet another step in Piskorski's pro-Kremlin activities in Poland. The party leadership united left-wing and right-wing activists. Vice-chairmen of the party included left-wing political commentator Jarosław Augustyniak, leader of the neo-fascist Falanga group Bartosz Bekier, pro-Assad businessman of Syrian origin Nabil Al Malazi, and member of the right-wing populist Self-Defence party Konrad Rękas.

Because of the ECAG's active involvement in politically biased election observation in Ukraine in previous years, one might have expected that the Opposition Bloc would invite them to observe local elections in Dnipropetrovsk and other cities and regions of interest to the party. However, Piskorski and his ECAG were major coordinators of international fake observation of the illegitimate referendum in Russia-occupied Crimea (16 March 2014) and

---

342   More on Piskorski's activities see Shekhovtsov, *Russia and the Western Far Right*, pp. 113-117.

illegitimate parliamentary elections in parts of eastern Ukraine (November 2014). Consequently, the road to Kyiv-controlled Ukraine was closed for him: if not for legal reasons, Piskorski himself and his ECAG became too toxic even for the Opposition Bloc.

Hence, instead of engaging with Piskorski, representatives of the Opposition Bloc reached out to a Latvian pro-Russian activist, Sergejs Blagoveščenskis. At that time, he positioned himself as the defender of the Russian language in Latvia and was supportive of the now defunct Latvian political party "Harmony Centre" (Saskaņas Centrs), which claimed to represent the interests of Russians in Latvia.[343] Although less infamous than Piskorski, Blagoveščenskis had had experience in organising and participating in fake election monitoring missions. In 2010, he took part in the observation mission of CIS-EMO at the 2010 Ukrainian regional elections.[344] The same year, he registered his own association in Latvia, "Political Initiative", one of the aims of which was "election monitoring at the local and international level",[345] and, in 2012, he brought an observation mission of "Political Initiative" to monitor Ukrainian parliamentary elections. Earlier that year, Blagoveščenskis had joined Piskorski and other pro-Kremlin activists in observing Russian presidential elections. Ironically, although "Political Initiative" was registered in Latvia, the country's Central Election Commission refused to accredit its observation mission to monitor the 2012 constitutional referendum on the amendments to the Constitution of the Republic of Latvia.[346]

Blagoveščenskis used the brand of "Political Initiative" to bring an 18-strong observation mission, apparently put together by

---

343 Sergey Blagoveshchenskiy, "Obrashchenie k deputatam XI Seyma ot Tsentra Soglasiya", *blago.lv*, 16 December (2011), http://blagolv.blogspot.com/2011/12/xi.html; Sergey Blagoveshchenskiy, "Latviyskaya demokratiya v deystvii", *blago.lv*, 17 February (2012), http://blagolv.blogspot.com/2012/02/blog-post.html.

344 In 2010-2011, he contributed at least two pieces for the CIS-EMO website, in which he criticised, from the pro-Russian point of view, Latvian methods of integrating Russian speakers into the larger Latvian society.

345 "Politiskā iniciatīva", *Lursoft*, https://company.lursoft.lv/en/politiskainiciativa/40008159599.

346 Blagoveshchenskiy, "Latviyskaya demokratiya v deystvii".

Niedźwiecki using Piskorski's contacts, to Ukraine in 2015. Apart from Niedźwiecki and Blagoveščenskis himself, the mission included, in particular, six members of the German far-right party Alternative for Germany (Alternative für Deutschland, AfD)[347] and three members of the Hungarian party Jobbik,[348] which at that time could also be described, in terms of ideology, as far-right.[349] Other observers from "Political Initiative" either had previous experience participating in fake election monitoring or represented pro-Russian parties. (Surprisingly, the mission also included Stanislav Berkovec, a member of the Czech parliament, who, in March 2014, joined Piskorski's "monitoring mission" at the "Crimean referendum".[350] Kyiv should have sanctioned him as it did many other European politicians who had been present at the "referendum" as "observers", and his unhindered participation in the "Political Initiative" mission in Ukraine in 2015 demonstrated that Ukraine's abilities to trace hostile elements were, at least at that time, limited.)

The aim of the "Political Initiative" mission in Ukraine was to endorse elections in case of the victory of the Opposition Bloc representatives, and condemn them in case of their defeat or unconvincing electoral performance. The mission split into two major teams. One team, including Niedźwiecki and AfD members, went to Dnipropetrovsk to observe the two rounds of the mayoral elections held on 25 October and 15 November 2015 respectively. The other team, including Jobbik members, went to Mariupol to monitor the city council elections held on 29 November 2015.

The Opposition Bloc's Oleksandr Vilkul won the first round of the elections in Dnipropetrovsk by securing 37.94% of the vote, while Borys Filatov obtained 35.77% of the vote. The following day,

---

347 Ludwig Flocken, Corinna Herold, Olaf Kießling, Rainer van Raemdonck, Thomas Rudy, and Christina Schade.
348 Zoltán Magyar, Tamás Gergő Samu, and Balázs Szabó.
349 Starting in 2016-2017, Jobbik has undergone an ideological transformation, shifting closer to the centre right, so it can no longer be considered a far-right party.
350 "Evropeyskie nablyudateli v Sudake: Zdes'vsyo ne tak, kak nam pokazyvaut'", *Sudak*, 16 March (2014), https://web.archive.org/web/2014 0319105617/http://sudak.me/articles/politic/evropeiskie-nablyudateli-v-su dake-zdes-vse-ne-tak-kak-nam-pokazyvayut.html.

the AfD's Rainer van Raemdonck declared that the elections had been held "in compliance with the European standards" and that "Political Initiative" observers had not detected any serious or grave violations of the electoral process.[351]

The reactions to the second round of the elections on the part of the "Political Initiative" mission were different. On the voting day, in the morning, the Ukrainian media published a statement signed by several members of the mission (Niedźwiecki, Berkovec, Andrzej Dariusz Dołecki, Thomas Rudy, and Ludwig Flocken), warning of alleged provocations against the candidate who had won the first round of the elections, i.e. the Opposition Bloc's Oleksandr Vilkul.[352] In particular, the statement said:

> Unfortunately, we are compelled to say that we have been informed by a credible source about mass provocations in the making aimed at the disruption of the electoral process. We know that some people were specifically hired—many of them having a criminal past—and were instructed to attack members of electoral commissions, burst into polling stations, damage the ballots and use other illegal means to disrupt the elections. [...] They were paid a large honorarium to turn themselves voluntarily in to the police and claim that they were working on behalf of one of the mayoral candidates. We also know that these claims are manipulative and aimed at precluding the front-runner in the elections to win in a lawful manner.[353]

The "credible source" mentioned in the statement was most likely political activist Ivan Krasikov, who at that time supported Vilkul.[354] In a comment publicised by the *Segodnya* newspaper, owned by Akhmetov's Media Group Ukraine, two days before the statement of "Political Initiative", Krasikov said that "the elections [would] be disrupted at the polling stations where, potentially,

---

351 "Mestnye vybory v Dnepropetrovske proshli v sootvetstvii s evropeyskimi normami, mezhdunarodnye nablyudateli", *Most Dnepr*, 26 October (2015), https://most-dnepr.info/news/politics/127114_mestnie_vibori_dnepropetrovske.htm.

352 "V Dnepropetrovske v den' vyborov ozhidayutsya provokatsii protiv lidera izbiratel'noy gonki—mezhdunarodnye nablyudateli", *Golos UA*, 15 November (2015), https://golos.ua/news/v-dnepropetrovske-v-den-vyborov-ozhidayutsya-provokatsii-protiv-lidera-izbiratelnoj-gonki-mezhdunarodnye-nablyudateli.

353 Ibid.

354 "Lyudi khotyat videt' merom Dnepropetrovska opytnogo menedzhera,—ekspert", *Dnepr Glavnoe*, 6 November (2015), https://glavnoe.dp.ua/articles/ljudi-hotjat-videt-mjerom-dnepropetrovska-opytnogo-menedzhera-jekspert-2/.

Oleksandr Vilkul [would] be winning. These people may claim that they represent Vilkul".[355] No other source ever suggested that the elections would be disrupted by a false-flag operation aiming at discrediting Vilkul; hence it is viable to suggest that the statement was either inspired by Krasikov's commentary or even coordinated with the Opposition Bloc's consultants. Eventually, none of the actions that Krasikov and "Political Initiative" warned of took place.

The Opposition Bloc's Oleksandr Vilkul lost the second round of the elections: his rival, Borys Filatov, obtained 52.31% of the vote, while Vilkul secured 44.92%. The day after the elections, at a press conference of the "Political Initiative" mission, Niedźwiecki declared that the second round of the elections could not be considered democratic or conforming to the European standards, in particular because he believed that 80 thousand votes had been allegedly bought by the team of one of the candidates (i.e. Filatov).[356] Furthermore, Niedźwiecki said that "Political Initiative" observers would appeal to the Council of Europe and European Parliament in order to re-run the elections in Dnipropetrovsk,[357] as if those institutions had authority to set elections in Ukraine.

There is no evidence that the Council of Europe gave credence to Niedźwiecki's criticism of the elections in Dnipropetrovsk, or that he ever voiced it to the Council of Europe. However, on 14 December 2015, during a plenary debate in the European Parliament, the AfD's MEP Marcus Pretzell used his 1-minute intervention to read out a statement on the elections in Dnipropetrovsk, in which he—with a reference to unnamed "election observers"—briefly

---

355   "Aktivisty ozhidayut provokatsiy na vyborakh mera Dnepropetrovska", *Segodnya*, 13 November (2015), https://www.segodnya.ua/regions/dnepr/aktiv isty-ozhidayut-provokaciy-na-vyborah-mera-dnepropetrovska--667037.html. It should be stressed here that it is impossible to say whether any candidate is winning at any polling station before the votes are counted.

356   "Vybory v Dnepropetrovske nel'zya priznat' demokratichnymi i sootvetstvuyush-chimi evropeyskim standartam, — mezhdunarodnye nablyudateli", *Dnepr vecherniy*, 16 November (2015), https://dv-gazeta.info/dneprnews/vyiboryi-v-dnepropet rovske-nelzya-priznat-demokratichnyimi-i-sootvetstvuyushhimi-evropeyskim-sta ndartam-mezhdunarodnyie-nablyudateli.html.

357   "Vybory v Dnepropetrovske proshli v sootvetstvii s afrikanskimi, a ne demo-kraticheskimi standartami, — Yanush Nedzvetskiy", *Gorod.dp.ua*, 16 November (2015), https://gorod.dp.ua/news/110851.

repeated all Niedźwiecki's points on the second round of the elections in Dnipropetrovsk.[358] However, instead of calling for a re-run of the elections, Pretzell raised questions about the use of the EU's funds in Ukraine, thus implicitly disputing rapprochement between Ukraine and the EU—fully in line with the narrative pushed both by the Opposition Bloc and the Kremlin to undermine the post-revolutionary authorities in Ukraine.

However, it was not surprising that, in his criticism of Ukraine, Pretzell did not mention the city council elections in Mariupol, also observed by the "Political Initiative" mission coordinated by Niedźwiecki. At their press conference, members of the "Political Initiative" mission declared that they had not noticed any gross violations of the electoral process in Mariupol.[359] Their conclusion was predictable: following the elections, the Opposition Bloc, to which the "Political Initiative" mission provided information support, secured more than 80% of the seats in the city council. Because of this outcome, the conduct of the elections did not require any criticism.

Operation Dnipropetrovsk 2: The Brussels connection

The "Political Initiative" mission was not the only organisation that called on the international community not to recognise the results of the mayoral elections in Dnipropetrovsk—so did the election observation mission of the Brussels-based Foundation for Democracy and Governance (FDG). For a better understanding of the subject of this report, it is important to discuss this mission too.

---

358 "Ausführungen von einer Minute (Artikel 163 GO)", *European Parliament*, 14 December (2015), https://www.europarl.europa.eu/doceo/document/CRE-8-2015-12-14-INT-1-260-0000_DE.html.

359 "Mezhdunarodnye nablyudateli ne uvideli narusheniy na vyborakh v Mariupole (VIDEO)", *0629.com.ua*, 29 November (2015), http://www.0629.com.ua/news/1045017; "Urny dlya golosovaniya ne dolzhny byt' prozrachnymi,—vengerskiy nablyudatel'", *Mariupol TV*, 29 November (2015), https://web.archive.org/web/20220218211709/https://mariupol.tv/news/elections/mariupol/7551/urny_dlya_golosovaniya_ne_dolzhny_byt_prozrachnymi_vengerskij_nablyudatel_video.html.

The FDG was officially registered in April 2015 by Belgian consultant Grégory Mathieu with the aim "to promote, protect and defend human rights, democracy and the rule of law wherever they are violated, and particularly in African states".[360] Despite the fact that it was officially registered only in 2015, the FDG had been active as early as 2013, which is permitted under Belgian law.

In the beginning of October 2015, just a few weeks before the regional elections in Ukraine, Mathieu expanded the scope of the activities of the FDG to include, among other activities, "participation and organisation of electoral observation missions".[361] The same month, Mathieu co-founded yet another Brussels-based organisation, called "International Foundation for Better Governance" (IFBG), that featured, among its founders, a Ukrainian individual Nadia Borodi.[362] Borodi was, at that time, a girlfriend of Oleh Voloshyn, a former spokesperson for the Foreign Ministry of Ukraine during Yanukovych's rule and a member of the Opposition Bloc; they would get married in 2016.

It was Borodi and Voloshyn who coordinated the trip of the FDG's mission to Ukraine to observe the regional elections. The mission was headed by Mathieu and consisted of 20 monitors,[363] eight of whom went to observe the elections in Dnipropetrovsk.[364] Like the observers from the "Political Initiative" mission, the FDG's monitors saw no grave violations during the first round of mayoral elections won by the Opposition Bloc's Vilkul.[365] However, when

---

360 "Fondation pour la Demokratie et la Gouvernance", *Moniteur Belge*, 23 April (2015), http://www.ejustice.just.fgov.be/tsv_pdf/2015/05/06/15064393.pdf.
361 "Fondation pour la Demokratie et la Gouvernance", *Moniteur Belge*, 7 October (2015), http://www.ejustice.just.fgov.be/tsv_pdf/2015/10/16/15146510.pdf.
362 "International Foundation for Better Governance", *Moniteur Belge*, 21 October (2015), http://www.ejustice.just.fgov.be/tsv_pdf/2015/10/30/15153076.pdf.
363 "Fundatsiya za demokratiyu ta upravlinnya", *Tsentral'na vyborcha komisiya*, 25 October (2015), https://www.cvk.gov.ua/pls/vm2015/pvm065pt001f01=100 pt162f01=175.html.
364 "Ot demokratichnosti provedeniya vyborov v Dnepropetrovske budet zaviset' vozmozhnost' privlecheniya investitsiy v gorod,—evropeyskie nablyudateli", *Gorod.dp.ua*, 24 October (2015), https://gorod.dp.ua/news/110031.
365 "Mezhdunarodnye nablyudateli o tom, kak proshli mestnye vybory v Dnepropetrovskoy oblasti (FOTO)", *Most Dnepr*, 26 October (2015), https://mostdnepr.info/news/press/127125_mezhdunarodnie_nablyudateli_tom.htm.

Vilkul lost the second round, the rhetoric of the FDG's mission dras-
tically changed. Speaking at an FDG press conference, its representative Richard Andrew Balfe (Lord Balfe of Dulwich) declared
that Filatov's team had bought up to 80 thousand votes — the same
number mentioned by Niedźwiecki — and called on the international community not to recognise Filatov's victory in the mayoral
elections in Dnipropetrovsk.[366]

At the same press conference, Balfe also said that, during his
visit to Dnipropetrovsk, he had been attacked by "Filatov's fighters",[367] while Mathieu added that "the incident [could] have [nega-
tive] consequences for Ukraine's international image".[368] A witness
of the incident told the author of this report that it indeed took
place: three masked thugs confronted Balfe and his companions, including Borodi, when they went out for dinner in Dnipropetrovsk.
The thugs menacingly declared that they were Filatov's supporters
and demanded that the observers leave Dnipropetrovsk. Neither
Balfe nor his companions could be visually identified as Vilkul's
supporters or even people having anything to do with the elections.
Moreover, during the incident Borodi started filming the thugs, but
they did not raise any objections. The entire situation looked like a
ruse orchestrated by Voloshyn to instil an impression of lawless-
ness and intimidation surrounding the electoral failure of the pro-
Russian the Opposition Bloc's Vilkul candidate. It is unclear
whether Voloshyn's apparent stunt influenced Balfe in terms of his
attitude towards Russia or Ukraine, but speaking to the Russian
state-controlled media in 2018, he would deny the Russian invasion

---

366 "Nablyudateli iz Zapadnoy Evropy razoblachili skhemu skupki golosov v
      pol'zu Filatova na vyborakh mera Dnepropetrovska", *Golos.ua*, 21 November
      (2015), https://web.archive.org/web/20151122173552/http://ru.golos.ua/p
      olitika/nablyudateli_iz_zapadnoy_evropyi_razoblachili_shemu_skupki_golo
      sov_v_polzu_filatova_.
367 Ibid.
368 Pyotr Likhomanov, "Ugrozhayut lordu. Mezhdunarodnye nablyudateli ne
      priznali vybory v Dnepropetrovske", *Rossiyskaya gazeta*, 17 November (2015),
      https://rg.ru/2015/11/17/dnepr-site-anons.html.

of Crimea and try to whitewash the Russian occupation of Georgian regions of Abkhazia and South Ossetia.[369]

The similarities between the statements of the observers of the "Political Initiative" and FDG, as well as the direct link between the FDG's coordinator Nadia Borodi and the leadership of the pro-Kremlin Opposition Bloc, suggest that both international, supposedly independent missions were in fact controlled by the political consultants of the Opposition Bloc. After their candidate's defeat in the elections in Dnipropetrovsk, the Opposition Bloc's objective was to discredit Ukraine in the eyes of the international community to the benefit of the Kremlin. It was hardly a coincidence that the official newspaper of the Russian government, *Rossiyskaya gazeta*, when covering the second round of the mayoral elections in Dnipropetrovsk, cited only the representatives of the "Political Initiative" and FDG,[370] despite the fact that there were other missions monitoring regional elections in Ukraine, including much more numerous and significantly more established observation missions of the Office for Democratic Institutions and Human Rights of the Organisation for Security and Cooperation in Europe (OSCE ODIHR) and the European Network of Election Monitoring Organisations (ENEMO).[371]

Niedźwiecki and the Zmiana experience

On 24 November 2015, during Russia's military operation in defence of the dictator Bashar al-Assad's regime in the course of the Syrian civil war, a Russian attack aircraft violated Turkish airspace

---

369 "Chlen Palaty lordov: vossoedinenie Kryma s RF bylo logichnym", *TASS*, 1 February (2018), https://tass.ru/mezhdunarodnaya-panorama/4921054.

370 Likhomanov, "Ugrozhayut lordu".

371 As mentioned above, the "Political Initiative" mission consisted of 18 observers, while the FDG's mission had 20 monitors. At the same time, the OSCE ODIHR mission had 727 observers, while the mission of ENEMO consisted of 398 monitors. See "Ofitsiyni sposterigachi vid vseukrayins'kykh gromadskikh organizatsiy, inozemnykh derzhav ta mizhnarodnykh organizatsiy", *Tsentral'na vyborcha komisiya*, 25 October (2015), https://www.cvk.gov.ua/pls/vm2015/pvm063pt001f01=100.html.

near the Syria-Turkey and was shot down by a Turkish fighter jet.[372] Russia denied the downed aircraft had violated Turkish airspace and condemned the incident, while Russian President Vladimir Putin went so far as to say that it was "a stab in the back carried out by the accomplices of terrorists", implying that Turkey was somehow cooperating with the terrorists from Islamic State of Iraq and Syria (ISIS).[373]

The shootdown of the Russian aircraft led to a significant deterioration of relations between Moscow and Ankara. Russia introduced a range of economic sanctions against Turkey, and initiated a campaign to discredit Turkey along Putin's statement, linking Ankara to Islamist terrorists. In Poland, Piskorski's Zmiana became one of the pro-Kremlin organisations that supported Moscow's line in its conflict with Ankara. On 28 November 2015, Niedźwiecki, as a member or sympathiser of Zmiana, joined a small protest co-organised by his party and another Polish far-right organisation, Camp of Great Poland (Obóz Wielkiej Polski, OWP), in front of the Turkish Embassy in Warsaw.[374] Following the official Russian narrative, the Zmiana and OWP declared that Turkey was cooperating with ISIS, and Zmiana called on the Polish government to condemn Turkey's "act of aggression" and — since both Poland and Turkey are NATO members — distance itself from Turkey's "actions in support of the de-facto terrorist groups operating in Syria".[375]

This anti-Turkish protest was not the only Zmiana activity that Niedźwiecki joined.

---

372 Tulay Karadeniz, Maria Kiselyova, "Turkey Downs Russian Warplane near Syria Border, Putin Warns of 'Serious Consequences'", *Reuters*, 24 November (2015), https://www.reuters.com/article/us-mideast-crisis-syria-turkeyidUS KBN0TD0IR20151124.

373 "Turkey Downing of Russia Jet 'Stab in the Back' — Putin", *BBC*, 24 November (2015), https://www.bbc.co.uk/news/world-middle-east-34913173.

374 "Protest pod ambasadą Turcji", *Zmiana*, 8 December (2015), https://web.ar chive.org/web/20160524204519/http://partia-zmiana.pl/2015/12/08/prote st-pod-ambasada-turcji/; "Warszawa: pikieta pod ambasadą Turcji", *Obóz Wielkiej Polski*, 28 November (2015), https://www.owp.org.pl/index.php/dzi alalnosc/2015/439-warszawa-pikieta-pod-ambasada-turcji.

375 "Protest pod ambasadą Turcji".

On 8 March 2015, he participated in the party's anti-NATO protest in Warsaw.[376]

On 27 April 2015, Niedźwiecki, together with other Zmiana activists and neo-fascists from Falanga, took part in a demonstration welcoming a group of ten motorcyclists from the pro-Putin "Night Wolves" biker gang that planned to travel to Poland (but were blocked from entering the country by the Polish authorities).[377]

On 2 May 2015, Niedźwiecki made a speech at an event aimed at discrediting post-revolutionary Ukraine by exploiting the tragic events in Odessa on 2 May 2014, when dozens of people died as a result of deadly clashes between pro-Ukrainian and pro-Russian activists (see below).[378]

And on 15 February 2016, Niedźwiecki participated in an anti-American costumed demonstration of Zmiana held by the Ronald Reagan Monument in Warsaw on the US Presidents' Day.[1379]

As would be stated by the Polish Internal Security Agency (Agencja Bezpieczeństwa Wewnętrznego, ABW) later, Piskorski, as the leader of Zmiana, organised many such events in direct cooperation with the Russian intelligence services:

> Since an unspecified date no later than 2013, [Piskorski] had been participating, in Warsaw, other Polish cities, and in Russia, in the activities of the Russian civilian secret intelligence. In particular, the applicant had had multiple operational meetings in Russia with identified agents of the Foreign Intelligence Service ("FSB") and Federal Security Service ("SVR") who worked under the cover of official representatives of Russian non-governmental organisations. [Piskorski], aware of the real status of those persons, had accepted operational assignments in the context of Russian "information warfare" in order to disseminate theories in Russia's interests and manipulate social attitudes in Poland. [He] had accepted funds for the realisation of those operations as well as remuneration. [...] [Piskorski] had led to the creation of a

---

376 "Partia ZMIANA. 8 Marca 2015, Warszawa", *YouTube*, 18 March (2015), https://www.youtube.com/watch?v=yurh1eDfxpk.

377 Janusz Gabriel Niedźwiecki: "'Nocne Wilki' dostały 'misia'", *Olsztyn.com.pl*, 28 April (2015), https://www.olsztyn.com.pl/artykul,janusz-gabriel-niedzwiecki-nocne-wilki-dostaly-misia,18544.html.

378 "02 05 2015 rocznica zbrodni w Odessie", *YouTube*, 3 February (2016), https://www.youtube.com/watch?v=_3dZpvq0eBo.

379 "Dzień antyprezydencki w Warszawie 15 02 2016", *YouTube*, 16 February (2016), https://www.youtube.com/watch?v=y-lpncQZwNc.

political party, "Change", and its associations "Ukrainian Committee" and "Kresy Trusteeship" (Powiernictwo Kresowe), all of which organisations were controlled and funded by Russian secret services. The applicant had used these organisations to carry out his operational activities (demonstrations and pickets) aimed at antagonising Polish-Ukrainian relations.[380]

The ABW arrested Piskorski on 18 May 2016 and charged him with the offence of taking part in the operations of Russia's intelligence against Poland. (It is to him, to Niedźwiecki's "associate", that the Press Department of Poland's National Public Prosecutor's Office referred to when publishing a notice on Niedźwiecki's arrest by the ABW.) Piskorski's associates from Zmiana started an active campaign calling for his release; Niedźwiecki, however – instead of joining them – distanced himself from Zmiana and did not participate in any protests in support of the arrested party leader.

Operation Odessa

In spring 2014, following the annexation of Crimea, the Kremlin dramatically stepped up its support for pro-Russian separatist movements in southern and eastern parts of Ukraine. One of the Ukrainian places that Moscow targeted via a wide network of agents of influence was Odessa.

In response to the separatist activities, pro-Ukrainian activists held a unity march in Odessa on 2 May 2014. Pro-Russian separatists attacked the march with stones, cold weapons and firearms, but pro-Ukrainian activists retaliated. Amid the fierce clashes, two pro-Ukrainian activists and four pro-Russian separatists were killed or mortally wounded.[381] But the major incident on that day took place at the Odessa House of Trade Unions, where 42

---

380 "Decision. Application no. 80959/17. Mateusz Andrzej PISKORSKI against Poland", *European Court of Human Rights*, 22 October (2019), https://hudoc. echr.coe.int/app/conversion/docx/pdf?filename=PISKORSKI+v.+POLAND. pdf&id=001-198662&libra ry=ECHR&logEvent=False. Note, however, the mistake in providing incorrect Russian abbreviations for the Foreign Intelligence Service (should be SVR) and Federal Security Service (should be FSB).

381 "Accountability for Killings in Ukraine from January 2014 to May 2016", *Office of the United Nations High Commissioner for Human Rights*, https://www. ohchr.org/Documents/Countries/UA/OHCHRThematicReportUkraineJan20 14-May2016_EN.pdf.

people,[382] including both pro-Russian separatists and accidental non-combatants, died in a fire that most likely erupted as a result of an exchange of Molotov cocktails between pro-Ukrainian activists and pro-Russian separatists who had holed up in the House. While both sides of the conflict seem to be responsible for the deadly fire,[383] Russia blamed the incident exclusively on the post-revolutionary Ukrainian authorities and compared the fire to the Nazi crimes during the Second World War.[384]

Since that day, Moscow and its allies kept on exploiting the deadly fire in Odessa in attempt to discredit Ukraine and post-revolutionary Ukrainian authorities domestically and internationally. To achieve this objective, Moscow and pro-Kremlin Ukrainian forces engaged with foreign journalists, academics, activists and politicians to bring them to Odessa around the commemorative date, or organised propaganda events outside of Ukraine – in key countries of the EU, as well as at international institutions. The aim of these activities – often hosted by pro-Kremlin agents of influence or front organisations – was to convince European political elites to

---

382 Ibid.
383 According to the report of the International Advisory Panel, constituted by the Secretary General of the Council of Europe, the fire was predominantly started by the people inside, rather than outside of, the House of Trade Unions: "At about 7.45 p.m. a fire broke out in the Trade Union Building. Forensic examinations subsequently indicated that the fire had started in five places, namely the lobby, on the staircases to the left and right of the building between the ground and first floors, in a room on the first floor and on the landing between the second and third floors. Other than the fire in the lobby, the fires could only have been started by the acts of those inside the building. The forensic reports did not find any evidence to suggest that the fire had been pre-planned. The closed doors and the chimney effect caused by the stairwell resulted in the fire's rapid spread to the upper floors and a fast and extreme rise in the temperature inside the building". See "IAP Report on Odesa Events", *Council of Europe*, 4 November (2015), http://rm.coe.int/CoERMPublicCommonSearchServices/Display DCTMContent?documentId=090000168048851b. See also the results of the independent journalistic investigation of the developments in Odessa on 2 May 2014: Vladislav Balinsky, Tatyana Gerasimova, Sergey Dibrov, Vladimir Sarkisyan (eds), *Odessa. 2 maya 2014-go: Kak eto bylo: Materialy i dokumenty nezavisimogo zhurnalistskogo rassledovaniya "Gruppy 2 maya"* (Odessa: 2016), https://2may group.blogspot.com/p/blog-page.html.
384 "Churkin: te, kto szhigal lyudey v Odesse, ne ukraintsy, eto fashisty", *RIA Novosti*, 4 May (2014), https://ria.ru/20140504/1006493342.html.

stop supporting Ukraine in its struggle against the Russian aggression.

In 2016, pro-Kremlin activists organised several Odessa-related events to disseminate anti-Ukrainian propaganda on the international level. In several contexts, the central figure in these events was a Ukrainian citizen, Viktoriya Machulko. She is the president of the so-called "Council of Mothers of May 2", an organisation that — at least at that time — was supported by the Opposition Bloc.

On 12 March that year, Machulko took part in a panel discussion that took place in Wrocław and was moderated by Jacek Cezary Kamiński.[385] The latter is the chairman of the Ukrainian Committee mentioned in the ABW's charges against Piskorski upon his arrest. Kamiński is also a co-founder of the International Institute of the Newly Established States, a Russian front organisation in Poland that Kamiński co-founded with one of Piskorski's Russian handlers, Aleksey Martynov.[386]

On 21 March, Machulko took part in a conference titled "Ukraine: Maidan, Odessa — Two Years Later", held at the Palace of Nations of the United Nations Office at Geneva. The conference was organised by a fake NGO named "Human Rights Agency",[387] and — apart from Machulko and Kamiński featured several European activists, including Xavier Moreau.[388] Moreau is a dual French-Russian citizen who owns the Moscow-based consultancy Sokol Holding and was instrumental in establishing relations

---

385 "Social Forum of Eastern Europe Discussed Topical Issues of the Region's Life", *FACT.International*, 13 March (2016), https://web.archive.org/web/201808 26073650/http://fact.international/2016/03/social-forum-of-eastern-europe-discussed-topical-issues-of-the-region-s-life/.

386 Anton Shekhovtsov, "More Evidence the Polish Center for Geopolitical Analysis Was a Russian Front", *Tango Noir*, 15 November (2020), https://www.tango-noir.com/2020/11/15/more-evidence-the-polish-center-for-geopolitical-analysis-was-a-russian-front/.

387 Tatyana Gerasimova, "Pod imenem OON v Zheneve proveli ukrainophobskuyu konferentsiyu. Znayut li ob etom v OON", *Dumskaya*, 25 March (2016), https://dumskaya.net/post/pod-imenem-oon-v-zheneve-proveli-ukra inof/author/.

388 "Sovet materey Odessy predstavil OON materialy o tragedii 2 maya v Dome profsoyuzov", *RT*, 22 March (2016), https://russian.rt.com/article/154824.

between Russian actors and the French far-right National Front (Front National) renamed National Rally (Rassemblement National) in 2018 of Marine Le Pen.

On 2 May, several foreign journalists and activists, including Bruce Gagnon, Phil Wilayto and Regis Tremblay from the US-based United National Antiwar Coalition, took part in commemorative events in Odessa at the invitation of Machulko's "Council of Mothers of May 2".[389] Wilayto also accompanied Machulko to the European Parliament in Brussels,[390] where she presented a pro-Kremlin interpretation of the events in Odessa at a roundtable organised by three MEPs, namely Tatjana Ždanoka and Andrejs Mamikins from Latvia, and Yana Toom from Estonia.[391] All three MEPs are known for their support of authoritarian regimes. Ždanoka was a member of Piskorski's "monitoring mission" at the "Crimean referendum", while Mamikins "urged Latvia to forget the Russian occupation of Crimea [...] with the aim of improving the economic situation of Latvia and the Baltic region".[392] Ždanoka and Toom would travel to Damascus to express support for Syrian dictator Bashar al-Assad.[393] And all three MEPs would regularly vote against resolutions of the European Parliament criticising Russia's aggressive behaviour and violation of human rights.

The Opposition Bloc's Oleh Voloshyn was also actively involved in organising commemorative events in Odessa in 2016. With these events, Voloshyn followed the same pattern as in

---

389 "Reports from the UNAC Delegation to Odessa for the May 2nd Memorial to Those Killed at the House of Trade Unions on May 2, 2014", *United National Antiwar Coalition*, https://www.unacpeace.org/odessarpt.html.

390 Ibid.

391 Lauri Laugen, "Väljaanne EU Today kirjutab Kremli mõjust europarlamendile Yana Toomi näitel", *Delfi*, 5 May (2016), https://www.delfi.ee/artikkel/744 35473/valjaanne-eu-today-kirjutab-kremli-mojust-europarlamendile-yana-too mi-naitel.

392 "MEP Mamikins: Forgetting Crimea Occupation Would Improve Our Economic Situation", *The Baltic Times*, 18 March (2017), https://www.balticti mes.com/mep_mamikins__forgetting_crimea_occupation_would_improve_ our_economic_situation/.

393 Maïa de La Baume, "Push to Crack Down on Rogue European Parliament Missions", *Politico*, 4 July (2017), https://www.politico.eu/article/push-to-crack-down-on-rogue-european-parliament-missions/.

Dnipropetrovsk in 2015: he engaged with Grégory Mathieu and Janusz Niedźwiecki to arrange visits of foreign politicians to Odessa.
First, with the help of Mathieu, Voloshyn brought Denis Ducarme, a member of the Belgian Reformist Movement (Mouvement
réformateur), to Odessa. On 2 May 2016, Ducarme paid a visit to
the Orthodox mass for the victims of the Odessa fire,[394] but when
Voloshyn suggested Ducarme lay floral tributes to the victims at
the location of the deadly incident, the Belgian politician, according
to a witness familiar with the situation, declined to follow the sug-
gestion, possibly realising the extremely politicised nature of the
action. Ducarme reportedly also became angry at Voloshyn's plans
to use him in the Ukrainian political games, and that downgraded
the IFBG's relations with Voloshyn and contributed to the decision
of the organisation's leadership to remove Borodi from the IFBG
team.

Niedźwiecki appeared in Odessa in July accompanying two
Polish senators, Jan Rulewski and Jerzy Wcisła, representatives of
the Civic Platform (Platforma Obywatelska), the main opposition
party in Poland at that time. Officially, Rulewski and Wcisła were
invited to Odessa by Machulko's "Council of Mothers of May 2",
but a closer look into their visit reveals a different picture.

Their trip was initiated by the Opposition Bloc,[395] which—following the Kremlin's line—exploited the tragic events in Odessa to
attack the Ukrainian pro-Western government. Voloshyn turned to
Niedźwiecki and asked him to coordinate the visit of the two Polish
senators to Odessa. The "Council of Mothers of May 2" (and its official invitation for Rulewski and Wcisła) was used only as a
smokescreen to conceal the political agenda of the Odessa visit—
perhaps not so much for the Ukrainian observers but rather for the
Polish senators who might otherwise have been put off by the idea

---

394 "V pamyat' o tragedii v Odesse mitropolit Agafangel sovershil panikhidu v
      Svyato-Uespenskom muzhskom monastyre", *Soyuz pravoslavnykh zhurnalistov*,
      4 May (2016), https://spzh.news/ru/news/29884-v-pamyat-o-tragedii-v-od
      esse-mitropolit-agafangel-sovershil-panikhidu-v-svyato-uspenskom-odessko
      m-mu.
395 "V Odesse Avtomaydan blokiroval v otele dvukh pol'skikh senatorov", *Evrop-
      eyskaya pravda*, 13 July (2016), https://www.eurointegration.com.ua/rus/
      news/2016/07/13/7052054/.

of being used by the pro-Kremlin propaganda machine. To confuse Rulewski and Wcisła, representatives of Machulko's "Council" even claimed they cooperated with the Brussels-registered IFBG.[396] That sounded respectful and revealed no immediate connection to Ukraine—the Polish senators hardly knew that it had been co-founded by Nadia Borodi, a girlfriend of a member of the Opposition Bloc's Oleh Voloshyn. However, the reference to the IFBG by the representatives of Machulko's "Council" — was not only manipulative but also illegitimate: by that time, Borodi had been removed from the IFBG, while the organisation itself had nothing to do with the Polish senators' visit to Odessa.

Although Niedźwiecki denied that it was the Opposition Bloc that organised the Polish senators' trip to Ukraine, Niedźwiecki communicated exclusively with representatives of this party during his visit to Odessa. Ukrainian activists who revealed the political agenda behind Rulewski's and Wcisła's trip published videos featuring Niedźwiecki and the two Polish senators in the company of Igor Shavrov (deputy head of the Opposition Bloc in Chornomorsk) and Irina Kovalish (the Opposition Bloc's then press secretary in the Odessa region), as well as Borodi and Voloshyn.[397]

One Ukrainian organisation also claimed that Rulewski and Wcisła were going to participate in a joint press conference with the representatives of the Opposition Bloc, but this claim cannot be verified by independent sources and seems false: the Opposition Bloc aimed at concealing, rather than highlighting, its involvement in

---

396 "Pol'ski senatory i separatizm v Odesi", *PolUkr*, July (2016), http://www. polukr.net/uk/blog/2016/07/polski-senatory-i-separatyzm/. When answering a question as to who organised their trip, Rulewski could only say that it was a foundation registered in Brussels. See "Sryv press-konferentsii odesskikh separatistov i pol'skikh politikov", *YouTube*, 14 July (2016), https://www.you tube.com/watch?v=6Dfj9bGPB6I. On his Facebook page, however, he indirectly confirmed that he had been told of the IFBG's alleged involvement, see Jan Rulewski, "Odessa. Wpuszczono do nas media", *Facebook*, 13 July (2016), https://www.facebook.com/permalink.php?story_fbid=1065900940165083& id=889618367793342.

397 "Rabota po vyyavleniyu podgotovki Oppoblokom separatistskoy konferentsii", *YouTube*, 13 July (2016), https://www.youtube.com/watch?v=ZfO ojWFzvwU; "Sryv press-konferentsii odesskikh separatistov i pol'skikh politikov".

organising the Odessa visit of the two Polish senators, hence the use of Machulko's "Council of Mothers of May 2" and IFBG as smokescreens. Nevertheless, some Ukrainian nationalists believed the claims about the press conference, and blocked the entrance to the hotel where the two Polish senators were staying in order to prevent them from participating in the presumed event.[398] Commenting on the blockade, the Opposition Bloc's MP Mykola Skoryk warned that it would lead to "an international scandal"[399] — which perhaps was the aim of the Opposition Bloc — but it never broke out, despite the attempts of the Polish edition of the Russian state-controlled Sputnik website to cause a stir.[400] Rulewski and Wcisła did manage to meet with a few people whose relatives had been killed in Odessa in 2014,[401] but those meetings were not widely publicised.

The substitute

As mentioned above, Niedźwiecki distanced himself from Zmiana and did not participate in its campaign calling for the release of Piskorski. It is fair to assume that Niedźwiecki's decisions in this regard were underpinned by two major considerations. On the one hand, his previous political experience and further activities suggest that he was never a staunch political activist and was engaged in various political projects as long as they served his personal objectives; in this sense, links to arrested Piskorski felt toxic and damaging to his reputation. On the other hand, in comparison to the domestic developments, his cooperation with the Opposition Bloc,

---

398 "Odesskiy 'Avtomaydan' zablokiroval inostrantsev v otele, chtoby sorvat' aktsiyu na Kulikovom pole", *Dumskaya*, 13 July (2016), https://dumskaya.net/news/odesskiy-avtomaydan-zablokiroval-inostrantcev-v-060351/.

399 "Nardep Skorik: Blokirovanie radikalami senatorov pol'skogo Senata v Odesse grozit mezhdunarodnym skandalom", *Slovo*, 13 July (2016), http://www.slovo.odessa.ua/news/13067-nardep-skorik-blokirovanie-radikalami-senatorov-polskogo-senata-v-odesse-grozit-mezhdunarodnym-skandalom-foto.html.

400 Leonid Sigan, "Prawa człowieka po ukraińsku", *Sputnik*, 1 September (2016), https://pl.sputniknews.com/20160901/prawa-czlowieka-po-ukrainsku-3803693.html.

401 Jerzy Wcisła, "Jestem w Warszawie", *Facebook*, 14 July (2016), https://www.facebook.com/jurek.wcisla/posts/10204957517936364.

bankrolled by Ukrainian oligarchs, apparently seemed to him more beneficial and lucrative.

Nevertheless, Niedźwiecki would keep some ties to members of Zmiana when expected benefits outweighed potential risks. One example of this calculated approach was Niedźwiecki's trip to Russia in August 2016 in the company of Zmiana's vice president Jarosław Augustyniak and the party secretary Tomasz Jankowski. All three of them, together with a few other Polish activists,[402] in fact, were simply accompanying a more prominent Polish politician, Janusz Korwin-Mikke, on his visit to Moscow and Chechnya's capital Grozny. The delegation also featured a now late far-right German journalist Manuel Ochsenreiter[403] and an Italian pro-Kremlin media activist Eliseo Bertolasi.

At that time, eccentric far-right politician Korwin-Mikke was a Member of the European Parliament (MEP), and, by the time of his trip in August 2016, had already participated in several events that can be seen as advancing the interests of the Kremlin and other authoritarian regimes. On 30 November – 1 December 2014, Korwin-Mikke took part in the International Conference on Combating Terrorism and Religious Extremism held in Damascus, Syria.[404] The conference, greeted by Syrian Prime Minister Wael Nader al-Halqi, was characteristically illiberal, and featured, among many other guests, Piskorski, Zmiana's future vice president Nabil Al Malazi,[405] British neo-fascist Nick Griffin, and a delegation of the American pro-Kremlin and anti-Semitic magazine *Veterans Today*.[406] In

---

402   Marcin Skalski, Jan Wsół, and Bartosz Bieszczad.
403   More on Manuel Ochsenreiter see the chapter "The German Connection: Far-Right Journalist Manuel Ochsenreiter in the Service of the Russian Propaganda Machine" in this book.
404   [Janusz Ryszard Korwin-Mikke], "Oświadczenie o udziale posłów w wydarzeniach organizowanych przez strony trzecie i na zaproszenie stron trzecich", *European Parliament*, 10 December (2014), https://www.europarl.europa.eu/epdat/124879_28-11-2014.pdf.
405   See more on Nabil Al Malazi in Mariusz Sepioło, "Putin's Orchestra: The Supporter", *VSquare*, 10 March (2022), https://vsquare.org/putins-orchestra-the-supporter/.
406   Lamiat Sabin, "What on Earth is Nick Griffin Doing in Syria?", *Independent*, 1 December (2014), https://www.independent.co.uk/news/world/middle-east/what-earth-nick-griffin-doing-syria-9895196.html; "Syrian Counterterrorism

December 2015, Korwin-Mikke illegally visited Russia-annexed Crimea and met with the Russian occupation authorities.[407] In March and May 2016, he visited Moscow to take part in programmes of the Russian state-controlled TV channels Russia-1 and NTV.[408]

Korwin-Mikke's trip to Russia in August 2016 was officially organised by the Centre for Russian-Polish Dialogue and Reconciliation, headed at that time by Yuriy Bondarenko. According to Łukasz Wenerski and Michal Kacewicz, Bondarenko was in close contact with Piskorski and the two had been in regular communication since 2015.[409] It seems viable to assume that had Piskorski not been arrested in May 2016, he would have likely accompanied Korwin-Mikke to Russia in August that year. In this respect, Niedźwiecki, who – like Zmiana's leader – spoke relatively good Russian, acted as Piskorski's substitute during Korwin-Mikke's trip to Moscow and Grozny. The participation of Ochsenreiter, a close ally of Piskorski, in that trip further supports this assumption.

Niedźwiecki's visit to Russia in August 2016 apparently became the beginning of his "Russian career" as a substitute for Piskorski, who would be released on bail only in May 2019.

Conference Attracts U.S. Anti-Semites", *Anti-Defamation League*, 4 December (2014), https://www.adl.org/blog/syrian-counterterrorism-conference-attracts-us-anti-semites.

407 [Janusz Ryszard Korwin-Mikke], "Oświadczenie o udziale posłów w wydarzeniach organizowanych przez strony trzecie i na zaproszenie stron trzecich", *European Parliament*, 14 March (2017), https://www.europarl.europa.eu/epdat/124879_09-12-2015.pdf; "Deputat EP: vinit' v energoblokade Kryma vsekh ukraintsev nel'zya", *RIA Novosti*, 11 December (2015), https://ria.ru/2015 1211/1340346788.html.

408 [Janusz Ryszard Korwin-Mikke], "Oświadczenie o udziale posłów w wydarzeniach organizowanych przez strony trzecie i na zaproszenie stron trzecich", *European Parliament*, 21 March (2016), https://www.europarl.europa.eu/epdat/124879_05-03-2016.pdf; [Janusz Ryszard Korwin-Mikke], "Oświadczenie o udziale posłów w wydarzeniach organizowanych przez strony trzecie i na zaproszenie stron trzecich", *European Parliament*, 31 March (2016), https://www.europarl.europa.eu/ep-dat/124879_17-05-2016.pdf.

409 Łukasz Wenerski, Michal Kacewicz, *Russian Soft Power in Poland: The Kremlin and Pro-Russian Organizations*, ed. by Lóránt Győri (Budapest: Political Capital, 2017), p. 29, https://www.politicalcapital.hu/pc-admin/source/documents/ PC_NED_country_study_PL_20170428.pdf.

In March 2017, Niedźwiecki launched the website of the European Council on Democracy and Human Rights (ECDHR). The ECDHR presented itself as a non-profit, non-governmental organisation "supporting democratic institutions and practices around the world" and engaged in "promotion of the values of European Charter of Fundamental Rights, and the European Convention of Human Rights".[410] As in the case of Piskorski's ECAG,[411] election monitoring was declared one of the main activities of the organisation.[412]

At first, however, the ECDHR re-published elections-related articles from a wide variety of sources, ranging from the reputable *The Economist* to the Russian state-controlled RT. But later in 2017, the ECDHR started its first election observation project, recruiting people to monitor elections in Russia on the so-called "single voting day".[413]

Niedźwiecki sent out invitations to an unidentified number of politicians, journalists and activists, inviting them to join a monitoring mission to observe the 2017 Russian elections. In inviting potential observers, Niedźwiecki mentioned that the expenses related to the trip to Russia would be covered by the Russian Peace Foundation.[414]

In recent years, the Russian Peace Foundation (RPF) has been instrumental in organising politically biased international election observation. The organisation is headed by Leonid Slutsky, the

---

410 "About Us", *European Council on Democracy and Human Rights*, https://web.ar chive.org/web/20171114114849/http://ecdhr.eu/.
411 "Statut stowarzyszenia", *Europejskie Centrum Analiz Geopolitycznych*, https:// web.archive.org/web/20101129124600/http://geopolityka.org/pl/informac je/71-statutstowarzyszenia.
412 "About Us", *European Council on Democracy and Human Rights*.
413 A single voting day is a day (the second Sunday in September every year) when Russian authorities hold municipal, regional and, when relevant, parliamentary elections. President Vladimir Putin signed the law introducing a single voting day in 2012. See Natalya Krainova, "Putin Signs Law Creating Single Voting Day in September", *Moscow Times*, 3 October (2012), https://www.themoscowtimes.com/2012/10/03/putin-signs-law-creating-single-voting-day-in-september-a18260.
414 Kenan Habul, "SD-topp kritiseras för bjudresa till Ryssland", *Aftonbladet*, 14 September (2017), https://www.aftonbladet.se/nyheter/samhalle/a/RLAlO/sd-topp-kritiseras-for-bjudresa-till-ryssland.

chair of the Committee on International Affairs of the Russian State Duma. In March 2014, the day after the "Crimean referendum", Slutsky became one of the first seven Russian nationals sanctioned by the US for their involvement in the annexation of Crimea.[415] Although Slutsky had been involved in Russian malign activities in Europe well before 2014, particularly in his capacity as a member of the Parliamentary Assembly of the Council of Europe, he became especially active since the start of the Russian war against Ukraine. Over the years, Slutsky engaged with Western politicians and activists to inform them of Kremlin narratives on international affairs, arranged trips of Moscow-friendly politicians to Russia and Russia-annexed Crimea, and organised events advancing the Kremlin agenda. Much of the expenses related to these activities were covered by the RPF.[416]

As the RPF coordinated fake election observation missions involving foreign individuals, it cooperated with Piskorski's ECAG — Slutsky and Piskorski had known each other since at least November 2014, when they brought "an observation mission" to the Russia-occupied territories in eastern Ukraine.[417] However, since Piskorski was arrested in May 2016, Slutsky needed another European partner who would substitute him as a recruiter and coordinator of fake election monitors, and Niedźwiecki became such a partner.

It is reasonable to suggest that Slutsky established operational contact with Niedźwiecki, at the latest, in the period between the latter's visit to Russia, in August 2016, together with Korwin-Mikke,[418] and summer 2017, when Niedźwiecki started sending out

---

415 Executive Order 13661 — Blocking Property of Additional Persons Contributing to the Situation in Ukraine", *Federal Register*, Vol. 79, No. 53, 19 March (2014), https://www.govinfo.gov/content/pkg/FR-2014-03-19/pdf/2014-06141.pdf.
416 "'Natsiki', granty v SShA i tayny vizit Enrike Iglesiasa: Kak fond deputata Slutskogo ishchet 'druzey Kremlya' po vsemu miru", *Dossier Center*, 5 April (2021), https://dossier.center/slutsky/.
417 Halya Coynash, "An 'Election' amid Kalashnikovs, Cabbages and Moscow's Fascist Fans", *Kharkiv Human Rights Protection Group*, 3 November (2014), https://khpg.org/en/1414979120.
418 Slutsky's RPF paid for several trips of French politicians to Russia and Russia-annexed Crimea and Sevastopol. Commenting on the words of Korwin-Mikke, who in August 2015 said that he was thinking of visiting Crimea, Slutsky welcomed the idea. See "Deputat o vozmozhnom vizite pol'skogo deputata v

invitations to potential election monitors. Furthermore, while at the moment it seems impossible to verify the assumption, there are grounds for assuming that operational contact between Slutsky and Niedźwiecki was established before March 2017 (i.e., the time of the ECDHR's launch), and that the very idea of launching the ECDHR came from Slutsky. For the latter, Niedźwiecki substituting for Piskorski was not sufficient: without Piskorski, the ECAG — as an EU-registered institutional framework functioning as a front of Russian malign influence — became disabled and had to be substituted too; hence the need for the ECDHR.

In September 2017, Russian media reported that 27 "international experts" from 12 countries would monitor the Russian elections during the single voting day on 10 September that year.[419] There is no evidence that Niedźwiecki invited all 27 observers, but it was confirmed that Pavel Gamov, a Russia-born MP from the Swedish far-right Sweden Democrats (Sverigedemokraterna, SD) party, went to Russia to monitor the elections at Niedźwiecki's invitation. Gamov also told the Swedish media that the same invitation was sent to all members of the European parliamentary group "Europe of Freedom and Direct Democracy" (EFDD), of which the SD was a member then.[420]

Gamov's visit to Russia was marked by a series of scandals. According to a rather entertaining report in the right-wing populist *Nyheter Idag*, the Swedish MP was drinking hard during his trip to Russia and was constantly fighting with Russian organisers, demanding from them to pay his bar bills and provide him with a separate hotel room for the girls that he met, threatening otherwise

---

Krym: ES khochet pravdu", *RIA Novosti*, 14 August (2015), https://ria.ru/20150814/1183591706.html. At the moment, it remains unclear whether it was Slutsky who eventually arranged the Polish MEP's visit to Crimea in December 2015. Slutsky could have contacted Korwin-Mikke through Piskorski. But if he did, it clearly facilitated establishing contact between Slutsky and Niedźwiecki when the latter travelled to Moscow together with Korwin-Mikke in August 2016.

419 "Za vyborami v Rossii budut nablyudat' 27 mezhdunarodnykh ekspertov", *RIA Novosti*, 8 September (2017), https://ria.ru/20170908/1502089440.html.

420 Patrik Dahlin, "Pavel Gamov (SD): Jag är inte Putinist", *Upsala Nya Tidning*, 13 September (2017), https://unt.se/nyheter/uppsala/pavel-gamov-sd-jag-ar-inte-putinist-4754655.aspx.

to tell the media about the irregularities at the elections — an observation he could not have possibly made, as he tried to blackmail the
organisers the night before the actual voting day.[421] Also during the
trip, Gamov repeatedly harassed his female assistant (and party
member), and that became one of the major reasons — along with
the fact that the SD had not authorised his participation in the observation of the Russian elections — he was asked to leave the party
following revelations of his behaviour in Russia.[422]

Niedźwiecki himself was observing the elections in Russia's
Udmurt Republic, together with Slovak MP and future Health Minister Marek Krajčí; as expected, both praised the conduct of the elections.[423]

Despite the blunder with Gamov, Niedźwiecki's work as a coordinator of fake election observation was presumably evaluated
well by Slutsky, and Niedźwiecki was again tasked with recruiting
potential observers for the presidential election that would take
place in Russia and Russia-annexed Crimea and Sevastopol on 18
March 2018.

On 1 January 2018, Niedźwiecki published a post on the EC-
DHR website saying that, "following an invitation from the Russian
Peace Foundation", his organisation would deploy an election observation mission to monitor the 2018 Russian presidential election.[424] (For some reason, Niedźwiecki would delete the post in
2020.) The same month, he started sending out letters inviting European politicians to observe the presidential election.[425] As was the
case in 2017, Niedźwiecki invited them on behalf of both the

421 Chang Frick, "Den svenska diplomaten", *Nyheter Idag*, 8 November (2017),
     https://nyheteridag.se/den-svenska-diplomaten/.
422 "Sweden Democrat Quits Party after Unauthorized Russia Trip", *The Local*, 10
     November (2017), https://www.thelocal.se/20171110/sweden-democrat-
     asked-to-leave-party-over-unauthorized-russia-trip-harassment-allegations.
423 "Vybory v Udmurtii podveli pod standarty demokratii", *Lenta*, 10 September
     (2017), https://lenta.ru/news/2017/09/10/udmurtia_standard/.
424 "Electoral Monitoring Mission in Russia. March 2018", *European Council on De-
     mocracy and Human Rights*, 1 January (2018), http://ecdhr.eu/project/electoral-
     monitoring-mission-in-russia-march-2018/ [no longer available].
425 Iida Tikka, Suvi Turtiainen, "Suomalaisia kansanedustajia yritetään naruttaa
     vaalitarkkailijoiksi Venäjälle — hämärän kutsun taustalla puolalaisjärjestö", *Yle*,
     25 January (2018), https://yle.fi/uutiset/3-10039429.

ECDHR and Slutsky's RPF, which he described in his letters as "our Russian partner and official host of this electoral monitoring mission". He promised that "all travel and accommodation expenses" would be covered by the organisers, and mentioned that they would be inviting "around 150 parliamentarians, politicians and experts from all around the world". The same number of observers was mentioned in the Russian media, with a reference to sources in the State Duma.[426]

However, the actual number of international observers invited by the Russian parliament was higher: the lower (State Duma) and upper (Federation Council) houses of the Federal Assembly of the Russian Federation invited a total of 482 monitors,[427] of whom 43 observed the presidential election in Russia-annexed Crimea and Sevastopol.[428] Several Russian organisations not formally affiliated with the Russian authorities, in particular, CIS-EMO, RPF, the Civic Control Association and the National Social Monitoring, actively participated in recruiting and coordinating foreign observers who were officially invited by the Federal Assembly. None of these developments was publicised, and at the moment it is difficult to estimate how many observers invited by the Russian parliament to observe the presidential election were coordinated by Niedźwiecki's ECDHR. One confirmed case is French MEP Joëlle Bergeron, who belonged to the EFDD group in the European Parliament: she observed the Russian presidential election in annexed

---

426   Dmitriy Laru, Angelina Galanina, Tatyana Baykova, "Bolee 150 inostrannykh deputatov posetyat prezidentskie vybory v Rossii", *Izvestiya*, 22 January (2018), https://iz.ru/697617/dmitrii-laru-angelina-galanina-tatiana-baikova/bolee-150-inostrannykh-deputatov-posetiat-prezidentskie-vybory-v-rossii.

427   "Inostrannye (mezhdunarodnye) nablyudateli na vyborakh Prezidenta Rossiyskoy Federatsii 18 marta 2018 goda", *Tsentral'naya izbiratel'naya komissiya Rossiyskoy Federatsii*, http://cikrf.ru/analog/prezidentskiye-vybory-2018/nablyudenie-za-vyborami/mezhdunarodnoe-nablyudenie/mejd_nablyudateli.php.

428   Valentina Egorova, "Svoimi glazami", *Rossiyskaya gazeta*, 18 March (2018), https://rg.ru/2018/03/18/za-vyborami-v-rf-sledilo-rekordnoe-chislo-mezh dunarodnyh-nabliudatelej.html.

Sevastopol.[429] Curiously, Bergeron's visit went completely unreported by the Russian media—in stark contrast to that of many other Western politicians and activists who observed the illegitimate election in Crimea and Sevastopol, and whose work garnered extensive coverage by the Russian media with the intention to demonstrate that at least some Westerners recognised the Russian status of the annexed Ukrainian territories.[430]

Back in Ukraine

Niedźwiecki's collaboration with Russian actors did not hinder his cooperation with the Opposition Bloc. In fact, there was an element of synergy in Niedźwiecki's collaboration with the two parties, as he became a go-to person when it came to organising and coordinating participation of European politicians in authoritarian propaganda events.

One prominent example of Niedźwiecki's crossover activities is a British politician Nathan Gill, who, at the time of his engagement with Niedźwiecki, was MEP from the British Eurosceptic UKIP and a member of the EFDD group.

In spring 2018, Niedźwiecki coordinated Gill's visit to Ukraine on behalf of Oleh Voloshyn and Nadia Borodi. The latter both, in their turn, acted on behalf of Oleksandr Vilkul—the same Oleksandr Vilkul who competed and lost against Borys Filatov at the mayoral elections in Dnipropetrovsk in 2015. The idea behind Gill's trip to Ukraine, which was reportedly funded by Vilkul's "Ukrainian Perspective" Fund,[431] was that he would accompany Vilkul and Voloshyn during the "Victory March" that would take

---

429 [Joëlle Bergeron], "Déclaration de participation des députés à des manifestations organisées par des tiers", *European Parliament*, 14 March (2018), https://www.europarl.europa.eu/mepdat/124740_TRAV_LEG8_1001770_FR.pdf.

430 Anton Shekhovtsov, "Foreign Observation of the Illegitimate Presidential Election in Crimea in March 2018", *European Platform for Democratic Elections*, 3 April (2018), https://www.epde.org/en/news/details/foreign-observation-of-the-illegitimate-presidential-election-in-crimea-in-march-2018-1375.html.

431 [Nathan Gill], "Declaration of Members Attendance Pursuant to an Invitation at Events Organised by Third Parties", *European Parliament*, 27 September (2018), https://www.europarl.europa.eu/mepdat/124965_TRAV_LEG8_1002264_EN.pdf.

place in the Ukrainian cities of Kryvyi Rih and Dnipro on 9 May 2018. Especially after the start of the Russian military aggression against Ukraine in 2014, the "Victory March", being a celebration of the Soviet victory in the so-called "Great Patriotic War" (1941-1945), became increasingly associated with the pro-Russian sentiment in Ukraine because of the political use of the war memory by the Kremlin.[432]

Gill was no stranger to pro-Kremlin activities. Since 2016, he had been providing commentary to the Russian state-controlled RT TV channel, criticising the EU's sanctions imposed on Russia for its war against Ukraine[433] or backing Moscow's line about alleged contacts between Ankara and ISIS.[434]

In September 2018, Gill was invited to take part in the Moldo-Russian Economic Forum that would take place in Moldova's capital Chișinău on 20-22 September that year. The person who invited Gill was Andrey Nazarov, co-chairman of the All-Russian Public Organisation "Business Russia", as well as a chairman of the Board of the Yalta International Economic Forum Foundation, an organisation that had been in charge of organising annual business events in Russia-annexed Crimea. According to Gill's official declaration of participation in events organised by third parties,[435] his expenses related to the trip to Moldova (flights and hotel) were paid by the ECDHR, although he intentionally or unintentionally provided incorrect details about the organisation. In his declaration about the

---

432   On the role of the "Great Patriotic War" in the construction of Russian post-Soviet national identity, see Olga Malinova, "Political Uses of the Great Patriotic War in Post-Soviet Russia from Yeltsin to Putin", in Julie Fedor, Markku Kangaspuro, Jussi Lassila, Tatiana Zhurzhenko (eds), *War and Memory in Russia, Ukraine and Belarus* (Cham: Palgrave Macmillan, 2017), pp. 43-70; Galia Ackerman, *Le régiment immortel: la guerre sacrée de Poutine* (Paris: Premier Parallèle, 2019).

433   "Anti-Russia Sanctions: 'EU Should Stop Playing Games of Washington'", *RT*, 24 July (2017), https://www.rt.com/op-ed/397353-eu-us-russia-sanctions/.

434   "Turkey's Alleged ISIS Support: 'Absolutely Horrendous'", *RT*, 25 March (2016), https://www.rt.com/op-ed/337219-turkey-evidence-isis-support/.

435   [Nathan Gill], "Declaration of Members Attendance Pursuant to an Invitation at Events Organised by Third Parties", *European Parliament*, 27 September 2018, https://www.europarl.europa.eu/mepdat/124965_TRAV_LEG8_1002263_EN.pdf.

trip to Chişinău, he gave a number in the EU Transparency Register that belonged to the European Centre for Democracy and Human Rights, a Brussels-based lobbying organisation, the acronym of which coincided with Niedźwiecki's ECDHR but which was "seeking to promote human rights and democracy in the Gulf region with a particular focus on Bahrain and Saudi Arabia".[436] Gill's panel at the Moldo-Russian Economic Forum was titled "Moldova: Between East and West". It was moderated by Manuel Ochsenreiter and featured — besides Moldovan and Russian speakers — Michael Harms, Executive Director of the Committee on Eastern European Economic Relations in Berlin; Maria Antoniou, then a member of the Hellenic Parliament from the Greek centre-right "New Democracy" party and participant of the fake monitoring mission at the 2018 Russian presidential election; and Siegbert Droese, then a member of the German Bundestag from the German far-right AfD.[437]

Niedźwiecki's ECDHR also reportedly paid for the Ukrainian trip of Gill and his fellow British EFDD MEPs Jonathan Arnott and David Coburn (though it is unlikely that ECDHR would use its own money for this purpose).[438] Officially, they went to Kyiv at the end of October 2018 on a "fact finding trip" to meet with journalists from the 112 Ukraine and NewsOne TV channels, as well as with representatives of the National Council of Television and Radio

---

436 "About Us", *European Centre for Democracy and Human Rights*, https://www.ec-dhr.org/?page_id=127. To clarify the confusion, the author of this report wrote several email messages to the European Centre for Democracy and Human Rights, but none of them was ever answered.

437 "Program of the Moldo-Russian Economic Forum", https://www.europarl.eu ropa.eu/mepdat/attach/124965_1242d397-d718-4971-a116-8b04969f7040_3. docx.

438 [Nathan Gill], "Declaration of Members Attendance Pursuant to an Invitation at Events Organised by Third Parties", *European Parliament*, 15 January (2019), https://www.europarl.europa.eu/mepdat/124965_TRAV_LEG8_1002474_ EN.pdf; [Jonathan Arnott], "Declaration of Members Attendance Pursuant to an Invitation at Events Organised by Third Parties", *European Parliament*, 15 January (2019), https://www.europarl.europa.eu/mepdat/124958_TRAV_LEG8_ 1002475_EN.pdf; [David Coburn], "Declaration of Members Attendance Pursuant to an Invitation at Events Organised by Third Parties", *European Parliament*, 17 January (2019), https://www.europarl.europa.eu/mepdat/124967_TRAV_ LEG8_1002479_EN.pdf.

Broadcasting of Ukraine, "in order to see the situation around the vote carried out by the Rada regarding closing TV channels in Ukraine"[439] and "gain information towards a potential European Parliament resolution on freedom of the press in Ukraine".[440]

The vote mentioned by the three British MEPs was the vote in the Ukrainian parliament on 4 October 2018, when Ukrainian MPs overwhelmingly voted in favour of sanctioning a number of Ukrainian media channels, including 112 Ukraine and NewsOne, as part of the measures of protecting the Ukrainian society and state from "aggressive influence of destructive propaganda", hampering calls for "violation of sovereignty and territorial integrity of Ukraine", and countering other malign influence operations.[441]

Until 2014, both channels were considered a media arm of the Party of Regions, and after the PoR's collapse, they became a media arm of the Opposition Bloc. However, as one expert observed, while 112 Ukraine and NewsOne had been criticised for publicising pro-Russian contents, until 2018 positions of hosts and guests remained relatively balanced. Yet when the two channels were acquired in 2018 by individuals close to the arguably major pro-Kremlin Ukrainian politician and businessman Viktor Medvedchuk (Putin happens to be the godfather of Medvedchuk's daughter), their congruence with the Kremlin's anti-Ukrainian propaganda became too obvious to ignore.[442]

In fear of losing their main TV channels, representatives of the Opposition Bloc decided to engage with the European community in hope that it would exert pressure on Ukraine's then President Petro Poroshenko, whose signature was needed to enact the sanctions against 112 Ukraine and NewsOne proposed by the Ukrainian parliament. The Ukrainian trip of three British EFDD MEPs was just the beginning of the Opposition Bloc's extensive campaign in

---

439 [Gill], "Declaration of Members Attendance", 15 January (2019).
440 [Arnott], "Declaration of Members Attendance".
441 "Proekt Postanovy pro skvalennya propozitsiy shchodo zastosuvannya personal'nykh spetsial'nykh ekonomichnykh ta inshykh obmezhuval'nykh zakhodiv (sanktsiy)", *Verkhovna Rada Ukrainy*, 3 October (2018), http://w1.c1.rada.gov.ua/pls/zweb2/webproc4_1?pf3511=64731.
442 See Georgy Chizhov, "Pro-Kremlin Influence in the Ukrainian Media", *The Kremlin's Influence Quarterly*, No. 1 (2020), pp. 63-71.

support of its TV channels. Niedźwiecki played the role of a coordinator and facilitator in several activities related to this campaign. Apart from covering the cost of Gill's trip to Kyiv as well as that of the other two British MEPs, where the three took part in a TV programme hosted by Nadia Borodi,[443] Niedźwiecki accompanied senior managers of 112 Ukraine and NewsOne, as well as Voloshyn and Borodi, to Strasbourg to meet with their allies among MEPs in February 2019. The aim of the trip was to create the International Editorial Board of the two channels. The board would consist of six people: Gill, Coburn, German MEP Arne Gericke (European Conservatives and Reformists Group), Voloshyn, and two managers of 112 Ukraine: general producer Artem Marchevs'ky and CEO Egor Benkendorf.[444] The idea behind the creation of the board was that the inclusion of three MEPs would make it harder for the Ukrainian authorities to sanction 112 Ukraine and NewsOne. In his declaration as a MEP, Gill claimed that his position on the editorial boards of the two Ukrainian channels was unremunerated.[445]

In September 2019, Niedźwiecki's ECDHR declared that, together with their Ukrainian partners, namely 112 Ukraine, NewsOne, Zik TV and the National Union of Journalists of Ukraine, they "prepared a comprehensive report describing the problem of freedom of speech and growing threats to the activity of journalist [sic] in Ukraine 2018-2019".[446] The report, titled "Attack on the Freedom

---

443 Borodi worked as a host at NewsOne TV channel from September 2016 until January 2018, then went to work as a host at 112 Ukraine in September 2018, see "Nadezhda Sass", Zik, https://web.archive.org/web/20220120205914/https://zikua.news/ru/person/6.

444 "Telekanaly '112 Ukraina' i NewsOne sozdali mezhdunarodny redaktsionny sovet", 112ua.tv, 13 February (2019), https://web.archive.org/web/2021102 3152710/https://112ua.tv/glavnye-novosti/telekanaly-112-ukraina-i-newson e-sozdali-mezhdunarodnyy-redakcionnyy-sovet-480480.html.

445 [Nathan Gill], "Declaration of Members' Financial Interests", European Parliament, 2 July (2019), https://www.europarl.europa.eu/mepdif/124965_DFI_LEG9_rev0_EN.pdf.

446 "Support for Freedom of Speech and Media in Ukraine", European Council on Democracy and Human Rights, 30 September (2019), https://web.archive.org/web/20201230020549/http://ecdhr.eu/project/support-for-freedom-of-speech-and-media-in-ukraine/.

of Speech and Growing Threats to the Activity of Journalists in Ukraine in 2018-2019",[447] aimed to show to European politicians the "problem" that "Ukrainian journalists [were] dealing with" and "to undertake solidarity actions condemning censorship, violation of the freedom of speech, political pressure and violence against journalist [sic] in Ukraine".[448] As one might expect, the report mentioned neither Russia's annexation of Crimea, nor its occupation of parts of eastern Ukraine or persistent threats to Ukraine's sovereignty—developments that had a direct bearing on Ukraine's national security and its regulation of information space in the face of the ongoing Russian aggression.

The ECDHR claimed that the report had been presented in the European Parliament in September, and that Niedźwiecki's organisation and its Ukrainian partners had held, on the basis of the report, "over 60 meetings with Members of European Parliament representing all political groups" in the European Parliament, and had "received support for [their] actions from most of them".[449] Curiously, the presentation, if indeed held, was unreported by the media, including 112 Ukraine and NewsOne. Yet another related "semi-clandestine" event, formally organised by the ECDHR and devoted to "violence against journalists and restrictions to free speech in Ukraine", was held in the European Parliament in Strasbourg on 18 December. Four MEPs took part in the event, namely Gill, Tatjana Ždanoka, James Wells (Brexit Party/non-attached) and Shaffaq Mohammed (UK Liberal Democrats/Renew Europe group); the main participants also included Borodi, Niedźwiecki and Voloshyn.[450]

---

447 "Attack on the Freedom of Speech and Growing Threats to the Activity of Journalists in Ukraine in 2018-2019. Report for the Meeting of the European Parliament on September 16, 2019", European Council on Democracy and Human Rights, https://web.archive.org/web/20220121002022/http://ecdhr.eu/wp-content/uploads/2020/08/Attack-on-the-freedom-of-speech-and-media-in-Ukraine-2019.pdf.
448 "Support for Freedom of Speech and Media in Ukraine".
449 Ibid.
450 "'Bely' shum: kak karmannye SMI kuma Putina pytayutsya diskreditirovat' Ukrainu v Evrope", *Informatsionnoe soprotivlenie*, 21 December (2019), https://sprotyv.info/rassledovaniya/belyj-shum-kak-karmannye-smi-kuma-putina-pytajutsya-diskreditirovat-ukrainu-v-evrope.

The fact that the events organised/coordinated by Niedźwiecki's ECDHR and held in the European Parliament in September and December 2019 were predominantly unreported in the media can be explained by the apparent lack of intention on the part of the Opposition Bloc to reveal any details of its engagement with European politicians as part of the campaign to prevent the introduction of sanctions against 112 Ukraine and NewsOne. While it is always difficult to assess the efficiency of influence operations such as the one conducted by the Opposition Bloc — considering many other intervening factors — it must be noted that President Poroshenko eventually decided not to enact the sanctions; they were introduced only in February 2021 by Ukraine's next president, Volodymyr Zelensky.[451]

In the bleak spotlight

As evidenced above, Niedźwiecki's Ukrainian handlers treated him predominantly as a coordinator and facilitator of contacts between representatives of the Opposition Bloc and European politicians. Probably because of the failed "Operation Odessa" and Niedźwiecki's too obvious association with Polish anti-Ukrainian political activists, even the Opposition Bloc rarely, if ever, engaged with Niedźwiecki as a commentator or opinion maker. After 2016, he became too toxic for them in the Ukrainian information space, but he was still useful as an operations manager working behind the scenes.

The nature of Niedźwiecki's collaboration with Russian actors was slightly different: they regarded him both as an organiser/recruiter and commentator/expert.

Already in November 2017, Niedźwiecki took part in the convention of the Russian National-Bolshevik movement "Essence of Time", founded by a Russian left-wing ultranationalist Sergey Kurginyan, who sent volunteers to fight against Ukrainian forces in Russia-occupied parts of eastern Ukraine. Apart from Niedźwiecki, several other foreign guests participated in the convention, in

---

451 "Ukaz Prezidenta Ukrainy No. 43/2021", *Prezident Ukrainy*, 2 February (2021), https://www.president.gov.ua/documents/432021-36441.

particular: Tatjana Ždanoka; Giulietto Chiesa, a late former Italian MEP and long-time associate of Russian fascist Alexander Dugin; Zakhari Zakhariev, a member of the Bulgarian Socialist Party; Iñaki Irazabalbeitia, a former MEP from the Basque separatist party "Aralar"; and Dimitris Konstantakopoulos, editor of the Greek anti-globalist and anti-Western Defend Democracy Press website.[452] Niedźwiecki delivered a short speech at the convention,[453] and later contributed an article on the "crisis of the Left" to the newspaper *Sut' vremeni*.[454]

Niedźwiecki would meet Ždanoka and Chiesa again the following month at the Eleventh European Russian Forum, an annual meeting of Russian officials and representatives of Russian diasporas, which took place in the European Parliament in Brussels in December 2017.[455] Ždanoka organised the meeting and also moderated it, together with Anton Ilyin, an advisor to the chair of the Russian World Foundation, one of the major instruments of the Kremlin's influence operations in countries with significant Russian-speaking communities. The forum hosted more than 20 politicians, journalists, academics and activists, and was addressed by Vladimir Chizhov, the Permanent Representative of the Russian Federation to the European Union in Brussels.[456]

In May 2018, against the background of Niedźwiecki's active collaboration with Slutsky, the former started reaching out to his European contacts and inviting them to participate in the

---

452 "Torzhestvenny s'yezd 'Suti vremeni' zavershilsya", *Krasnaya vesna*, 7 November (2017), https://rossaprimavera.ru/news/ce80440c.
453 Yanush Nidzvetskiy [Janusz Niedźwiecki], "Vystuplenie Yanusha Nidzvetskogo", *Sut' vremeni*, No. 253-254, 18 November (2017), https://rossaprimavera.ru/article/fb989857; "Zapis' pryamoy translyatsii Torzestvennogo zasedaniya SV 7.11.2017", *Sut' vremeni*, 7 November (2017), https://eot.su/node/22633.
454 Yanush Nidzvetskiy [Janusz Niedźwiecki], "Levye v kolossal'nom krizise", *Sut' vremeni*, No. 253-254, 18 November (2017), https://rossaprimavera.ru/article/c7173ae6.
455 Before his arrest, Piskorski used to attend the European Russian Forum, so here, again, Niedźwiecki substituted Piskorski as a "Russia-friendly Pole" participating in a pro-Kremlin event.
456 "V Bryussele prokhodit XI Evropeyskiy russkiy forum", *Russkoe pole*, 4 December (2017), http://russkoepole.de/ru/news-18/4209-v-bryussele-prokhodit-xi evropejskij-russkij-forum.html.

International Forum "Development of Parliamentarism", which would take place in Moscow on 4-5 June 2018. Niedźwiecki sent out letters of invitation on behalf of Chairman of the State Duma Vyacheslav Volodin, who acted as host and official organiser of the Forum, while the letters were signed by Volodin's deputy, Pyotr Tolstoy. Over 500 politicians from across the globe took part in the forum; Niedźwiecki himself participated, together with another Polish politician, Jacek Wilk, a non-attached far-right member of the Polish Sejm.[457]

While the Russian pro-Kremlin media had occasionally engaged with Niedźwiecki before 2018, publishing his comments on the incident in Odessa in 2016,[458] Russian elections, or joint Russian-Belarusian military manoeuvres,[459] he became a regular commentator for a number of Russian state-controlled media channels starting from the second half of 2018. In particular, his commentary on various socio-political issues was published in the Polish and Latvian editions of Sputnik, as well as the web resources of the Rossiya Segodnya news agency and its subsidiaries. Russian media would usually refer to Niedźwiecki as a "Polish expert", "Polish politician" or "Polish political scientist", and turn to him for his ideas on the developments in Ukraine. He would typically provide views benefitting the Opposition Bloc and, starting in 2019, the Opposition Platform—For Life (Opozytsiyna platforma—Za zhyttya), a party that replaced the Opposition Bloc as the major pro-Russian party in Ukraine.

On 21 March 2019, Niedźwiecki took part, via a video-link, in a press conference at the Rossiya Segodnya press centre, discussing

---

457 Grażyna Garboś, "'Kiedy walczą ze sobą dwa słonie, to najbardziej cierpi trawa'. A trawa to my", *Sputnik*, 6 June (2018), https://pl.sputniknews.com/20180606/rozwoj-parlamentaryzmu-forum-moskwa-polska-wspolpraca-sputnik-8109253.html.

458 Marina Baltacheva, "'Politsiya tol'ko smotrela'", *Vzglyad*, 13 July (2016), https://vz.ru/society/2016/7/13/821289.html.

459 "Pol'skiy publitsist: neponyatno, zachem 'Zapad-2017' vydayut za nechto nebyvaloe", *Radio Sputnik*, 9 September (2017), https://radiosputnik.ria.ru/20170919/1505098922.html.

forthcoming presidential elections in Ukraine.[460] The press conference was moderated by Iskander Khisamov, the editor of the
"Ukraina.ru" website owned by Rossiya Segodnya. On this occa-
sion, the discussants predicted social turmoil would follow the elections, regardless of who won — thus pushing a typical Kremlin message on Ukraine as an unstable and erratic state. Niedźwiecki's own
message was different yet still similar: according to him, no elected
Ukrainian president would be able to solve Ukraine's problems.[461]

Perhaps inspired by his engagement with Russian media,
Niedźwiecki decided — or was nudged — to start his own media. On
26 August 2020, he registered the web address InternationalAf-
fairs.eu for what became known as *International Affairs* magazine.
The magazine claimed it was based in Brussels; the address it provided,[462] however, allowed for opening a virtual office for a fee
starting from €99 per month.[463] The website of this anti-American,
anti-Ukrainian and pro-Kremlin magazine was never fully developed, with sections, such as "About Us", containing the "Lorem ip-
sum" placeholder text. Nevertheless, it was more or less regularly
updated predominantly by users named "Marta Piekarska" and
"James Cornwell", with Niedźwiecki and Polish far-right author
Ronald Lasecki being irregular contributors.

The following month, on 3 September 2020, Niedźwiecki registered two more web addresses, BrusselsDaily.eu and Eu-
ropaTimes.info, evidently attempting to develop a media network
of propaganda resources, but they were never developed before
Niedźwiecki was arrested.

---

460 "Kampaniya po vyboram Prezidenta Ukrainy — na finishnoy pryamoy", *Rossiya
     segodnya*, 21 March (2019), http://pressmia.ru/special_ukrainianfile/201903
     21/952282077.html.
461 "Pol'skiy politolog: pobeditel' vyborov na Ukraine ne reshit problemy strany",
     RIA Novosti, 21 March (2019), https://ria.ru/20190321/1552000073.html.
462 "Contact", *International Affairs Magazine*, https://web.archive.org/web/202012
     29211157/https://internationalaffairs.eu/contact/.
463 "Virtual Offices", *Servcorp*, https://www.servcorp.be/en/virtual-offices/pric
     es-locations/brussels/bastion-tower/.

Working on the side

In addition to participation in various projects of Russian and pro-Russian Ukrainian politicians, Niedźwiecki ECDHR was also involved in a few side-projects, predominantly in the area of election observation.

For example, in June 2019, the ECDHR website claimed that Niedźwiecki participated in a short-term election observation mission at the early local elections in the Mexican state of Puebla.[464]

But arguably the largest election observation mission that Niedźwiecki organised before his arrest was an 18-strong mission of the ECDHR at the early parliamentary elections in Azerbaijan, held on 9 February 2020. That was a high-profile mission: it featured 12 members of parliament from six European countries and two regional legislators from Germany.

According to the International Election Observation Mission formed by the OSCE ODIHR, OSCE PA and PACE, "the restrictive legislation and political environment prevented genuine competition in the 9 February 2020 early parliamentary elections in Azerbaijan, despite a high number of candidates. Some prospective candidates were denied the right to stand, but candidate registration process was otherwise inclusive. Voters were not provided with a meaningful choice due to a lack of real political discussion".[465] Nevertheless, the overwhelming majority of other international organisations and individual monitors—who had been carefully selected by the authoritarian regime of President Ilham Aliyev—endorsed the parliamentary elections.[466] Niedźwiecki's ECDHR was one of those organisations.

---

464 "Electoral Observation Mission in Mexico. June 2019", *European Council on Democracy and Human Rights*, 6 July (2019), https://web.archive.org/web/20220121013822/http://ecdhr.eu/project/electoral-observation-mission-in-mexico-june-2019/.

465 "Azerbaijan, Early Parliamentary Elections, 9 February 2020: Statement of Preliminary Findings and Conclusions", *OSCE*, 10 February (2020), https://www.osce.org/odihr/elections/azerbaijan/445759.

466 For more on the international observation of the 2020 Azerbaijani elections, see Anton Shekhovtsov, "Problematic International Observation of the Azerbaijani 2020 Parliamentary Elections", *European Platform for Democratic Elections*, 6 April

In fact, members of the ECDHR's mission started to praise the elections even before the voting process officially ended. For example, Bavarian regional parliamentarian Uli Henkel of the German far-right AfD declared that the Azerbaijani government manifested openness and transparency in the organisation and conduct of the early parliamentary elections.[467] His fellow party member Ulrich Singer said that he had heard of no complaints about the elections at the polling stations they visited.[468] Věra Procházková, a Czech MP from the populist ANO 2011 party, and Manol Genov, an MP from the Bulgarian Socialist Party, who, in 2017, was charged with vote-buying,[469] spoke highly of the organisation of the elections, too.[470]

Two days after the elections, the ECDHR published a report concluding that the mission had not registered any violations of the electoral legislation that could affect the results of the elections, and that the elections had been held in compliance with the electoral laws of Azerbaijan and universally recognised democratic norms.[471]

Conclusion

Over the course of five years, Polish national Janusz Gabriel Niedźwiecki had transformed from an activist of a marginal and non-registered far-right party into a coordinator of pro-Kremlin

(2020), https://www.epde.org/en/news/details/problematic-international-observation-of-the-azerbaijani-2020-parliamentary-elections-2615.html.

467 A. Mamedov, B. Rustambekov, "Vlasti Azerbaydzhana organizovali otkrytye dosrochnye parlamentskie vybory—deputat Landtaga", *Interfax Azerbaijan*, 9 February (2020), http://interfax.az/view/791827.

468 "Nemetskiy deputat: 'Nikakikh zhalob na vybory k nam ne postupalo'", *Haqqin*, 9 February (2020), https://haqqin.az/news/169667.

469 "Bulgaria: Bulgarian Anti-Corruption Unit Charges MP Manol Genov with Votebuying", *Regional Anti-Corruption Initiative*, 13 July (2017), http://www.rai-see.org/bulgaria-bulgarian-anti-corruption-unit-charges-mp-manol-genov-with-vote-buying/.

470 Mamedov, Rustambekov, "Vlasti Azerbaydzhana organizovali"; A. Mamedov, B. Rustambekov, "Vybory v Azerbaydzhane prokhodyat spokoyno—mezhdunarodnye nablyudateli", *Interfax Azerbaijan*, 9 February (2020), http://interfax.az/view/791851.

471 "Observers: Elections Were Held with No Violations", *Axar*, 11 February (2020), https://en.axar.az/news/politics/444200.html.

activities and, ultimately, into an agent of Moscow's influence—albeit an unimpressive one, as by the time of his arrest in May 2021 none of his projects had effectively taken off.

This transformation is not unique: a significant number of far-right politicians, especially of anti-American persuasion, engage in pro-Kremlin activities. Moreover, as our previous research shows,[472] the same far-right politicians often take part in fake election observation in support of authoritarian regimes, leaders or political forces, and this participation deepens their ties to Russian politicians, officials and, sometimes, intelligence services. Indeed, it is joining politically biased observation missions that has, for many a European politician, become an entry point into a larger area of Moscow's malign influence operations and other active measures.

To a certain extent, Niedźwiecki followed the path of another Polish national, namely Mateusz Piskorski: the latter also started out as a marginal far-right militant, then embarked on fake observation missions, and eventually became heavily involved in Moscow's disinformation and propaganda efforts—involvement that led to Piskorski's arrest by the Polish security services in 2016.

In fact, the major reason Russian politicians and officials enlisted Niedźwiecki's services in the first place was that they needed a Polish pro-Russian activist to replace Piskorski as "our man in Poland". Due to his detention, the latter could no longer deliver services to Moscow. Niedźwiecki was Piskorski's forced substitute, but he never reached the operational level of the latter.

---

472 Shekhovtsov, *Russia and the Western Far Right*, pp. 101-131.

7. The German Connection
Far-Right Journalist Manuel Ochsenreiter in the Service of the Russian Propaganda Machine

Introduction

"He was a real warrior. He has chosen his camp and stayed in it till the end. He was my publisher, my friend, my son. He was convinced German patriot. Brave and bold. He has sacrificed his life to the Multipolar Idea. He was enemy of open society and atlanticism. He has chosen the Greatest Europe, the Eurasia, the Pluriversum". These lines are from a short obituary,[473] which Russian fascist Alexander Dugin wrote (in poor English) for a German journalist Manuel Ochsenreiter who reportedly died of a heart attack on 18 August 2021.[474]

Much of what Dugin wrote about Ochsenreiter was actually true, although a less engaged observer would probably use slightly different terms, like "far-right" instead of "patriot", or "illiberal" instead of "enemy of Atlanticism", or "Putin's Russia" instead of "the Greatest Europe". But what Dugin definitely failed, understandably, to mention was that Ochsenreiter was directly involved in numerous—public and covert—influence operations aimed at advancing Moscow's foreign policy interests across Europe. Although Ochsenreiter is presumably dead, the story of his last years reveals typical tactics and mechanisms of Russian malign influence in Europe.

---

473 Alexandr Dugin, "My very good friend Manuel Ochsenreiter is dead", *Facebook*, 20 August (2021), https://www.facebook.com/alexandr.dugin/posts/pfbid 02T5stW2XWcFpET5XV1j2N6C8KrCjKpKACLRBp3n42ZL1o2fVy1BMqfTNq Y3VjuRgRl.
474 "In eigener Sache: ZUERST!-Chefredakteur Manuel Ochsenreiter ist tot", *Zuerst!*, 21 August (2021), https://zuerst.de/2021/08/29/in-eigener-sache-zue rst-chefredakteur-manuel-ochsenreiter-ist-tot/.

A Dugin fan-boy

Ochsenreiter had been active in German far-right circles since the 1990s. In 2011, he became an editor-in-chief of the German far-right magazine *Zuerst!* (At first!), which — in the words of its editorial staff (probably Ochsenreiter himself) — was "committed only to the life and survival interests of the German people and the precious heritage of our European culture".[475]

At that time, Ochsenreiter was known in the far-right environment for his reports on the Arab Spring and the Syrian civil war. To his credit, he personally travelled across the Middle East, and although his views on the topics he covered were ideologically marked by illiberalism, anti-Americanism and, in the case of Syria, support for Bashar al-Assad, his reporting was founded on firsthand experiences. It was in Syria in 2014 when Ochsenreiter, while doing a report for *Zuerst!*, suffered his first heart attack, which severely undermined his health from then onwards.

According to an account from a person who communicated with Ochsenreiter in 2009-2012, the latter expressed no pro-Kremlin stances until spring 2012.[476] But it was most likely his interest in the Syrian civil war that led Ochsenreiter to his encounter with the works of Dugin who — following the official Russian line — was against the Arab Spring and supported Assad. Apparently, Ochsenreiter and Dugin met in person for the first time in Freiburg, Germany, in December 2012, when Dugin visited the house of the influential yet politically controversial German philosopher Martin Heidegger (1889-1976).[477] Ochsenreiter used the opportunity to interview Dugin for *Zuerst!*, and that was the beginning of Ochsenreiter's long-standing infatuation for Dugin's neo-Eurasianism, a form of a fascist ideology centred on the idea of building a totalitarian, Russia-dominated Eurasian Empire.

---

475   "Über uns", *Zuerst!*, https://web.archive.org/web/20130326111023/http://www.zuerst.de/uber-uns/.

476   Dmitry Khmelnitsky, "Berlinskie evraziytsy", *Kasparov.ru*, 11 December (2017), http://www.kasparov.ru/material.php?id=5A2E71F54706A.

477   "Reportaje sobre Dugin en revista alemana ZUERST!", *The Fourth Political Theory*, http://www.4pt.su/es/content/reportaje-sobre-dugin-en-revista-aleman a-zuerst.

Since then, Ochsenreiter had interviewed Dugin several times for his magazine and his own blog, and likely used the pretext of interviews to have the possibility to spend more time communicating with Dugin, who became an inspirational figure for him. In the beginning of 2013, Ochsenreiter contributed a piece on German politics towards Syria to *Journal of Eurasian Affairs* published by Dugin's neo-Eurasianist movement and mimicking international scientific journals.[478] In that piece, Ochsenreiter criticised Berlin for its opposition to Assad and for depending "on the so called 'western community', on NATO, and on Washington's political guidelines".

Dugin's influence on Ochsenreiter cannot be overestimated: Ochsenreiter would even refer to him as a "long-time paternal friend", while Dugin, in his obituary, called Ochsenreiter his "spiritual son".[479] According to Dugin, who is an Orthodox Christian, Ochsenreiter converted from Catholicism to Christian Orthodoxy, and Dugin participated in the conversion ceremony.

In late December 2013, when Dugin assisted Russian ultranationalist businessman Konstantin Malofeev (sanctioned by the EU and US) in developing his own media project, he recommended Ochsenreiter as a German figure who could be involved in Russian influence operations in Europe. However, in his internal memorandum to Malofeev, Dugin shamefully misspelled the name of his "spiritual son", giving an awkward Romanised version of the Russian pronunciation of Ochsenreiter's name: "Ohzenrayter".

A Russian media darling

Ochsenreiter's articles and commentary would be regularly published on Malofeev's website "Katehon" edited by Dugin. But it was a different Russian media resource that turned Ochsenreiter, who was then practically unknown even at home outside of the far-

---

478 Manuel Ochsenreiter, "The Bandhog of the West. Germany's Politiccs towards Syria", *Journal of Eurasian Affairs*, Vol. 1, No. 1 (2013), pp. 94-97.
479 Christian Fuchs, Paul Middelhoff, Fritz Zimmermann, "Putins AfD-Truppe", *Zeit Online*, 17 August (2017), https://www.zeit.de/2017/34/osteuropa-wahlbeobachtung-afd-wladimir-putin/seite-2.

right environment, into a real star of Russian international propaganda. RT, which was until 2009 known as Russia Today,[480] engaged with Ochsenreiter already in 2012, and since then would refer to him as a "German journalist",[481] "investigative journalist",[482] "Syria expert",[483] and "Middle East expert".[484] For RT, Ochsenreiter would talk about the US spying on European allies, the CIA's alleged involvement in the Syrian civil war, and other — real or imagined — issues that could give RT an opportunity to use a German national to depict the US in an unfavourable light.

Ochsenreiter was apparently the only Western journalist at the illegitimate "referendum" in Russia-occupied Crimea in March 2014 — a referendum that was followed by the illegal annexation of that Ukrainian peninsula by Russia. During his stay in Crimea, Ochsenreiter interviewed Johann Gudenus, a now disgraced Austrian politician who had been primarily responsible for the pro-Russian turn of the far-right Freedom Party of Austria (Freiheitliche Partei Österreichs, FPÖ) in 2007-2008.[485]

Gudenus was one of a few dozen European politicians invited by the Russians to provide international "legitimacy" to the otherwise illegitimate Crimean "referendum". In his interview to Ochsenreiter, Gudenus expectedly denied the Russian military

---

480   More on RT see Anton Shekhovtsov (ed.), *RT in Europe and beyond: The Wannabe Elite of the Anti-Elites* (Vienna: Centre for Democratic Integrity, 2022).

481   "Germany Begins Deployment of Patriot Missiles to Turkey", *RT*, 8 January (2013), https://www.rt.com/news/germany-turkey-missiles-patriot-565/.

482   "UN Anti-Spying Draft Resolution Completely Ignores 'National Sovereignty' Issue", *RT*, 9 November (2013), https://www.rt.com/op-ed/spying-resolution-national-sovereignty-460/.

483   "US Military Intervention in Syria Is Not off the Table", *RT*, 14 September (2013), https://www.rt.com/op-ed/us-syria-crisis-intervention-867/.

484   "Moderate Syrian Opposition Are 'Phantoms,' Have No Influence on the Ground", *RT*, 9 January (2014), https://www.rt.com/op-ed/moderate-syrian-oppostion-phantoms-346/.

485   See Anton Shekhovtsov, "Ending the Schwarzer Tango with Moscow: The Freedom Party of Austria and the Embrace of Neutralism", *Stockholm Centre for Eastern European Studies* (2022), https://sceeus.se/en/publications/ending-the-schwarzer-tango-with-moscow-the-freedom-party-of-austria-and-the-embrace-of-neutralism/.

occupation of Crimea in the run-up to the "referendum".[486] So did Ochsenreiter himself in an interview to the Russian state-controlled (yet now defunct) "Voice of Russia" website on 21 April 2014,[487] although on 17 April of that year Vladimir Putin had himself admitted to the deployment of Russian special operations units and troops in Crimea.[488]

RT also used Ochsenreiter's commentary in its bid to justify the annexation of Crimea, and the year 2014 in general saw a surge of Ochsenreiter's comments for RT.[489] In numerous interviews and reports, he offered his views on the situation in Ukraine from a pro-Russian and anti-American perspective. Tellingly, however, only the English-language version of RT — and, to a much lesser extent, its Spanish-language version — featured commentary or reports from Ochsenreiter. English- and Spanish-speaking audiences, unlike the German one, would hardly be aware of Ochsenreiter's far-right — and thus problematic — credentials.

Expanding the network

In the context of Russia-related activities, Ochsenreiter would have probably just remained a commentator for the Russian media and a Dugin fan if not for the acquaintance with arguably the most infamous Polish pro-Kremlin activist, Mateusz Piskorski.

Piskorski had been active in the Russian far-right circles since the early 2000s and was, at some point, close to Dugin's neo-Eurasianist movement. However, it did not take long for Piskorski to realise that the Russian far right had limited, if any, financial

---

486 "A Strong Russia Is Good for Europe!", *Manuel Ochsenreiter — Journalist*, 18 April (2014), https://web.archive.org/web/20180222111923/http:/manuelochsenreiter.com/blog/2014/4/18/a-strong-russia-is-good-for-europe.

487 "Crimea: No Russian Invasion, Happy People — Manuel Ochsenreiter", *The Voice of Russia*, 21 April (2014), https://web.archive.org/web/20150107212936/http:/sputniknews.com/voiceofrussia/2014_04_21/Crimea-No-Russian-invasion-happy-people-Manuel-Ochsenreiter-9307/.

488 "Putin Admits Russian Forces Were Deployed to Crimea", *Reuters*, 17 April (2014), https://www.reuters.com/article/russia-putin-crimea-idUSL6N0N921H20140417.

489 Adam Holland, "RT's Manuel Ochsenreiter", *The Interpreter*, 21 April (2014), https://web.archive.org/web/20140322030326/https:/interpretermag.com/rts-manuel-ochsenreiter/.

resources to cover foreign pro-Russian activities. Thus, Piskorski started cooperating with Russian operators of pro-Moscow activities who had the Kremlin's backing.

One of those operators was Aleksey Kochetkov, who specialised in organising and coordinating fake election observation aimed at advancing the Kremlin's interests by imitating credible election monitoring. For Piskorski, fake election observation became an important point of entry into the professional pro-Kremlin circles in Russia. In 2007, he registered his own organisation under the name "European Centre for Geopolitical Analysis" (Europejskie Centrum Analiz Geopolitycznych, ECAG) taken from a non-functioning organisation registered by Kochetkov and his then spouse Marina Klebanovich in 2004.

The ECAG became arguably the most important organisation that organised fake election observation missions in Russia and Eastern Europe. And it was Piskorski and his ECAG—together with the Belgium-based Eurasian Observatory for Democracy and Elections run by Luc Michel, a fringe Belgian far-right activist—that were tasked with coordinating the majority of "international observers" at the Crimean "referendum" in March 2014.

It seems likely that Ochsenreiter met Piskorski for the first time at the Crimean "referendum", and that was a pivotal meeting for both of them. Through Ochsenreiter, Piskorski was able to expand his network in Germany and Austria, while Ochsenreiter obtained, with Piskorski's help, access to a wider range of contacts in Russia.

Having established a strong partnership, Piskorski and Ochsenreiter would often participate in joint activities. On 28 September—1 October 2014, both of them took part in the second instalment of the anti-Semitic "New Horizon" conference in Tehran, where Piskorski was talking on "the Israeli lobby in Poland", and Ochsenreiter—on "the Israeli lobby in Germany".[490] And a month

---

490 "New Horizon—The 2nd Annual International Conference of Independent Thinkers & Film Makers", *New Horizon*, https://web.archive.org/web/20141002194931/http:/newhorizon.ir/index.php?option=com_content&view=article&id=159&Itemid=139.

later, in the beginning of November 2014, Piskorski took Ochsenreiter to Russia-occupied parts of eastern Ukraine to "observe" illegitimate "parliamentary elections" in the "Donetsk People's Republic".

On 19 June 2015, in Warsaw, Ochsenreiter and Piskorski took
part in the debate "Poland and Germany in the era of US hegemony" that was co-organised by Piskorski's ECAG and the Polish
neo-fascist Falanga group.[491] Falanga's two representatives, Bartosz
Bekier and Michał Prokopowicz, participated in the debate too, and
Ochsenreiter's contact with Falanga's activists would play a crucial
if not fateful role in his later life, of which more is discussed below.

A Kremlin protest in Germany

As Piskorski was engaged in Russian active measures aimed at discrediting, undermining and subverting the pro-Western aspira-
tions of Ukraine after the 2014 democratic revolution, he collaborated with several Russian operators of malign influence. One of his
Russian handlers since 2015 was Sargis Mirzakhanian. At that time,
Mirzakhanian was a minor official at the Central Office of the State
Duma (Russian parliament) and was involved in coordinating information operations against Ukraine.[492]

Documents seen by the author suggest that Mirzakhanian and
Piskorski organised a protest against the politics of US President
Barack Obama and Turkey's President Recep Tayyip Erdoğan in
February 2016. Mirzakhanian and his assistant Stepan Mantsurov
communicated the main slogans for the protests to Piskorski, as
well as providing pictures for posters. Slogans proposed by the
Russians included "Against Obama's black business", "Erdoğan

---

491 "Debata geopolityczna / Geopolitical debate—Manuel Ochsenreiter vs. Ma-
     teusz Piskorski", *Facebook*, 19 June (2015), https://www.facebook.com/even
     ts/1009743369127317.
492 See more on Mirzakhanian and his activities in Martin Laine, Cecilia Anesi, Lo-
     renzo Bagnoli, Tatiana Tkachenko, "Kremlin-Linked Group Arranged Pay-
     ments to European Politicians to Support Russia's Annexation of Crimea", *Or-
     ganized Crime and Corruption Reporting Project*, 3 February (2023), https://
     www.occrp.org/en/investigations/kremlin-linked-group-arranged-paymen
     ts-to-european-politicians-to-support-russias-annexation-of-crimea.

produces oil for Obama", "Erdoğan and Obama are a threat to peaceful Europe", "Erdoğan is a new Hitler", and "Stop feeding ISIS".

The protest took place in Berlin in front of the Rotes Rathaus, the Berlin town hall, on 28 February 2016. The event failed to attract many people, but, according to the internal documents as well as photographic evidence, not only did Ochsenreiter participate in the protest, he also spoke there.

In addition to Ochsenreiter, several other people were planned to speak in Berlin, including Madeleine Feige and Viktor Seibel from the Pegida movement, Jürgen Elsässer of the far-right *Compact* magazine, and Markus Frohnmaier of the youth wing of the far-right Alternative for Germany (AfD). Frohnmaier did hang around the demonstration, but did not speak there.

The following day, Ochsenreiter attended a much larger demonstration in Dresden organised by the Pegida movement that gathered around three thousand people. Ochsenreiter and his associates brought Russian posters to the demonstration and recorded Ochsenreiter's short speech in the crowd with the posters in the background. Although the gathering was a regular one of Pegida's anti-Islamist "Montagsdemos" (Monday demonstrations), Mirzakhanian used the guidelines for the Berlin protest, as well as quotations from Ochsenreiter, Frohnmaier and Feige, to mispresent the demonstration – in his press release for the Russian media[493] – as specifically targeting Obama and Erdoğan.

Fighting the "anti-Russian sanctions"

On 11 May 2016, several Russian media ran a story about members of the AfD preparing a resolution on the lifting of the "anti-Russian sanctions" to be sent to the Baden-Württemberg state parliament.[494]

---

493 "V Germanii proshel miting protiv politiki dvoynykh standartov Obamy i Erdogana", *EurAsia Daily*, 1 March (2016), https://eadaily.com/ru/news/2016/03/01/v-germanii-proshel-miting-protiv-politiki-dvoynyh-standartov-obamy-i-erdogana.

494 Darya Tsoy, "Nemetskie deputaty trebuyut otmenit' antirossiyskie sanktsii", *Izvestiya*, 11 May (2016), https://iz.ru/news/613049; Anastasiya Novikova,

The story cited Udo Stein, a member of the Baden-Württemberg state parliament, saying: "The sanctions have to be lifted. They turned out to be useless and harmful for our German economy".

Few readers, however, knew that the story was a result of the influence operation conducted by a trio of Mirzakhanian, Piskorski and Ochsenreiter. As properties of the documents seen by the author reveal, already on 5 May 2016, Ochsenreiter drew up two documents. One was called "A small question [*Kleine Anfrage*] of the AfD faction" and inquired about the impact of the "anti-Russian sanctions" on the economy of Baden-Württemberg. The other document was called "Member of the state parliament Udo Stein: 'Strengthen Baden-Württemberg — end anti-Russian sanctions!'" and dated 10 May.

All evidence shows that, rather than asking for a real quotation from Stein, Ochsenreiter wrote both documents himself from beginning to end, and then cleared them with Stein. He then forwarded the documents to Piskorski, who sent them to Mirzakhanian on 8 May. On 10 May, Piskorski supplemented the two documents with a document titled "Sanctions-Russia-Campaign.doc" that was most likely — as the document's metadata show — written by Ochsenreiter too. The third document gave figures on the alleged damage that the "anti-Russian sanctions" inflicted on the economy of Baden-Württemberg and gave more presumed quotations from Stein and Frohnmaier.

The same day, Mirzakhanian sent Russian translations of Ochsenreiter's documents to his contacts in the Russian media, adding that Stein and Frohnmaier would hold a press conference on the need to lift the "anti-Russian sanctions" on 11 May and giving Frohnmaier's phone number so the Russian media could request additional information from him. Curiously, a little less than a year later, Frohnmaier would marry the author of the story about him and Stein, Russian journalist Daria Tsoy, published in the *Izvestiya* newspaper.

"Nemetskie deputaty potrebovali otmenit' antirossiyskie sanktsii", *Komsomolskaya pravda*, 11 May (2016), https://www.kp.ru/online/news/2388500/.

At the end of May 2017, when Mirzakhanian presented an organisation which he helped found, Hemingway Partners, he included the media story on the AfD's resolution on the lifting of the "anti-Russian sanctions" in the list of the projects implemented by that organisation.

Mirzakhanian's correspondence seen by the author suggests that Russian operatives were also likely involved in producing a special issue of Ochsenreiter's *Zuerst!* magazine specifically attacking "anti-Russian sanctions". In June 2016, Mirzakhanian sent a project of the special issue to Mantsurov. The project described *Zuerst!* as a magazine "popular among European German-speaking opposition politicians and public figures" and claimed that copies of the printed version of the magazine were sent to all members of the Bundestag, to all offices of the AfD, and to the FPÖ in Austria. The project also focused on three major features of the special issue that would be published in July of that year: interviews with the AfD's MEP Marcus Pretzell, the AfD's member of the Saxony state parliament Jörg Urban, and the FPÖ's Johann Gudenus — all criticising "anti-Russian sanctions". The budget of the special issue was estimated at €12,000. The fact that the project describing *Zuerst!* and the contents of the special issue were written in Russian and were exchanged between Russian operatives of malign influence suggests that they, at the very least, considered financing it, but there is no evidence that any Russian actor paid any money for the publication of the issue.

Operating a Romanian MEP

On 18 May 2016, the Polish Internal Security Agency (Agencja Bezpieczeństwa Wewnętrznego, ABW) arrested Piskorski and later charged him with the offence of taking part in the operations of Russia's intelligence against Poland. Piskorski's work was very important for Russian pro-Kremlin actors, and it took at least two persons to substitute him as an operator of Russian malign influence in Europe after his arrest. One person was Piskorski's associate, a Polish activist Janusz Niedźwiecki, who would also be handled by

Mirzakhanian and be arrested by the ABW on 31 May 2021.[495] The other person was Piskorski's partner Marina Klebanovich, whom he "stole" from his former Russian associate Aleksey Kochetkov — that was apparently one the major reasons why Piskorski and Kochetkov ended cooperation with each other around ten years earlier.

Correspondence between Klebanovich and Ochsenreiter seen by the author suggest that, in September 2016, Ochsenreiter wrote a text on "the economic situation in Ukraine" on behalf of Romanian MEP Laurenţiu Rebega, who, at that time, was a member of the far-right Europe of Nations and Freedom group. Ochsenreiter presumably received Rebega's authorisation for the text and then sent it to Klebanovich. The latter forwarded the text to Mirzakhanian, adding a line saying "3.000 Euros" to the e-mail message, which can be understood as a fee that Mirzakhanian or his superiors had to pay for the service.

Since the text concerned Ukraine, Mirzakhanian forwarded it to a Russian team that conducted malign influence operations specifically against Ukraine. The team made up a typical false news story using parts of Ochsenreiter's text. The story reported on "an international economic forum" in Ukraine's capital Kyiv that presumably called for restoring economic relations with Russia, and featured a presumed quote from Rebega implying that he had participated in the forum too, although there is no evidence that he had.

The quote asserted that Ukraine was "not on the road of economic success", and, since "neither the EU nor NATO nor the USA" would support Ukraine forever, the quote urged the country to return to "the old Ukrainian-Russian partnership" as "the new solution for a stable future growth" of Ukraine's economy.

---

495 See more on Niedźwiecki in the chapter "The Rise and Fall of a Polish Agent of the Kremlin Influence: The Case of Janusz Niedźwiecki" in this book.

Mirzakhanian sent the story to his contacts to plant it in a number of Ukrainian media sources[496] and publish it in the Russian media too.[497]

In another related piece, the above-mentioned Russian team went as far as to entirely fake a quote from Rebega, allegedly saying that Ukraine needed to adopt a special law for the Russian language. The piece was, again, published in the Ukrainian and Russian media.

Since the "quote" was not authorised by Rebega, the publication of that false news story triggered an angry reaction from Ochsenreiter. In a series of messages to Klebanovich, he wrote:

> [Rebega] never said that!!!!! Please control that!!!! [...] This is an attack against my network. MEP totally upset and might fire assistant. S. unprofessionalism makes us look all like idiots. I am not going to accept that. [...] [The piece] is published over and over again since yesterday. It is really a mess. Call you tomorrow.

The blunder with the false story, however, did not undermine Rebega's relations with either Ochsenreiter or Russian malign influence operators.

In January 2017, in his report on the conference of the Europe of Nations and Freedom group in Koblenz, Ochsenreiter gave a surprisingly long quote from Rebega's speech at the conference, which can be interpreted as Ochsenreiter's intention to keep Rebega firmly

---

496   See, for example, "Na mezhdunarodnom forume v Kieve prizvali nachat' vosstanovlenie ekonomicheskikh svyazey s Rossiey", *Golos UA*, 21 September (2016), https://web.archive.org/web/20160922151143/http:/ru.golos.ua/un category/na_mejdunarodnom_forume_v_kieve_prizvali_nachat_vosstanovle nie_ekonomicheskih_svyaze; "Na mezhdunarodnom forume v Kieve prizvali nachat' vosstanovlenie ekonomicheskikh svyazey s Rossiey", *Ukrayinski novyny*, 21 September (2016), https://ukranews.com/news/450395-na-mezhdu narodnom-forume-v-kyeve-pryzvaly-nachat-vosstanovlenye-ehkonomychesk ykh-svyazey-s-rossyey.

497   See, for example, "Uchastniki foruma v Kieve vystupili za vosstanovlenie ekonomicheskikh otnosheniy Ukrainy i RF", *Interfax*, 21 September (2016), https://www.interfax.ru/world/529330; "SMI: uchastniki foruma v Kieve prizvali vlasti k sotrudnichestvu s Rossiey", *RIA Novosti*, 21 September (2016), https://ria.ru/20160921/1477545745.html; "Uchastniki Mezhdunarodnogo foruma v Kieve prizvali vosstanovit' ekonomicheskie svyazi s RF", *TASS*, 21 September (2016), https://tass.ru/mezhdunarodnaya-panorama/3642292.

within his network.[498] And on 2 April 2017, Ochsenreiter accompanied Rebega and several other European far-right politicians, as well as Russian MP Alexander Yushchenko of the Communist Party of the Russian Federation, at a pro-Kremlin conference titled "End the economic sanctions against Russia" that took place in the German town of Freiberg.[499]

Rebega's readiness to cooperate with Russian stakeholders earned him an invitation to the Third Yalta International Economic Forum that took place in Russia-annexed Crimea on 20-22 April 2017. Mirzakhanian played a role in the decision to invite Rebega to the Forum: Mirzakhanian's boss Andrey Nazarov was the chair of the Board of the Yalta International Economic Forum Foundation, while Mirzakhanian himself was responsible for media contacts to the Forum. The official invitation to the Forum came from the head of the Russian occupation government in Crimea, Sergey Aksyonov.

Not only did Rebega attend the conference, he was also interviewed for *Delovoy krym* (Business Crimea) magazine and quoted by the Russian state-controlled RT website in one of its reports on the Yalta International Economic Forum.[500]

A fake "election observer"

While Ochsenreiter was not part of the "international observation mission" at the "referendum" in Crimea in 2014, becoming close colleagues with Piskorski, who was the main coordinator of numerous politically-biased election observation missions, necessarily drew Ochsenreiter into that area too.

---

498 Manuel Ochsenreiter, "A Historical Chance for Europe—and Most Probably the Last One", *Free West Media*, 23 January (2017), https://freewestmedia.com/2017/01/23/a-historical-chance-for-europe-and-most-probably-the-last-one/.
499 "International Conference against Anti-Russian EU Sanctions", *Free West Media*, 19 April (2017), https://freewestmedia.com/2017/04/19/international-conference-against-anti-russian-eu-sanctions/.
500 Roman Tikhonov, "Krym, sanktsii i breksit: RT pobesedoval s uchastnikami delovogo foruma v Yalte", *RT*, 21 April (2017), https://russian.rt.com/russia/article/381366-yalta-forum-interviu-ekonomika-sankcii-krim.

In autumn 2014, as Russia occupied parts of eastern Ukraine and formed two internationally unrecognised entities on the occupied territories, the "Donetsk People's Republic" (DPR) and "Lugansk People's Republic" (LPR), the Kremlin needed to legitimise the new "authorities" of the "republics". To that end, Moscow decided to conduct "elections" in the DPR and LPR—elections that were deplored as "unconstitutional" by UN Secretary-General Ban Ki-moon.[501] And in order to add "legitimacy" to the "elections", the Kremlin invited "international observers" to "monitor" them.

Russian stakeholders tasked Piskorski with coordinating an "international observation mission", and Piskorski brought several "monitors", including Ochsenreiter, to the occupied Ukrainian territories. The aim of the "mission" was to imitate credible election monitoring and declare the "elections" legitimate, peaceful and democratic, and Ochsenreiter expectedly praised the conduct of the "elections" in the Russian media.[502]

Among Russian stakeholders who coordinated the "international observation mission" at the "parliamentary elections" in the DPR and LPR was EU- and US-sanctioned Russian MP Leonid Slutsky and the Agency for Strategic Communications co-founded by Vadim Samodurov and Oleg Bondarenko. In January 2018, Bondarenko would be denied entry to the Schengen area at Poland's request,[503] which could possibly be a result of the investigation into the activities of Piskorski who was in Polish jail at that time.

As relations between Ochsenreiter and Russian malign influence operators developed, he decided to register an organisation that would become a "respectable" front for his pro-Kremlin and far-right activism. In spring 2016, Ochsenreiter, Markus Frohnmaier and Thuringian AfD member Thomas Rudy founded

---

501 "Secretary-General Deplores Unconstitutional Elections Called by Armed Rebel Groups in Ukraine", *United Nations*, 29 October (2014), https://press.un.org/en/2014/sgsm16291.doc.htm.

502 "Nablyudatel' ot FRG: vybory v LNR prokhodyat bez narusheniy i provokatsiy", *RIA Novosti*, 2 November (2014), https://ria.ru/20141102/1031408598.html.

503 "Rossiyskomu politologu zapretili v'yezd v ES po trebovaniyu Pol'shi", *TASS*, 14 January (2018), https://tass.ru/politika/4872891.

the German Center for Eurasian Studies,[504] which was officially registered on 2 August 2016.[505] Ochsenreiter was appointed director of
the organisation, while Piskorski became its vice director.[506]

Using the cover of the German Center, Ochsenreiter brought
the AfD's Rudy and Udo Stein to the DPR as "international observers" to "monitor" "primary elections". In autumn the same year,
Ochsenreiter, again, travelled to occupied eastern Ukraine to "observe" the "primaries".

In-between his travels to "monitor" the "primaries", Ochsenreiter "observed" the Russian parliamentary elections that took
place on 18 September 2016. In a series of email exchanges seen by
the author, Ochsenreiter and Klebanovich discussed, on 18-19 September, the publication of Ochsenreiter's article on the Russian elections (the exchange was edited for better clarity):

> Klebanovich: Answer me as soon as possible if you write something in
> *Zuerst* and *Zeit-Fragen*.
> Ochsenreiter: *Zuerst*! (online + print), *Wochenblick* (print), German Center
> (English, online), Nortexa (online). Which do you want of these?
> K: *Zuerst*, but you remember, only 1500 to share. Do you agree?
> O: Will be online tomorrow.
> K: Great! Only they ask to send it first here to read before. Possible?
> O: Of course. Send it tonight to you.
> K: :))
> O: Please check and give me "green light" tomorrow. Our online guys are
> sometimes a bit slowly — so it might be online at Wednesday if the "go" by
> you comes very late tomorrow.

Klebanovich cleared Ochsenreiter's text with Mirzakhanian, and it
appeared in *Zuerst*! on 20 September.[507] As can be understood from

---

504 Katja Riedel, Andrea Becker, Georg Heil, Sebastian Pittelkow, "Die Russland-
     Verbindungen der AfD", *Tagesschau*, 16 August (2017), https://www.tagess
     chau.de/inland/afd-russland-101.html.
505 "Deutsches Zentrum für Eurasische Studien e.V.", *Geschäftskatalog*, http://
     geschaftskatalog.eu/en/germany-business/deutsches-zentrum-fur-eurasische
     -studien-e-v-bahiedi.
506 "Board", *German Center for Eurasian Studies*, https://web.archive.org/web/
     20160711213843/http://germancenter.net/staff/department/board/.
507 "Wahl der Staatsduma in Rußland: Putins 'Einiges Rußland' mit überwältigen-
     dem Sieg", *Zuerst*!, 20 September (2016), https://zuerst.de/2016/09/20/
     zuerst-chefredakteur-manuel-ochsenreiter-zur-wahl-der-neuen-staatsduma-
     in-russland/.

the communications, as well as other similar exchanges between Ochsenreiter and Klebanovich seen by the author, the fee for the publication of Ochsenreiter's article was €1,500 Euros, which he would need to share with Klebanovich for her service as an intermediary between him and Mirzakhanian.

But Ochsenreiter would perform the role of an "election observer" outside of Russia and Russia-occupied territories too. On February 2017, together with the AfD and FPÖ delegations, Ochsenreiter "observed" the "constitutional referendum" in the "Nagorno-Karabakh Republic" – a territory disputed by Azerbaijan and Armenia, but internationally recognised as part of Azerbaijan.

Operation *"Our candidate"*

There was a reason why Markus Frohnmaier, the founder of the AfD's youth wing in Baden-Württemberg, Young Alternative for Germany, appeared so often alongside Ochsenreiter and as part of the Russian malign influence operations.

In the beginning of April 2019, a joint investigation by the BBC, *Der Spiegel*, the ZDF and *La Repubblica* revealed that Russian stakeholders considered supporting Frohnmaier as a candidate in the 2017 German parliamentary elections.[508] The investigation was based on two documents. One document was a letter sent by Petr Premyak, an assistant to Russian MP Viktor Shreider, which suggested to officials dealing with foreign policy issues at the Russian Presidential Administration to consider providing support to Frohnmaier. The other document, apparently written by Ochsenreiter, detailed Frohnmaier's election campaign and asked for Russian support.

Frohnmaier has been in contact with Russian actors at the latest since 2014. In particular, that year he got acquainted with Daniil Bisslinger, who at that time was an attaché in the foreign policy

---

508 "Has Russia Infiltrated the German Parliament?", *BBC*, 5 April (2019), https://www.bbc.co.uk/programmes/p075kx70.

office at the Russian Embassy to Germany.[509] In March 2015, Frohnmaier was a guest at the meeting of the association "Franco-Russian Dialogue" co-chaired by Russian Railways CEO Vladimir Yakunin and French right-wing politician Thierry Mariani, who was then a member of the centre-right Union for a Popular Movement (Union pour un mouvement populaire, UMP).[510] And in April 2015, Frohnmaier took part in a meeting in Belgrade with the leaders of the youth organisation of the Russian ruling party "United Russia", Alexander Galkin and Vladislav Artyomov — the meeting was hosted by Serbian far-right politician Miroslav Parović and also featured Pierre Gentillet from Mariani's more nationalist wing of the UMP.[511]

Ochsenreiter knew Frohnmaier since at least 2015,[512] and Ochsenreiter apparently saw a lot of potential in the young far-right politician. As the relations between Ochsenreiter and his Russia-related network developed, he presumably decided to introduce Frohnmaier to that network via Piskorski.

On 7 March 2016, Piskorski sent a message to Mirzakhanian and his assistant Mantsurov, seen by the author, in which he described Frohnmaier as "our candidate". The message also contained an article from *Die Zeit* that reported on Frohnmaier's pro-Russian activism.[513]

All further developments point to the fact that Mirzakhanian and his team became interested in Frohnmaier. After his introduction to the Russian operatives, Frohnmaier was immediately

509 Markus Frohnmaier, "Dialog statt Konfrontation", *Facebook*, 10 August (2014), https://www.facebook.com/frohnmaier/photos/a.1414533632130119/14649 56093754539/.
510 Markus Frohnmaier, "Zu Gast bei der Association Dialogue Franco-Russe", *Facebook*, 28 March (2015), https://www.facebook.com/frohnmaier/posts/pfb id02xwjoyhMA8M8u4uGpcDyNfKXBhxhdVDvnHVSgkhEGQUmgMjjYm7Fh pZh673skkMMsl.
511 Markus Frohnmaier, "Mit Pierre Gentillet (UMP)", *Facebook*, 24 April (2015), https://www.facebook.com/frohnmaier/posts/pfbid037ZhiTWXQCf9Gdrz5 LjL4xhPv9zA2H9EVuQmKNKKto9SqgFnadeJrexAwJBH6Qm1jl.
512 Markus Frohnmaier, "Mit syrischen Freunden", *Facebook*, 6 June (2015), https://www.facebook.com/frohnmaier/photos/1599205410329606/.
513 Jochen Bittner, "Weg aus dem Westen", *Zeit Online*, 3 March (2016), https://www.zeit.de/2016/11/afd-jugend-markus-frohnmaier.

invited to take part in the Second Yalta International Economic Forum, which would take place in April 2016, along with several established European politicians invited by Mirzakhanian's team:
MEP Marcus Pretzell (AfD), the FPÖ's Mps Axel Kassegger and
Barbara Rosenkranz, Czech far-left MEP Jaromir Kohlíček, and Italian regional far-right politician Stefano Valdegamberi.

According to the above-mentioned joint investigation, on 3
April 2017, Petr Premyak sent a message to Sergey Sokolov who, at
that time, worked at the foreign policy department of the Russian
Presidential Administration. The message also had a six-page at-
tachment written in Russian and titled "Foreign Policy Activities"
that, as the message implied, was proposed to be considered by the
then head of the department, Alexander Manzhosin. At the same
time, Mirzakhanian's assistant Alexander Kirpichev would provide
more details on the proposed projects.

The authors of the six-page document suggested organising
protests in the EU to discredit those who stood "in opposition to
the foreign policy trends of the Russian Federation"; lobbying for
the lifting of the "anti-Russian sanctions" with the help of European
actors; and establishing closer ties with friendly European political
forces.[514]

Importantly, the document also contained a section on
Frohnmaier saying that he had a good chance of being elected to
the Bundestag in the 2017 German parliamentary elections and
needed support for his election campaign. As the authors of the
document put it, the aim of the endeavour was simple: "We will
have our own absolutely controlled MP in the Bundestag". The authors also promised to provide a detailed programme for
Frohnmaier's electoral campaign "by the end of the next week".

The following week, on 11 April 2017, Ochsenreiter drew up a
document titled "Frohnmaier election campaign / action plan
(draft)". The document, seen by the author, urged to provide

---

514   Melanie Amann, Stephan Heffner, Martin Knobbe, Ann-Katrin Müller, Jan
Puhl, Marcel Rosenbach, Alexander Sarovic, Jörg Schmitt, Wolf Wiedmann-
Schmidt, Anika Zeller, "Documents Link AfD Parliamentarian to Moscow",
Spiegel, 12 April (2019), https://www.spiegel.de/international/germany/doc
uments-link-afd-parliamentarian-to-moscow-a-1261509.html.

"material" and "media support" for Frohnmaier's electoral campaign, saying that during the campaign, the candidate would emphasise the following topics: "German independence and sovereignty", "good relations with the Russian Federation", "conservatism", and "criticism towards US".

The document also promised that Frohnmaier, as an MP in the Bundestag, would "immediately start operating in international policy field" and "be ready for cooperation in various fields of German-Russian relations". Frohnmaier would also head international delegations to Crimea, Donbass and Russian regions, and would frequently appear in the Russian media.

The same day on 11 April 2017, Mirzakhanian sent Ochsenreiter's draft on Frohnmaier's campaign to an email address likely jointly used by himself and currently unidentified members of his team.

At the time of the writing, there is no evidence that Ochsenreiter's "action plan" for Frohnmaier's election campaign was acted upon by any Russian stakeholders. Nevertheless, Frohnmaier was indeed elected to the Bundestag, and Ochsenreiter became his adviser in early September 2018. Frohnmaier continued being engaged in pro-Kremlin activities, such as participation in the fake "observation mission" for the 2018 Russian presidential election. While Frohnmaier, already as a German MP, would go to Russia to "observe" the election, Ochsenreiter would accompany yet another AfD MP, Bernhard Ulrich Oehme,[515] who "monitored" the illegitimate Russian presidential election in Russia-annexed Crimea.[516]

---

515 Anton Shekhovtsov, "Politically Biased Foreign Electoral Observation at the Russian 2018 Presidential Election", *European Platform for Democratic Elections*, 16 April (2018), https://www.epde.org/en/documents/details/politically-biased-foreign-electoral-observation-at-the-russian-2018-presidential-election-1423.html.

516 Anton Shekhovtsov, "Controversial 'International Observation' at the 2019 Regional Elections in Russia", *European Platform for Democratic Elections*, 8 October (2019), https://www.epde.org/en/documents/details/controversial-international-observation-at-the-2019-regional-elections-in-russia.html.

Between Russia and the AfD

In the rare media reports on Ochsenreiter, discussions of his links to the AfD have usually been limited to his work as an adviser to Frohnmaier in the Bundestag and his participation in events featuring AfD members. Documents seen by the author, however, reveal that in 2016, Ochsenreiter played a more significant role—at least in the AfD's relations with Russian actors.

According to an internal memorandum written by Kirpichev in May 2016, Mirzakhanian's team started cooperating with members and activists of the AfD in January 2016. The aim of the cooperation was to engage them in "projects concerning foreign policy issues important to Russia: settlement of the conflict in Ukraine, confrontation with Turkey, recognition of Crimea [as part of Russia], lifting of the anti-Russian sanctions". The memorandum mentioned Frohnmaier and Ochsenreiter as "party workers" who provided media commentary "for the benefit of Russian foreign policy".

Moreover, Kirpichev's memorandum asserted that Mirzakhanian's team had spearheaded a letter from the AfD's then leader Frauke Petry addressed to Putin. The Russian version of Petry's presumed letter to Putin was attached to the memorandum, and—in case it actually existed—represented the first instance of the AfD leadership expressing interest in cooperation with Putin's regime. In particular, the letter read:

> In connection to the wrong direction of European politics, [our] party is worried about the Russia-German relations. As a party, we reject the Berlin sanctions policies towards Moscow, [and] we make every effort to improve Russian-German relations. [...]

> Dear Mr. President, in this letter, I ask for a personal meeting with you in Moscow. I would like to talk to you on how we, as the "Alternative for Germany" party, can contribute to the normalisation of the Russian-German relations, so it would have a positive effect on both of our countries.

The text also featured a list of people of the AfD's delegation who Petry presumably wanted to accompany her to Moscow: Marcus Pretzell, Alexander Gauland, Frohnmaier, Sven Werner Tritschler, and Ochsenreiter—the latter was referred to as "a journalist with experience of working in Russia" who would accompany Petry to Moscow "in the capacity of a consultant".

In June 2016, Kirpichev wrote a note that claimed to detail Petry's expectations from her visit to Moscow: (1) meeting the head of the Russian state, (2) meeting the Russian State Duma Chairman Sergey Naryshkin, (3) holding "closed-door negotiations" with an assistant or adviser to Yuriy Ushakov, who, at that time, was the Russian president's assistant on foreign policy issues, and (4) meeting "people who deal with the lifting of the sanctions".

Those expectations were evidently overambitious, if not straightforwardly ridiculous. Putin would generally be reluctant to meet a leader of a European opposition party if he wanted to maintain good relations with the authorities of that country, and he would not meet political figures without a thorough and usually long preparation for such a meeting on the part of his foreign policy team. For example, Marine Le Pen, the leader of the French far-right National Front, expressed her desire to meet "people in power" in Russia in 2011, and yet it took her and her party years of talks, negotiations and low-profile visits to arrange Le Pen's meeting with Putin six years later.

Meeting with Naryshkin, however, was more realistic: over the years, in his capacity as the chair of the Russian parliament, Naryshkin met several European politicians, including leaders of opposition parties.

Communications between Russian and German stakeholders concerning Petry's visit to Moscow show that Ochsenreiter was not only a potential participant in the AfD's delegation – he also drafted some of the communications. For example, he drafted a letter from Alexander Agapov, apparently one of Naryshkin's assistants, that was addressed to Petry and informed her of the rescheduling of her prospective visit to Moscow. The letter also mentioned Ochsenreiter as a person "in charge of the arrangements in Germany".

The revised schedule did not work for Petry, and Frohnmaier wrote a message to Naryshkin saying that Petry could not go to Moscow as she had to "attend the Federal Convention of Alternative for Germany". At the same time, Frohnmaier suggested to

Naryshkin that only Pretzell, Ochsenreiter and Frohnmaier himself would go to Moscow, but the idea did not seem to have resonated with the Russian side: the delegation would be too low-ranking for Naryshkin's status.

Petry, too, presumably wrote a letter to Naryshkin saying that she was "interested to discuss the current challenges in German-Russian relationships", in particular, "the sanctions regime" and "positive perspectives of a future better understanding" between Germany and Russia. Petry proposed to find a suitable date in October 2016 to meet with Naryshkin in Moscow.

It is currently unknown whether the communications about Petry's prospective meeting with Naryshkin continued any further, but on 22 September 2016, Putin appointed Naryshkin Director of Russia's Foreign Intelligence Service (also known as SVR),[517] and the latter's public meeting with Petry — in that particular capacity — became impossible.

Petry did visit Moscow later: accompanied by Pretzell and Julian Flak, Petry went to Russia in February 2017 and met with Naryshkin's successor as the State Duma chairman, Vyacheslav Volodin, as well as Volodin's deputy Pyotr Tolstoy, the now late leader of the far-right, misleadingly named Liberal-Democratic Party of Russia, Vladimir Zhirinovsky, the head of the State Duma foreign affairs committee, Leonid Slutsky, and the head of the State Duma committee on energy, Pavel Zavalny.[518]

As an investigation by *Frankfurter Allgemeine Zeitung* showed, Russian stakeholders would book a private jet for the AfD delegation and pay €25,000 for their trip.[519] However, there is currently no evidence as to whether Ochsenreiter or Mirzakhanian's team had anything to do with Petry's trip to Moscow in February 2017.

---

517 "Executive Order on Foreign Intelligence Service Director", *President of Russia*, 22 September (2016), http://en.kremlin.ru/events/president/news/52950.

518 "Vyacheslav Volodin vstretilsya s delegatsiey politicheskoy partii 'Alternativa dlya Germanii' (FRG) vo glave s liderom partii Frauke Petri", *Gosudarstvennaya duma*, 20 February (2017), http://duma.gov.ru/news/13216/.

519 "Russen bezahlten Privatflugzeug für AfD-Politiker", *Frankfurter Allgemeine Zeitung*, 21 May (2018), https://www.faz.net/aktuell/politik/russen-bezahl ten-privatflugzeug-fuer-afd-politiker-15600740.html.

The downfall

In the early morning hours of 4 February 2018, two Polish far-right activists, Adrian Marglewski and Tomasz Rafał Szymkowiak, attacked a building of the Hungarian Cultural Centre in the Ukrainian city of Uzhhorod, the home of a sizeable ethnic Hungarian community.[520] The two activists tried to set the building on fire and reported their efforts to a third Polish national, yet another far-right activist named Michał Prokopowicz—the very same Michał Prokopowicz who participated in the debate "Poland and Germany in the era of US hegemony" alongside Ochsenreiter and Piskorski in June 2015.

The aim of Marglewski and Szymkowiak was not simply to set the building on fire; rather, the main objective was to present the arson as a result of the attack of Ukrainian neo-Nazis in order to sour relations between Hungary and Ukraine. To that end, as instructed by Prokopowicz, the two perpetrators also painted swastikas and the number 88 (a neo-Nazi code standing for "Heil Hitler") on the walls of the Hungarian Cultural Centre. It was meant to be a typical false-flag attack.

Ukrainian law enforcement identified the perpetrators,[521] and the Polish ABW arrested all three activists on 22 February 2018. During the investigation, Prokopowicz confessed that the entire operation had been commissioned by Ochsenreiter. According to Prokopowicz, Ochsenreiter would pay €1,500 to hire five people to carry out the attack in Ukraine,[522] but Prokopowicz was able to find only two. Ochsenreiter paid Prokopowicz €500 in advance, while the rest was paid after the execution of the operation at a restaurant in the Tegel airport area where the two met on 7 February 2018. In

---

520 Rafał Pasztelański, "Polacy oskarżeni o terroryzm po spaleniu węgierskiej placówki na Zakarpaciu", *TVP Info*, 5 January (2019), https://www.tvp.info/40726696/polacy-oskarzeni-o-terroryzm-na-ukrainie.

521 "Sprobu pidpalu spilky uhortsiv v Uzhhorodi skoyily dvoye polyakiv—Moskal", *Evropeys'ka pravda*, 21 February (2018), https://www.eurointegration.com.ua/news/2018/02/21/7077866/.

522 Jonas Mueller-Töwe, Lars Wienand, Jonas Schaible, Sarah Orlos, "Mitarbeiter eines AfD-MdB soll Drahtzieher von Anschlag sein", *T-Online*, 14 January (2019), https://www.t-online.de/nachrichten/deutschland/id_84665294/ukraine-afd-mitarbeiter-soll-anschlag-initiiert-haben.html.

their turn, Marglewski and Szymkowiak were paid 1,000 Polish złoty (approximately €240 at that time) each by Prokopowicz.[523]

The story about Ochsenreiter's involvement became known to the media in January 2019. He expectedly denied his involvement in the arson attack in Ukraine, but, due to the scandal, Frohnmaier was compelled to terminate the employment contract with Ochsenreiter, who had worked for Frohnmaier in his Bundestag office since early September 2018.[524]

In January 2019, the Berlin Public Prosecutor's Office opened an investigation into incitement to serious arson against Ochsenreiter. The latter, however, disappeared. In August 2020, the Federal Prosecutor's Office would take over the investigation from Berlin and issue an arrest warrant; the investigation suspected Ochsenreiter of terrorist financing in combination with incitement to arson.[525]

In the beginning of September 2019, Ochsenreiter and Piskorski, who had been released on bail in May 2019, announced the start of the "revolutionary infotainment podcast about geopolitics" called "Die Guten Menschen [The good people] — Public Enemies of the Deep State".[526] The pro-Kremlin and vehemently illiberal podcast was said to be supported by *Zuerst!* and the "Free West Media" website run by two Swedish far-right activists, Vávra Suk and Sanna Hill, with identified links to Russian operatives.[527] The podcast premiered in November 2019, but the majority of its episodes ran in 2020; the last one was published on 14 December 2020.

---

523 Pasztelański, "Polacy oskarżeni o terroryzm".
524 Christian Fuchs, Daniel Müller, "AfD trennt sich nach Terrorvorwurf von Mitarbeiter", *Zeit Online*, 17 January (2019), https://www.zeit.de/politik/deut schland/2019-01/afd-politiker-manuel-ochsenreiter-brandanschlag-ukraine-terror-vorwurf.
525 Anton Shekhovtsov, "Vermittler zwischen AfD und Russland", *Tagesschau*, 29 September (2022), https://www.tagesschau.de/investigativ/ochsenreiter-afd-russland-101.html.
526 "The New Dissident Podcast", *Free West Media*, 7 September (2019), https://freewestmedia.com/2019/09/07/the-new-dissident-podcast/.
527 Anton Shekhovtsov, "Fake Election Observation as Russia's Tool of Election Interference: The Case of AFRIC", *European Platform for Democratic Elections*, 26 March (2020), https://www.epde.org/en/documents/details/fake-election-observation-as-russias-tool-of-election-interference-the-case-of-afric.html.

The description of the podcast on its Facebook page alleged that Ochsenreiter was based in the Moroccan city of Casablanca,[528] but there is no evidence to support that allegation. An obituary for Ochsenreiter in *Zuerst!* said that, since 2019 — the year when he disappeared from Germany following the opening of an investigation by the Berlin Public Prosecutor's Office against him — he had been living mostly in Moscow.[529] Based on the same report in *Zuerst!*, Ochsenreiter died in August 2021, after a week in a coma following a heart attack.

Apart from his involvement in the podcast with Piskorski, starting from 2019, Ochsenreiter effectively disappeared from the media space as a commentator. Even Russian media could no longer engage with him to push pro-Moscow narratives as, after the arson story, Ochsenreiter became too toxic even for the Russian propaganda machine. However, given his colourful life before 2019 as an operator and facilitator of Russian malign influence in Europe, there is little doubt that Ochsenreiter had been involved in covert operations during the period between 2019 and his reported death in summer 2021. At the request of Silvia Stöber from *tagesschau.de*, the Federal Foreign Office stated that, on 19 August 2021, the Russian authorities informed the German Embassy in Moscow that Ochsenreiter had died the day before.[530] The Federal Prosecutor's Office stopped the proceedings against Ochsenreiter in December 2021.

---

528 "Die Guten Menschen — Public Enemies of the Deep State", *Facebook*, https://archive.ph/7Wkmn.
529 "In eigener Sache: ZUERST!-Chefredakteur Manuel Ochsenreiter ist tot".
530 Shekhovtsov, "Vermittler zwischen AfD und Russland".

Post Scriptum

With the exception of the last chapter, "The German Connection", all other essays had originally been written before the beginning of the full-blown Russian invasion of Ukraine on 24 February 2022. The dramatic escalation of the Russian-Ukrainian war had a sobering effect on some pro-Kremlin figures, and they distanced themselves from their Russian contacts. For some, however, the genocidal efforts of the Russian troops in Ukraine changed nothing, and they continued to be involved in various pro-Kremlin activities.

The "Post Scriptum" provides an update on some of the activists, politicians, and other stakeholders that the essays featured in this book discussed. This update is necessarily limited in scope: while it seems important — given the extraordinary nature of the events — to follow up, where relevant, on some major figures mentioned in the chapters, it is unrealistic to do so with regard to all of them, so this final section focuses only on particular developments that I found intriguing, indicative or symptomatic against the background of the earlier discussions.

"Russian Election Interference in Africa: The Case of AFRIC"

Several investigations into the activities of the Association for Free Research and International Cooperation (AFRIC), as well as Facebook's actions taken against its presence on the social network, dealt a crushing blow to this Russian front organisation founded by the structures managed by Yevgeniy Prigozhin.

In April 2021, AFRIC, as well as associated organisations such as the International Anticrisis Centre and the Foundation for the Defence of National Values, were sanctioned by the US for conducting malign influence operations in Africa and Europe, as were

Russian individuals linked to those organisations: Yulia Afanasyeva, Petr Bychkov, Alexander Malkevich, and Taras Pribyshin.[531]

Aiming to gain in influence in Africa, Prigozhin's structures launched yet another project, "Africa Politology", but its operations appeared to be less public than those of AFRIC. The US sanctioned "Africa Politology" in January 2023.[532]

After the start of the full-blown Russian invasion of Ukraine in February 2022, Prigozhin himself became increasingly involved in building up the Wagner Group that played an important role in a number of Russian military operations.

"Russian Malign Influence Operations in Coronavirus-Hit Italy"

The Italian far-right party Northern League (Lega Nord, now also known as League or Lega), whose members were involved in a number of pro-Kremlin efforts, had somewhat distanced themselves from Moscow even before the escalation of the Russian-Ukrainian war, but the developments of 2022 had a game-changing effect on the party's leader, Matteo Salvini. The party condemned the Russian aggression, and eventually supported the sanctions against Russia and voted to send weapons to Ukraine to help the country fight off the Russian invasion.[533]

---

531 "Treasury Escalates Sanctions Against the Russian Government's Attempts to Influence U.S. Elections", *U.S. Department of the Treasury*, 15 April (2021), https://home.treasury.gov/news/press-releases/jy0126.

532 "Russia-related Designations and Designation Update; Central African Republic Designations; Transnational Criminal Organizations Designation; Global Magnitsky Designations; Issuance of Global Magnitsky General Licenses and Frequently Asked Questions, *U.S. Department of the Treasury*, 26 January (2023), https://ofac.treasury.gov/recent-actions/20230126.

533 Cecilia Biancalana, "Italy's Multiple Populisms Facing the Russo-Ukrainian War", in Gilles Ivaldi, Emilia Zankina (eds), *The Impacts of the Russian Invasion of Ukraine on Right-Wing Populism in Europe* (Brussels: European Center for Populism Studies, 2023), pp. 187-198 (192), https://doi.org/10.55271/rp0022.

"How to Fail a Malign Influence Operation: The Case of Russian Aid to Serbia"

Following the start of the full-blown invasion of Ukraine, Leonid Slutsky, the chair of the Committee on International Affairs of the Russian parliament, who had previously been involved in Russian malign influence operations linked to the COVID-19 pandemic, became one of the members of the Russian delegation in the short-lived Russian-Ukrainian "peace negotiations". And after the death of Vladimir Zhirinovsky, the founder of the Russian far-right, misleadingly named Liberal-Democratic Party of Russia, Slutsky replaced him as the leader of the party.

"The Rise and Fall of a Polish Agent of Kremlin Influence: The Case of Janusz Niedźwiecki"

Janusz Niedźwiecki's Ukrainian pro-Kremlin handlers Oleh Voloshyn and Nadia Borodi fled Ukraine several days before the full-blown invasion, and settled in Belarus. In March 2022, the UK sanctioned Voloshyn for his involvement "in destabilising Ukraine, or undermining, or threatening the territorial integrity, sovereignty or independence of Ukraine, namely by using his position of influence to promote, via the spreading of disinformation and pro-Russian narratives which support Russia's actions in Ukraine".[534] In February 2023, the Security Service of Ukraine charged Voloshyn with state treason, while the Ukrainian parliament revoked his parliamentary mandate.

Voloshyn's political patron Viktor Medvedchuk, who had been put under house arrest in May 2021, escaped his arrest a few days after the start of the invasion and tried to flee Ukraine. In April 2022, he was captured by the Security Service of Ukraine and, in September 2022, was sent to Russia in exchange for Ukrainian

---

534 "Consolidated List of Financial Sanctions Targets in the UK", *Office of Financial Sanctions Implementation*, 17 July (2023), https://assets.publishing.service. gov.uk/government/uploads/system/uploads/attachment_data/file/11709 61/Russia.pdf.

prisoners of war. The UK sanctioned Medvedchuk in April 2022 for his efforts to destabilise and undermine Ukraine.[535]

Following the invasion, Ukrainian politician Oleksandr Vilkul, who had held pro-Russian views and had used Voloshyn's and Niedźwiecki's services in his political career, distanced himself from Russia and adopted an unambiguously pro-Ukrainian position on the war. At the end of February 2022, he was appointed the Head of the Military Administration of Kryvyi Rih.

"The German Connection: Far-Right Journalist Manuel Ochsenreiter in the Service of the Russian Propaganda Machine"

No revelation about the pro-Kremlin efforts of Manuel Ochsenreiter, or his political relations with German MP Markus Frohnmaier, for whom Ochsenreiter sought Russian support, seemed to damage the latter's political career in any significant way.

In the course of 2022, unlike several other major European far-right parties, Frohnmaier's party, Alternative for Germany, emerged as the strongest pro-Kremlin far-right political force in the EU.

---

535 Ibid.

SOVIET AND POST-SOVIET POLITICS AND SOCIETY

Edited by Dr. Andreas Umland | ISSN 1614-3515

121 *Mykhaylo Banakh* | Die Relevanz der Zivilgesellschaft bei den postkommunistischen Transformationsprozessen in mittel- und osteuropäischen Ländern. Das Beispiel der spät- und postsowjetischen Ukraine 1986-2009 | Mit einem Vorwort von Gerhard Simon | ISBN 978-3-8382-0499-4

122 *Michael Moser* | Language Policy and the Discourse on Languages in Ukraine under President Viktor Yanukovych (25 February 2010–28 October 2012) | ISBN 978-3-8382-0497-0 (Paperback edition) | ISBN 978-3-8382-0507-6 (Hardcover edition)

123 *Nicole Krome* | Russischer Netzwerkkapitalismus Restrukturierungsprozesse in der Russischen Föderation am Beispiel des Luftfahrtunternehmens „Aviastar" | Mit einem Vorwort von Petra Stykow | ISBN 978-3-8382-0534-2

124 *David R. Marples* | 'Our Glorious Past'. Lukashenka's Belarus and the Great Patriotic War | ISBN 978-3-8382-0574-8 (Paperback edition) | ISBN 978-3-8382-0675-2 (Hardcover edition)

125 *Ulf Walther* | Russlands „neuer Adel". Die Macht des Geheimdienstes von Gorbatschow bis Putin | Mit einem Vorwort von Hans-Georg Wieck | ISBN 978-3-8382-0584-7

126 *Simon Geissbühler (Hrsg.)* | Kiew – Revolution 3.0. Der Euromaidan 2013/14 und die Zukunftsperspektiven der Ukraine | ISBN 978-3-8382-0581-6 (Paperback edition) | ISBN 978-3-8382-0681-3 (Hardcover edition)

127 *Andrey Makarychev* | Russia and the EU in a Multipolar World. Discourses, Identities, Norms | With a foreword by Klaus Segbers | ISBN 978-3-8382-0629-5

128 *Roland Scharff* | Kasachstan als postsowjetischer Wohlfahrtsstaat. Die Transformation des sozialen Schutzsystems | Mit einem Vorwort von Joachim Ahrens | ISBN 978-3-8382-0622-6

129 *Katja Grupp* | Bild Lücke Deutschland. Kaliningrader Studierende sprechen über Deutschland | Mit einem Vorwort von Martin Schulz | ISBN 978-3-8382-0552-6

130 *Konstantin Sheiko, Stephen Brown* | History as Therapy. Alternative History and Nationalist Imaginings in Russia, 1991-2014 | ISBN 978-3-8382-0665-3

131 *Elisa Kriza* | Alexander Solzhenitsyn: Cold War Icon, Gulag Author, Russian Nationalist? A Study of the Western Reception of his Literary Writings, Historical Interpretations, and Political Ideas | With a foreword by Andrei Rogatchevski | ISBN 978-3-8382-0589-2 (Paperback edition) | ISBN 978-3-8382-0690-5 (Hardcover edition)

132 *Serghei Golunov* | The Elephant in the Room. Corruption and Cheating in Russian Universities | ISBN 978-3-8382-0570-0

133 *Manja Hussner, Rainer Arnold (Hgg.)* | Verfassungsgerichtsbarkeit in Zentralasien I. Sammlung von Verfassungstexten | ISBN 978-3-8382-0595-3

134 *Nikolay Mitrokhin* | Die „Russische Partei". Die Bewegung der russischen Nationalisten in der UdSSR 1953-1985 | Aus dem Russischen übertragen von einem Übersetzerteam unter der Leitung von Larisa Schippel | ISBN 978-3-8382-0024-8

135 *Manja Hussner, Rainer Arnold (Hgg.)* | Verfassungsgerichtsbarkeit in Zentralasien II. Sammlung von Verfassungstexten | ISBN 978-3-8382-0597-7

136 *Manfred Zeller* | Das sowjetische Fieber. Fußballfans im poststalinistischen Vielvölkerreich | Mit einem Vorwort von Nikolaus Katzer | ISBN 978-3-8382-0757-5

137 *Kristin Schreiter* | Stellung und Entwicklungspotential zivilgesellschaftlicher Gruppen in Russland. Menschenrechtsorganisationen im Vergleich | ISBN 978-3-8382-0673-8

138 *David R. Marples, Frederick V. Mills (Eds.)* | Ukraine's Euromaidan. Analyses of a Civil Revolution | ISBN 978-3-8382-0660-8

139 *Bernd Kappenberg* | Setting Signs for Europe. Why Diacritics Matter for European Integration | With a foreword by Peter Schlobinski | ISBN 978-3-8382-0663-9

140 *René Lenz* | Internationalisierung, Kooperation und Transfer. Externe bildungspolitische Akteure in der Russischen Föderation | Mit einem Vorwort von Frank Ettrich | ISBN 978-3-8382-0751-3

141 *Juri Plusnin, Yana Zausaeva, Natalia Zhidkevich, Artemy Pozanenko* | Wandering Workers. Mores, Behavior, Way of Life, and Political Status of Domestic Russian Labor Migrants | Translated by Julia Kazantseva | ISBN 978-3-8382-0653-0

142 *David J. Smith (Eds.)* | Latvia – A Work in Progress? 100 Years of State- and Nation-Building | ISBN 978-3-8382-0648-6

143 *Инна Чувычкина (ред.)* | Экспортные нефте- и газопроводы на постсоветском пространстве. Анализ трубопроводной политики в свете теории международных отношений | ISBN 978-3-8382-0822-0

ibidem.eu